Assessing for Learning

Assessing for Learning

Librarians and Teachers as Partners

Second Edition
Revised and Expanded

VIOLET H. HARADA AND
JOAN M. YOSHINA

 LIBRARIES UNLIMITED

AN IMPRINT OF ABC-CLIO, LLC
Santa Barbara, California • Denver, Colorado • Oxford, England

Library of Congress Cataloging-in-Publication Data

Harada, Violet H.
    Assessing for learning : librarians and teachers as
partners / Violet H. Harada and Joan M. Yoshina. — 2nd ed.,
rev. and expanded.
        p. cm.
    Rev. ed. of: Assessing learning. 2005.
    Includes bibliographical references and index.
    ISBN 978-1-59884-470-2 (acid-free paper) — ISBN 978-1-59884-471-9
(ebook)   1. School libraries—United States—Evaluation.
2. Instructional materials centers—United States—Evaluation.
3. School librarian participation in curriculum planning—United
States.   I. Yoshina, Joan M.   II. Harada, Violet H. Assessing
learning.   III. Title.
    Z675.S3H264   2010
    027.8'0973—dc22   2010028713

ISBN: 978-1-59884-470-2
EISBN: 978-1-59884-471-9

14   13   12   2   3   4   5

This book is also available on the World Wide Web as an eBook.
Visit www.abc-clio.com for details.

Libraries Unlimited
An Imprint of ABC-CLIO, LLC

ABC-CLIO, LLC
130 Cremona Drive, P.O. Box 1911
Santa Barbara, California 93116-1911

This book is printed on acid-free paper ∞

Manufactured in the United States of America

Contents

Illustrations   xv

Acknowledgments   xxi

Introduction   xxiii
    Dispelling the Myths   xxiii
    Facing Challenges   xxv
    Organization of Book   xxvi

Chapter 1   What Needs to Happen in 21st-Century Schools?   1
    Challenges in Our Schools   1
    Talking the Right Talk: Standards Moving in
       the Same Direction   2
    Walking the Talk: Schools Becoming
       Learning Organizations   3
    Reflection and Assessment: Vital Parts of the
       Walk   6
    Implications for the Library Media Specialist   6
    Conclusion   8

Chapter 2   Assessment for Learning   9
    What Is Assessment?   9
    What's Happening with Assessment in
       Our Schools?   10
    How Does No Child Left Behind Affect
       Assessment?   12
    Do Effective Library Media Programs Make a
       Difference?   13

What Is the Library Media Specialist's Role?   15
   Benefits of Assessment   17
   Essential Questions for the Library Media
      Specialist   17
Conclusion   18

Chapter 3   Tools for Assessment: Checklists, Rubrics,
      and Rating Scales   19
Checklists   20
   What Is a Checklist?   20
   When Might We Use a Checklist?   20
   How Do We Construct a Checklist?   21
   How Do We Use a Checklist to Assess for
      Information Literacy?   22
Rubrics   22
   What Is a Rubric?   22
   When Might We Use a Rubric?   23
   How Do We Construct an Instructional
      Rubric?   24
   How Do We Use Rubrics to Assess for
      Information Literacy?   26
Rating Scales   29
   What Is a Rating Scale?   29
   When Might We Use a Rating Scale?   29
   How Do We Construct a Rating Scale?   29
   How Do We Use a Rating Scale to Assess for
      Information Literacy?   30
Conclusion   31

Chapter 4   Tools for Assessment: Conferences, Logs,
      Personal Correspondence, and Exit Passes   33
Conferences   33
   What Is a Conference?   33
   When Might We Use Conferences to Assess
      Learning?   33
   How Do We Structure the Conference?   35
   How Do We Use Conferences to Assess for
      Information Literacy?   36

Logs 38
What Is a Log? 38
When Might We Use Logs as Assessment Tools? 38
How Do We Facilitate the Use of Logs? 42
How Do We Use Logs to Assess for Information Literacy? 43
Personal Correspondence 47
What Is Personal Correspondence? 47
When Might We Use Personal Correspondence to Assess Learning? 48
How Do We Construct the Correspondence? 48
How Do We Use Personal Correspondence to Assess for Information Literacy? 50
Exit Pass 51
What Is an Exit Pass? 51
When Might We Use an Exit Pass? 52
How Do We Construct an Exit Pass? 52
How Do We Use an Exit Pass to Assess for Information Literacy? 53
Conclusion 55

Chapter 5 Tools for Assessment: Graphic Organizers 57
What Are Graphic Organizers? 57
Concept Maps 58
What Is a Concept Map? 58
When Might We Use a Concept Map? 58
How Do We Construct a Concept Map? 60
How Do We Use a Concept Map to Assess for Information Literacy? 61
Webs 65
What Is a Web? 65
When Might We Use a Web? 65
How Do We Construct a Web? 65
How Do We Use a Web to Assess for Information Literacy? 66
K-W-L Charts 68
What Is a K-W-L Chart? 68

When Might We Use a K-W-L Chart?   69

How Do We Construct a K-W-L Chart?   69

How Do We Use a K-W-L (or K-W-H-L) Chart
to Assess for Information Literacy?   70

Matrices   72

What Is a Matrix?   72

When Might We Use a Matrix?   72

How Do We Construct a Matrix?   73

How Do We Use a Matrix to Assess for Information
Literacy?   73

Conclusion   76

Chapter 6   Student Portfolios   77

What Is a Portfolio?   77

What Is a Digital Portfolio?   78

How Do Portfolios Differ from Other
Assessment Tools?   79

Why Use Portfolios?   80

Who Are the Audiences for Portfolios?   81

How Might the Library Media Specialist
Use Portfolios?   82

What Is a Process Folio and How
Is It Developed?   83

What Might a Process Folio Look Like?   84

Step 1: Determine Standards for Instruction
and Assessment and Agree upon Skills,
Dispositions, and Responsibilities to Address   85

Step 2: Develop Tools and Strategies to Assess
Achievement of the Standard   86

Step 3: Devise a Consistent Rating System for
Assessment Tools Used   87

Example A: Matrix for Identifying Resources   87

Example B: Checklist for Bookmaking   88

Step 4: Identify Samples of Student Work to
Include for Each Standard   88

Sample Work A: Completed Matrix   90

Sample Work B: Completed Checklist   90

Step 5: Include Samples of Student Reflections 93
Step 6: Prepare a Summary Sheet for the Process Folio 95
Getting Started 97
Conclusion 97

Chapter 7 Assessing for Critical Understanding 99
Defining Critical Understanding 99
Acquiring Critical Understanding 101
Developing Critical Understanding through Inquiry 103
Assessing for Critical Understanding 105
Scenario A: Assessing Ability to Connect New Learning to Prior Knowledge 105
Scenario B: Assessing Ability to Ask a Range of Questions to Focus the Search for Understanding 107
Scenario C: Assessing Ability to Consider Different Points of View toward a Controversial Issue Before Coming to a Conclusion 110
Scenario D: Assessing Ability to Identify Bias 111
Scenario E: Assessing the Ability to Draw Conclusions 113
Scenario F: Assessing Ability to Effectively Communicate Understanding 115
Conclusion 117

Chapter 8 Assessing for Dispositions 119
Defining Dispositions 120
Acquiring Dispositions 120
Assessing for Dispositions 121
Scenario A: Assessing for Initiative 122
Scenario B: Assessing for Flexibility 123
Scenario C: Assessing for Persistence 123
Scenario D: Assessing for Literary Appreciation 125
Scenario E: Assessing for Openness 126
Scenario F: Assessing for Social Responsibility 126
Using Portfolios 129
Conclusion 131

Chapter 9   Assessing for Tech-Integrated Learning   133
              Defining the Digital Landscape   133
              Acquiring Skills for Success in a Digital World 133
              Implications for Library Media Specialists   135
              Assessing for Tech-Integrated Learning   136
                  Scenario A: Assessing Online Discussions   136
                  Scenario B: Assessing Blogs   137
                  Scenario C: Assessing Podcasts and Vodcasts 138
                  Scenario D: Assessing Wikis   140
                  Scenario E: Assessing Digital Narratives   141
                  Scenario F: Assessing Wiki Pathfinders   144
              Conclusion   146

Chapter 10   Outcome-Based Approach: Elementary
              Grade Example   147
              Outcome-Based Approach   147
              Summary of Project   150
              Sample Lessons   151
                  *Lesson 1: Finding Information in a Variety
                      of Sources*   151
                  Outcomes Desired   151
                      Standards and Performance Indicators   151
                      Disposition/Responsibility   151
                      Product/Performance   152
                  Assessment   154
                      Learning Goal   154
                      Assessment Criteria   154
                      Self-Assessment Strategies   154
                      Tools for Collecting, Recording, and
                          Quantifying Data   154
                  Learning Plan   154
                  *Lesson 2: Developing Criteria to Assess
                      Student Books*   157
                  Outcomes Desired   157
                      Standards and Performance Indicators   157
                      Disposition/Responsibility   158
                      Product/Performance   158

Assessment   158

   Learning Goal   158

   Assessment Criteria   158

   Self-Assessment Strategies   159

   Tools for Collecting, Recording, and
      Quantifying Data   160

Learning Plan   162

Conclusion   164

Chapter 11   Outcome-Based Approach: Middle School
  Example   165

Outcome-Based Approach   165

Summary of Project   166

Sample Lessons   167

Lesson 1: Asking the Right Questions   167

Outcomes Desired   167

   Standards and Performance Indicators   167

   Disposition/Responsibility   168

   Product/Performance   168

Assessment   168

   Learning Goal   168

   Assessment Criteria   168

   Self-Assessment Strategies   168

   Tools for Collecting, Recording, and
      Quantifying Data   168

Learning Plan   169

*Lesson 2: Selecting and Evaluating
  Resources*   170

Outcomes Desired   170

   Standards and Performance
     Indicators   170

   Disposition/Responsibility   170

   Product/Performance   170

Assessment   170

   Learning Goal   170

   Assessment Criteria   170

   Self-Assessment Strategies   170

                    Tools for Collecting, Recording, and
                        Quantifying Data   173
                    Learning Plan   175
                 Conclusion   179

Chapter 12   Outcome-Based Approach: High School
             Example   181
             Outcome-Based Approach   181
             Summary of Project   182
             Sample Lessons   183
                 Lesson 1: Evaluating Web Sites   184
                 Outcomes Desired   184
                    Standards and Performance Indicators   184
                    Disposition/Responsibility   184
                    Product/Performance   185
                 Assessment   185
                    Learning Goal   185
                    Assessment Criteria   185
                    Self-Assessment Strategies   186
                    Tools for Collecting, Recording, and
                        Quantifying Data   186
                 Learning Plan   187
                 *Lesson 2: Preparing an Annotated
                     Bibliography*   191
                 Outcomes Desired   191
                    Standards and Performance Indicators   191
                    Disposition/Responsibility   192
                    Product/Performance   192
                 Assessment   192
                    Learning Goal   192
                    Assessment Criteria   192
                    Self-Assessment Strategies   192
                    Tools for Collecting, Recording, and
                        Quantifying Data   194
                 Learning Plan   194
                 Conclusion   197

Chapter 13   Communicating Evidence of Learning   199
               How Can Assessment Data Be Used to
                    Support School-Wide Goals?   200
               Why Is It Important to Communicate Results?   200
               Communicating with Teachers   201
                    Step 1: Collect Evidence of Achievement   202
                    Step 2: Analyze Evidence   202
                    Step 3: Synthesize Findings   203
                    Step 4: Communicate Results   204
               Communicating with Principals and
                    School Councils   206
                    Step 1: Collect Evidence of Achievement   207
                    Step 2: Analyze Evidence   209
                    Step 3: Synthesize Findings   209
                    Step 4: Communicate Results   209
               Communicating with the Larger Community   212
                    Step 1: Collect Evidence of Achievement   213
                    Step 2: Analyze Evidence   214
                    Step 3: Synthesize Findings   216
                    Step 4: Communicate Results   217
               Making the Testing Connection   220
                    Step 1: Collect Evidence of Achievement   222
                    Step 2: Analyze Evidence   222
                    Step 3: Synthesize Findings   223
                    Step 4: Communicate Results   223
               Conclusion   224

References   225

Index   233

Illustrations

2.1 Linear model of relationships among curriculum, instruction, and evaluation 10

2.2 Dynamic model of relationships among curriculum, instruction, and assessment 11

2.3 Moving from a focus on resources to a focus on student learning 16

3.1 Questions used to create an observation checklist 21

3.2 Checklist for assessing access to information in various sources 23

3.3 Steps in creating a rubric 25

3.4 Rubric for note taking 27

3.5 Evidence to assess instructional targets for Bill of Rights unit 30

3.6 Rating scale for assessing targeted aspects of the inquiry process 31

3.7 Rating scale for self-assessing Bill of Rights presentation 32

4.1 Linking conferencing questions with instructional targets 35

4.2 Matching journal prompts with AASL *Standards for the 21st-Century Learner* 39

4.3 Learning log for primary research projects 41

4.4 Example of synthesis log A 42

4.5 Example of synthesis log B 42

4.6 Example of literary response log 43

4.7 Prompts for assessing aspects of information literacy 45

4.8 Using letters and notes to assess instructional goals 48

4.9 Template for invitation to a science fair 49

4.10 Template for guardians' response 49

4.11 Notes and letters used to assess the information
      literacy process   50
4.12 Prompts used on exit passes   52
4.13 Directions for read-in activity   53
4.14 Exit pass for read-in activity   54
4.15 Exit pass for inquiry process   54
5.1   Examples of organizers for different learning objectives   59
5.2   Steps in constructing a concept map   60
5.3   Concept map for the rain forest ecosystem   63
5.4   Concept map for howler monkey   64
5.5   Web for "How did the colonists live?"   67
5.6   Web showing contributions made by colonial
      tradespeople   68
5.7   Using the K-W-L chart to organize the research process   69
5.8   Basic K-W-L chart   70
5.9   K-W-H-L chart   70
5.10 K-W-H-L chart for pet project   71
5.11 Model for constructing a comparison matrix   74
5.12 Matrix for comparing candidates and issues   75
6.1   Portfolios versus other assessment measures   80
6.2   Use of portfolios by different audiences   81
6.3   Standards and assessment measures for wetlands unit   86
6.4   Matrix for identifying resources   87
6.5   Rating system for matrix   88
6.6   Checklist for assessing wetlands books   89
6.7   Rating system for checklist   90
6.8   Example of student-completed matrix for
      identifying resources   91
6.9   Example of student-completed checklist for
      assessing wetlands books   92
6.10 Example of student log for the wetlands unit   94
6.11 Example of student's summary sheet for the
      wetlands unit   95
7.1   Questions used to plan inquiry lessons   104
7.2   K-W-L chart for visit to salmon hatchery   107
7.3   Checklist for assessing interview questions   109

7.4 Response form for panel discussion on health care 111
7.5 Assessing news stories for bias 113
7.6 Map for assessing ability to draw conclusions 114
7.7 Rubric for assessing slide presentation 116
8.1 Postgallery walk: Questions to assess for initiative 122
8.2 Log prompts to assess for flexibility 123
8.3 Rating scale to assess for persistence 124
8.4 Reading tracker to assess for literary appreciation 125
8.5 Graphic organizer to assess diverse points of view
and conclusions 127
8.6 Rubric to assess for social responsibility 128
8.7 Portfolio prompts to assess dispositions 130
9.1 Rating scale to assess online collaborative teamwork 137
9.2 Rubric to assess blog entries 138
9.3 Rating scale to assess podcasts and vodcasts 139
9.4 Checklist to assess a wiki page 140
9.5 Rubric to assess a digital narrative 142
9.6 Reflection rubric to assess a wiki pathfinder 144
10.1 Conventional versus outcome-based planning 148
10.2 Relationship between standards and assessment 149
10.3 Standards and performance indicators addressed
in lesson 1 152
10.4 Organizer for identifying resources 153
10.5 Criteria for locating and evaluating a variety
of sources 154
10.6 Rating system for identifying resources 155
10.7 Learning plan for identifying information resources 156
10.8 Map of information sources 157
10.9 Standards and performance indicators addressed
in lesson 2 158
10.10 Criteria for evaluating student-created books 159
10.11 Checklist for assessing wetlands books 160
10.12 Learning plan for developing assessment criteria
with students 162
10.13 Lessons for grade 3 wetlands project: Focus,
outcome, task, and assessment 164

11.1   Standards and performance indicators addressed
       in lesson 1   167
11.2   Possible criteria for questions   168
11.3   Assessment rubric for generating questions   169
11.4   Learning plan for lesson on generating questions   171
11.5   Standards and performance indicators addressed
       in lesson 2   174
11.6   Criteria for assessing resources in different formats   174
11.7   Response sheet for assessing resources   175
11.8   Self-assessment tool for contributions to blog   176
11.9   Learning plan for selecting and evaluating resources   176
11.10 Lessons for grade 8 Holocaust unit: Focus, outcome,
       task, and assessment   180
12.1   Standards and performance indicators addressed
       in lesson 1   184
12.2   Criteria for evaluating Web sites   185
12.3   Tool for assessing Web sites   186
12.4   Learning plan for evaluating Web sites   188
12.5   Standards and performance indicators addressed
       in lesson 2   192
12.6   Criteria for assessing annotated bibliographies   193
12.7   Rubric for assessing annotated bibliographies   193
12.8   Learning plan for developing bibliographies   195
12.9   Lessons for senior project: Focus, outcome,
       task, and assessment   198
13.1   Steps involved in evidence-based assessment   200
13.2   Matrix for identifying resources (work sample)   203
13.3   Rubric for assessing the resource matrix
       (assessment tool)   204
13.4   Sample of grade 3 class profile   205
13.5   Alignment of standards and performance indicators
       for reading and information literacy   207
13.6   Literature response form   208
13.7   Sample of grade 8 class profile   210
13.8   Profile of achievement   212
13.9   Sample of tally sheet   214

13.10   Plan for presentation   215
13.11   Synthesizing data about the use of technology   216
13.12   Tallying data related to technology use   217
13.13   Percentage of students using technology to
        locate information   218
13.14   Percentage of students using technology to
        present information   219
13.15   Student attitudes toward technology   219
13.16   Example of student test results on analyzing
        primary sources   223

Acknowledgments

We extend our gratitude to Sharon Coatney, acquisitions editor at Libraries Unlimited, for encouraging us to update and expand our original work and for providing constructive feedback through the production of this manuscript.

We continue to express our warmest aloha to our fellow library media specialists and teachers in Hawaii and across the nation who have helped us shape our vision and thinking about the issue of assessment for learning. Special thanks go to Sandy Yamamoto and Carolyn Kirio, librarians at Kapolei High School in Hawaii, for assisting us with one of the new chapters in the book dealing with technology-related learning. We also have the deepest appreciation for the wisdom shared by so many library educators, especially Dr. Marjorie Pappas, who have been professional colleagues imparting both inspiration and insight on the topic of assessment.

Finally, we thank our spouses, Byron and Wayne, for their continuous encouragement and wholehearted support.

Introduction

The learning journey is fueled by one's ability to know about oneself as a learner. This critical concept undergirds the cultivation of young minds that "know how to plan, follow through with plans, modify plans when necessary, and evaluate the effectiveness of their planning" (Tomlinson 2008a, 30). Getting into this habit of effective thinking lies at the heart of the *Standards for the 21st-Century Learner* (American Association of School Librarians [AASL] 2007). In revising and updating our book *Assessing Learning: Librarians and Teachers as Partners* (Libraries Unlimited, 2005), we focused on how school library media specialists and other educators might work together to not only facilitate deeper learning but to assist students in developing the habits of mind and skills to own their personal learning.

DISPELLING THE MYTHS

The myths about assessment for learning that we described in the introduction of our original book still persist today and are worth mentioning below. They include:

"I have to teach the same skills year after year because the students don't seem to get them."

"I don't have time to give students quizzes and tests so I can't really assess their work."

"Assessment is not my responsibility because I don't grade the students. It's the teacher's job."

"My job is getting kids excited about reading and helping them with their research, not conducting assessment."

"My goal is producing lifelong learners. That is a long-term goal. It happens in the future and you can't assess these skills now."

We have heard variations of these comments repeated at meetings, workshops, conferences, and informal gatherings wherever library media specialists have a chance to network and exchange war stories. Let's revisit these comments for a moment and discuss some of the underlying myths that support them.

- "I have to teach the same skills year after year because the students don't seem to get them."
  - Myth 1: The fault lies with students, who are simply unable to learn.
  - Myth 2: Addressing these skills necessitates teaching them in the same way over and over again. Repetition, rather than assessment and modification of teaching strategies, is the most effective way to achieve more effective student learning.
- "I don't have time to give them quizzes and tests so I can't really assess their work."
  - Myth 3: The primary method of assessing student performance is through administration of traditional evaluation instruments such as paper and pencil tests.
- "Assessment is not my responsibility because I don't grade the students. It's the teacher's job."
  - Myth 4: Assessment and evaluation are one and the same. Since library media specialists don't usually give grades, they also don't assess students' work.
- "My job is getting kids excited about reading and helping them with their research, not conducting assessment."
  - Myth 5: Skills and attitudes that help students develop their abilities to read and use information do not require assessment.
- "My goal is producing lifelong learners. That is a long-term goal. It happens in the future and you can't assess these skills now."
  - Myth 6: Developing skills and dispositions for lifelong learning are *not* the focus of instruction in the library. These are attributes that learners somehow acquire (on their own) later in life.

If these myths actually drive current practices in the library media profession, we need to seriously rethink them. We need to "change our mental models about what we teach, how we teach it, and how we assess students' learning growth" (Costa and Kallick 2010, 211). In today's schools, assessment for student learning is every school professional's business *and* every student's business. If our goal is to engage students in ways that help them grow into confident, self-directed adult learners, we must demonstrate how our teaching contributes to this development. Not only is it critical to teach students *how to,* but it is equally crucial to assist them in measuring *how well* they demonstrate their learning. It is imperative that we help students become "masters of their own fate as learners" (Tomlinson 2008a, 30). Library media specialists are involved in daily assessment of many kinds, but there is a real need to conduct ongoing assessment of student progress and to report it in a manner that communicates the results to school staff, students, and parents (Kansas Association of School Librarians 2001).

FACING CHALLENGES

There is no doubt that library media specialists face formidable challenges in today's schools (Neuman 2000):

- Administrators and teachers have not fully accepted the increased instructional role of the library media specialist.
- Library media specialists themselves may be reluctant to assume this role.
- Additional training is essential for library media specialists to assess student outcomes in information literacy.

These challenges point to the fact that effecting change in the school is a complex endeavor. Making the transition is not an overnight process. The Kansas Association of School Librarians Research Committee (2001) describes this as a formidable undertaking likened to eating an elephant. One does it a bite at a time.

For library media specialists, a critical first bite is orienting themselves to the purposes of assessment and learning about possible strategies to develop their own assessment tools. This book reflects the following core beliefs:

- Assessment is a critical tool to help students determine their strengths and weaknesses and work on improvements.
- Assessment is an equally valuable means of analyzing and informing instruction.
- Assessment is *not* evaluation; it is infused throughout the learning and teaching experience rather than limited to final outcomes.
- Assessment is not an add-on; it is integral to effective teaching and learning.

ORGANIZATION OF BOOK

This revised and updated version of the book includes the following:

Chapter 1 provides a context for assessment in today's schools. It emphasizes the importance of schools perceiving themselves as learning organizations.

Chapter 2 examines the role of the library media specialist as a partner in assessment and the importance of viewing assessment as an essential component of the teaching-learning process.

Chapters 3 through 5 describe various tools for assessing student learning in the library media center and provide examples of their uses in integrated classroom-library instruction.

Chapters 6 introduces the notion of portfolios as a means of viewing learning over an extended period of time.

Chapters 7 through 9 are entirely new chapters that focus on assessing for critical understanding, dispositions, and technology-integrated learning.

Chapters 10 through 12 illustrate how teachers and library media specialists at the elementary, middle, and high schools might collaborate on units that are based on standards and desired learning outcomes.

Chapter 13 explores how assessment data from the library media center might be organized and shared with various stakeholder groups in a school community. It also explores how library media specialists might use results from high-stakes tests to help close learning gaps.

Our message is that library media specialists are vital partners in teaching. Their physical classrooms are their library media centers; however, their virtual learning centers extend to information and knowledge in the global community. As instructors, they need to ask themselves the following deep questions:

- What exactly does a lifelong learner do?
- How do we help to produce such learners?
- How can we prove that our teaching has made a difference?

This book invites library media specialists to delve into these questions and find meaningful answers that help them build a compelling case for the power of classroom-library partnerships for learning. Most importantly, the book focuses on how library media specialists and other educational partners might empower students to take charge of their own learning.

Costa and Kallick (2010) emphasize the importance of educating students for the "tests of life" and not a "life of tests" (225). They state:

> We must constantly remind ourselves that the ultimate purpose of evaluation is to have students learn to become self-evaluative. If students graduate from our schools still dependent upon others to tell them when they are adequate, good, or excellent, then we've missed the whole point of what self-directed learning is about. (Costa and Kallick 2010, 225)

CHAPTER 1

What Needs to Happen in 21st-Century Schools?

This chapter addresses the following:

- Challenges facing today's schools
- Standards and their role in reform
- Moving from change rhetoric to real change
- Why assessment is critical
- Role of library media specialists in making change happen

CHALLENGES IN OUR SCHOOLS

School systems are perennially under critical scrutiny for their failure to stem dropout rates and their inability to produce graduates ready to succeed in the workplace or move seamlessly into higher education. Statistics from the U.S. Department of Education (cited in Perkins-Gough 2008) are particularly dismal:

- Forty-three percent of all students attending public two-year academic institutions and 29 percent of those attending public four-year colleges reported they had to enroll in remedial courses.
- Only 56 percent who enrolled in four-year colleges received a degree within six years.

Even more damning is what high school students have to say about the quality of their secondary schooling. In "Diploma to Nowhere," a report funded by the Broad Foundation and the Gates Foundation (Strong American Schools 2008), almost 700 students were surveyed and their candid responses recorded. The majority indicated that they had taken the most challenging courses offered in their high schools and earned As and Bs. Yet all of them were required to enroll in remedial college courses! Students strongly stated they needed more engaging and rigorous instruction in high school.

What must happen in K–12 schools to change this picture? In the rest of this short chapter, we (1) discuss the importance of goals and standards that address the needs of today's students, (2) describe the transformation necessary in our schools to actualize these goals, (3) introduce the importance of reflection and assessment in meeting these goals, and (4) address the implications of the shifting learning paradigms for the library media specialist.

TALKING THE RIGHT TALK: STANDARDS MOVING IN THE SAME DIRECTION

Robert Sternberg (2008) states that if our goal is to promote excellence for all learners, we must rethink the core of the current learning paradigm. While the traditional three Rs are still important, he suggests that educators working with the community and families must focus on a new set of three Rs:

- Reasoning—providing a comprehensive set of higher-order skills for creative, analytical, and socially constructed learning
- Resilience—persisting in tasks and goals
- Responsibility—distinguishing right from wrong, common good over personal good, empathy for others, and right actions (Sternberg 2008, 15–19)

It's encouraging to note that Sternberg's thinking is mirrored in current content and performance standards. Marcia Mardis and Anne Perrault (2008) conducted an insightful analysis of standards from the Association for Supervision and Curriculum Development (2007), the International Society for Technology in Education (2007), the Partnership for 21st Century Skills (2007), and the American Association of School Librarians (AASL 2007). They reported that the new standards, regardless of origin, highlighted three distinguishing themes:

- *A conceptual framework for knowledge*—being curious, questioning deeply, and building higher-order relationships
- *An interdisciplinary perspective on knowledge construction*—shaping personal knowledge by constructing and reconstructing connections among ideas and concepts
- *A strong emphasis on the importance of affect in the learning process*—promoting empathy for other points of view, caring about what is being learned, and building self-efficacy

WALKING THE TALK: SCHOOLS BECOMING LEARNING ORGANIZATIONS

Standards, no matter how comprehensive and thoughtful, are simply statements of idealistic rhetoric unless school communities transform them into real, purposeful actions. Allison Zmuda and Violet Harada (2008) refer to this as committing to a "mission-centered mindset" with the learner in the center (2). Grant Wiggins and Jay McTighe (2008), who also support a learner-focused mission, bluntly state: "The mission of high school is not to cover content, but rather to help learners become thoughtful about, and productive with, content. It's not to help students get good at school, but rather to prepare them for the world beyond school" (36).

Jennifer Steele and Kathryn Boudett (2009) propose that schools need to become *learning organizations* skilled at creating, acquiring, and transferring knowledge and at modifying their behavior to reflect new knowledge and insights. Learning organizations change their behaviors and mindsets as a result of evidence-based practices and experiences. Importantly, they promote learning and leadership throughout the community. For schools, this involves not just the students as learners but the faculty, staff, administration, and families as well. Schools that are learning organizations recognize that genuine learning is composed of more than individual efforts. Such learning emerges and evolves from the interaction of people in groups and teams of different sizes. Cooperation, collaboration, trust, and respect are key elements in working together as a community of learners (Mitleton-Kelly n.d.). In schools that see themselves as learning organizations, stakeholder-participants talk about "being part of something larger than themselves, of being connected, of being generative" (Senge 1990, 13).

What do classrooms and library media centers look like in schools that are learning organizations? Jacqueline Brooks and Martin Brooks (1993) identify the following defining characteristics:

- Curriculum emphasizes big concepts rather than minute skills.
- Student questions are highly valued.
- Activities invite use of primary sources of data.
- Students are viewed as thinkers with emerging theories about the world.
- Adult mentors behave in an interactive manner, mediating the learning environment.
- Assessment is interwoven throughout the experience.
- Learning is often achieved in groups.

Ross Todd (2001b), David Conley (2008), and Arthur Costa (2008) provide further elaborations on the features of inquiry-focused centers of
learning:

- Learners take responsibility for solving problems and resolving
  conflicts.
- They have opportunities for testing, reviewing, and reflecting.
- They gather evidence systematically.
- They respect one another's traditions and cultures.
- They use resources from everywhere for collaborative learning.
- They feel connected, cared for, and trusted.
- They chart and measure their own learning gains.
- They celebrate learning successes.
- They experiment with educational technologies as tools for learn-
  ing.

In such centers of learning, Todd (2001b) maintains that adult facilitators exhibit the following behaviors:

- Facilitators use creative and imaginative approaches to instruction.
- They provide both virtual and physical spaces that link students
  with peers, staff, and community mentors.
- They provide opportunities for students to share their experi-
  ences with others.
- They contextualize learning experience through curriculum co-
  ordination.
- They provide processes to help students understand their
  strengths and weaknesses in learning.
- They show students how to think about their learning and learn-
  ing processes in a reflective way (Todd, quoted in Zmuda and
  Harada 2008, 17–20).

There are several critical action principles reflected in the best practices
of all schools functioning as learning organizations:

*Effective schools understand the profound difference between simply covering
the curriculum and teaching for understanding.*

They shift value structures from simply *acquiring* knowledge to the
active production of knowledge (Costa and Liebmann 1995). Importantly, all learners commit to a clear sense of purpose. William Damon
(2008) indicates that "purpose acts as a moral north star on the route
to excellence: it offers a steady beacon for inspiring and directing

students' best efforts over the long haul, within the classroom and beyond" (10).

They believe in the production of knowledge as not only an individually developed experience but as a socially constructed, dynamic learning process.

Learners recognize and value the power of collaborative knowledge building. They capitalize on the talents and experiences of team members to generate questions as well as solutions and to design products as well as to solve problems. They appreciate the synergy of the give-and-take and the building and rebuilding that is possible through active discourse and action. Schools that facilitate such learning recognize that technology enables social participation in ways unimaginable a scant decade ago. Web 2.0 applications, for example, allow for virtual participation, collaboration, and distribution of expertise. Groups are formed around shared interests to harness and transform collective intelligence (Knobel and Wilber 2009).

They believe that technology is a fundamental tool for learning and teaching.

In the mid-20th century, audio-visual aids were touted as revolutionary media that would change how classrooms were conducted. They turned out to be ancillary and dispensable aids that never lived up to the hype. This is not the case with the present digital innovations that have changed how people read, write, listen, and speak (Ohler 2009). Learning is no longer fixed in time and space; it is virtual and asynchronous. To an extent never possible before, learning can be self-motivated and self-regulated (Richardson 2009). Effective schools recognize the power of technology and devise creative ways to engage all stakeholders in sharing expertise and resources.

They foster a culture of reflection.

Effective schools invite an "academic awakening…a point of a-ha" when both adults and students see connections, relevance, and a personal need to pursue something (Damon 2008, 8). All seekers ask probing questions: *Why should this matter? How do I matter?* People discover that the heart of learning is the continual generation of questions that drive deeper thinking and inquiry. They recognize that learning itself is a journey propelled by reflective questions.

REFLECTION AND ASSESSMENT: VITAL PARTS OF THE WALK

The ability to examine practice and performance is foundational to change. All learners must engage in self-appraisals to effect genuine improvements in their work. All instructors must also look at their efforts against established criteria and guidelines to determine what is working well and what needs to be adjusted.

Reflection and assessment, therefore, are active processes essential to learning. Rather than *assessing learning*, which is summative in nature, there is a need to focus on *assessment for learning*, which involves an on-going examination of the teaching and learning process (Chappuis and Stiggins 2002). Research indicates that assessments that provide accurate, descriptive feedback to students and involve them in the process can improve learning in significant ways (Black and William 1998). Daniel Callison (2009) states that the management of inquiry involves reflective metacognition. This process includes "knowing about yourself and others as knowers, knowing about the task to be undertaken, knowing what strategies to apply to the task, and how to monitor one's own performance with respect to the task" (Callison 2009, 24).

IMPLICATIONS FOR THE LIBRARY MEDIA SPECIALIST

Empowering Learners (AASL 2009a), the current national guidelines for library media specialists, envisions librarians as *instructional partners* as well as *teachers*. Librarians need to seriously consider the ramifications of instructional partnerships. To be viable partners, librarians must be knowledgeable about key aspects of instructional design that include the following (Zmuda and Harada 2008):

- Recognizing the developmental nature of learners and the evolving and nonlinear nature of learning
- Differentiating learning experiences based on the learners' abilities and needs
- Designing instruction that challenges student engagement in their own learning
- Being responsive to learners with diverse cultural backgrounds and prior experiences
- Providing robust assessment and feedback and involving learners in the process

For this type of instruction to thrive, certain truths must be embraced:

Teaching can no longer exist in isolated silos.

Teachers, librarians, and vital support specialists must embrace a mission-stated commitment to work together. Administrators must provide the necessary resources, time, and incentives to enable these teaching partnerships. For librarians, this means taking a hard look at long-standing practices such as one-shot library orientations. William Badke (2009) refers to this as learning by "inoculation" that is separated from actual learning in the curriculum. He says this process of injecting students and sending them on their way rarely results in successful applications in future situations.

Librarians must go beyond teaching location and access.

The AASL *Standards for the 21st-Century Learner* (AASL 2007) makes it clear that while information literacy serves as a foundation for all subject matter taught, library media specialists must focus on learning that helps students in life, not just schooling. They need to facilitate inquiry that requires the thoughtful use of information. To do this, they must ask probing questions such as: What are you curious about and why? What information do you need to address your questions? How will you evaluate what you've found? How can you harness that information to provide the best answers to your questions? (Badke 2009, 58).

School librarians have traditionally taught students how to access an online public access catalog (OPAC), understand the Dewey organizational scheme in a library, retrieve information from a range of resources, and cite sources used in reports and research papers. These skills are still needed points of teaching; however, they are not enough. Today's library media specialists must grapple with some of the real problems with which students struggle. They must determine how best to collaborate with teachers in helping students deal with these challenges. Michael Cohen (2008) identifies some of these challenges as follows:

- Reading and comprehending complex information texts, not just literary works
- Synthesizing information from multiple informational and technical sources
- Drawing conclusions based on evidence from these sources
- Defining a researchable problem
- Evaluating the credibility and validity of data from a variety of sources
- Producing analyses that marshal evidence in support of clear purpose statements and related claims

Assessment is not an add-on if time permits; it is integral to learning.

Lorna Earl (2003) rightfully promotes *assessment as learning*. Carol Ann Tomlinson (2008a) states why it's so critical for students to become thoughtful and reflective learners:

> They understand how to capitalize on their learning strengths and how to compensate for their weaknesses. They know how to plan, follow through with plans, modify plans when necessary, and evaluate the effectiveness of their planning. Through these avenues, they come to believe that they are captains of their own fate as learners. (30)

For library media specialists to be true instructional partners, they must be actively engaged in assessment with students. They work with teachers to have students keep track of their own development and provide relevant and timely feedback. They provide opportunities for students to reflect on their work through a range of assessment strategies.

CONCLUSION

In this chapter, we discussed the need for new learning paradigms in 21st-century schools as an introduction to our book's focus on *assessment for learning* and *assessment as learning*.

We made a case for rethinking doing business as usual and diving into difficult and uncomfortable questions about what matters, what works, and how schools must move from functioning as "test prep centers" (Sternberg 2008, 19) to schools envisioning themselves as catalysts for intellectual inquiry and personal meaning making. This paradigm shift requires schools to move away from "simply marching through textbooks to teaching with meaning and transfer in mind" (Wiggins and McTighe 2008, 37).

The Partnership for 21st Century Skills (2008), a leading advocacy organization promoting the infusion of diverse skill sets for today's flexible and adaptable workforce, strongly recommends that assessment must be a priority in 21st-century schools. In the rest of this book, we share strategies for and examples of what assessment might look like when library media specialists participate as indispensable instructional partners.

CHAPTER 2

Assessment for Learning

This chapter addresses the following essential questions:

- What is assessment?
- What's happening with assessment in our schools?
- How does No Child Left Behind affect assessment?
- Do effective library media programs make a difference in student learning?
- What is the library media specialist's role in assessing for student learning?

WHAT IS ASSESSMENT?

Assessment is the process of "collecting, analyzing, and reporting data" that informs both student and instructor of the progress and the problems that the student encounters throughout a learning experience (Coatney 2003, 157). It differs from evaluation in that assessment is conducted as an ongoing activity that provides crucial *formative* information about what the student is learning and how that learning is taking place. Students compare their performance against established criteria; they know what is expected before they begin their work (Donham 1998). In contrast, evaluation is a *summative* activity that occurs at the end of a learning experience. Its primary intent is to place a value on the student's performance.

This book focuses on formative assessment. Susan Brookhart, Connie Moss, and Beverly Long (2008) contend that formative assessment "restores students' natural love of learning" (52). Its real power comes from student-to-teacher and student-to-student communication. This type of assessment convinces students that "teachers really want to understand what and how they think, rather than whether they know the right answers" (Brookhart, Moss, and Long 2008, 53). Carol Ann Tomlinson (2008b) further describes formative assessment as "informative assessment" that can be informal as well as formal (9). While checklists and rubrics may be developed and used, observations and conferences are less formal but equally valid approaches to assessment. The important thing to realize is that assessment is not separate from the curriculum and that it permits students to think for themselves and openly share their understandings.

WHAT'S HAPPENING WITH ASSESSMENT IN OUR SCHOOLS?

For almost three decades, assessment has been the intense focus of our nation's educational reform agenda. Rather than viewing curriculum, instruction, and assessment as having a linear relationship, the current perspective emphasizes an interactive, dynamic relationship among these three key elements. The contrastive models are depicted in Figures 2.1 and 2.2.

Cognitive learning theory and its constructivist approach to knowledge acquisition support this dynamic process. In this model captured in Figure 2.2, assessment is fully integrated with instructional outcomes and curriculum content (Herman, Aschbacker, and Winters 1992). This interactive concept of assessment is part of a larger paradigm shift in which learning and understanding are seen as a spiraling, student-focused process. In this process, assessment becomes critical in reshaping and reordering knowledge through action and reflection. The aim of assessment becomes *educating and improving* student performance, not merely *auditing* it (Wiggins 1998).

If we view assessment as a *learning tool* that serves both the instructor and student, there are two important underlying assumptions:

1. Students must be central partners in assessment.

By participating in assessment, students figure out what they are doing and where they are heading. Emerging brain research supports learning theories that propose we interpret the world through our men-

Figure 2.1
Linear model of relationships among curriculum, instruction, and evaluation.

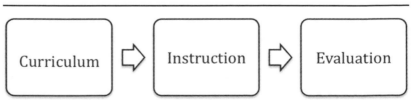

Figure 2.2
Dynamic model of relationships among curriculum, instruction,
and assessment.

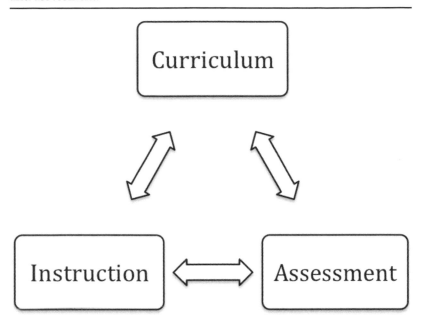

tal models (Pinker 1997). Therefore it is important to involve students from the beginning to help them shape anticipatory mental models of their learning. When students participate in the assessment process, they develop the following behaviors (Chappuis and Stiggins 2002):

- Students understand what is expected.
- They access prior knowledge.
- They have ownership over making the learning happen.
- They are able to give themselves, as well as others, descriptive feedback as they are learning.
- Assessment goes beyond *measuring*; it becomes *motivating*.

Tomlinson (2008b) captures the essence of self-assessment as follows:

When students clearly understood the learning objectives, knew precisely what success would look like, understood how each assignment contributed to their success, could articulate the role of assessment in ensuring their success, and understood that their work correlated with their needs, they developed a sense of self-efficacy that was powerful in their lives as learners. (13)

In spite of the benefits associated with self-regulated learning, researchers have reported that a majority of students are not adequately
self-regulating (Perry, Phillips, and Hutchinson 2006). This finding
is certainly not surprising when we realize that students have few
opportunities in school to regulate their learning (Parsons 2008). Reform efforts, therefore, must emphasize the importance of guiding
students to assume increasing levels of self-responsibility and self-
appraisal. Instructors must provide opportunities for students to reflect
on their work through various means—for example, exit cards, journal
entries, checklists, and rubrics—that aid them in thinking about their
strengths and identifying areas for improvement in their present and
future work. Self-assessment doesn't mean that students control decisions regarding what will or won't be learned. It means they discover
ways to identify how they learn best and how they can channel their
creative energies to empower themselves.

   2. Teachers must view assessment as integral and ongoing.

   As we stated in Chapter 1, instructors must not view assessment
as "an *add on* to the curriculum, something to be squeezed in, something for which time must be found. It must be seen as *a part* of
pedagogy rather than *apart* from it" (Adkison and Tchudi 2000, 3–4).
Seen in this light, assessment is an indispensable tool to inform and
strengthen teaching. It is integrated throughout the instruction rather
than limited to final outcomes. It takes place consistently and con-
stantly. Formative assessment accentuates students' strengths and
capitalizes on their interests and learning preferences. Tomlinson
(2008b) says that when educators build on students' "positive space,
the results are wonderful...students have a sense of possibility" (12).
In short, assessment becomes an empowering tool for learning and
teaching (Guskey 2003).

HOW DOES NO CHILD LEFT BEHIND AFFECT ASSESSMENT?

The landmark authorization of the No Child Left Behind (NCLB) Act
represented a sweeping overhaul of federal support for K–12 education in the United States based on schools meeting state content
standards. NCLB required that states implement comprehensive
accountability systems covering all students in the public schools. It
also necessitated annual testing of students against state standards
in reading, mathematics, and science. Sharon Coatney (2003) makes

a critical point that such testing has its place in "sorting and ranking schools, defining school improvement goals, and if used correctly, helping monitor and ensure school quality" (158). The individual states are responsible for determining their own tests and ensuring that these tests are aligned with the state's curriculum standards. Michael Eisenberg (2004) indicates that districts and states should take the initiative to show the relationship between information literacy skills instruction and student performance on these tests. They can do this by conducting an item analysis to determine the test's alignment with information literacy instruction (Eisenberg 2004).

Coatney (2003) maintains that this type of large-scale testing is usually "not very helpful in determining *individual student needs* or informing students about their *progress on specific learning goals*" (158). The upshot is that while standardized tests figure prominently in NCLB, this federal initiative also necessitates that assessment programs include *multiple measures* to appraise students' higher-order thinking skills (Education Commission of the States 2002).

Given that NCLB acknowledges learning as a complex and variegated process, a variety of assessment tools must be administered so that the results can be triangulated to ensure reliable data collection (Farmer 2003). Authentic assessment of performance in the classroom and the library media center is a critical measure of students' achievement and motivation (Callison 2003). In short, a balance between standardized tests for *accountability* purposes and school-level assessment for *improved teaching and learning* in the classrooms offers students a powerful way to demonstrate mastery of content, skills, and dispositions essential for their success in the larger community (Partnership for 21st Century Skills 2007).

DO EFFECTIVE LIBRARY MEDIA PROGRAMS MAKE A DIFFERENCE?

There is a growing body of research that indicates effective library media programs positively affect student achievement. Among the most widely cited research have been the numerous studies undertaken by Keith Curry Lance and colleagues (cited in Todd 2003). These surveys—involving hundreds of primary and secondary schools in states such as Colorado, Alaska, Pennsylvania, New Mexico, Oregon, and Texas—have empirically established the relationship of school library programs to student achievement. One common finding across these surveys has been a positive correlation between schools with professionally trained library media specialists and students' performance on achievement tests.

Students themselves voiced overwhelming support for school library media centers as important sources for learning in a survey commissioned by the Ohio Educational Library Media Association (Whelan 2004). Ross Todd and Carol Kuhlthau of Rutgers University's Center for International Scholarship in School Libraries conducted the study, which involved over 13,000 students in grades 3 to 12. Over 90 percent of the student respondents indicated that use of computers in the school library media centers improved their overall academic work. They also noted that instruction in the libraries helped them earn better grades on projects and assignments (88.5%) and assisted them with homework (74.7%) (Whelan 2004).

In the international arena, the Council for Museums, Archives and Libraries in Scotland has conducted equally critical research on the impact of libraries on learning (Williams and Wavell 2001). This investigation provided evidence that school libraries positively influenced a range of critical areas in the acquisition of information, including locating and using information, applying computer technology, strengthening reading comprehension, and developing study habits that encouraged independent learning.

In more recent research conducted in Delaware, Todd (2007) identified teaching foci of school librarians in the area of information literacy and the student learning outcomes resulting from the instruction. While over one-third of the librarians indicated that the instruction helped students become effective researchers, only 4.5 percent were able to articulate learning outcomes linked to curriculum standards and goals. Clearly, more professional development would be imperative to aid library media specialists in implementing evidence-based practice. In another study in New Jersey, Todd's (2007) analysis of students' writing tasks indicated that the students' overall knowledge of their topics increased with instruction but that this knowledge was largely factual. Reason and outcome statements did not substantially increase as students progressed, while cause/consequence and synthesis statements showed a small decline. Studies such as this investigation are extremely useful in determining what school librarians teach, how they teach, and how their teaching might be strengthened.

A powerful, systematic approach to examining teaching and learning in real-life contexts is participation in action research. Carol Gordon (2007) has written extensively on how to conduct action research.

She has also reported on actual studies involving school library media specialists and teachers serving as practitioner-researchers. She indicates: "Action research anchors the school library in the teaching and learning context of the school, enhancing its instructional role, and breaking down barriers between classroom and library" (177).

Library media specialists, as advocates for literacy and learning, must be active consumers of this research. They must have current knowledge of what the research is saying and how this research might help them improve their local situations. There are many avenues to access this information. David Loertscher and Blanche Woolls (2002), Lesley Farmer (2003), Ken Haycock (1999), and Nancy Thomas (2004) have compiled useful research summaries. *School Library Media Research* (http://www.ala.org/aasl/slmr) provides online access to current scholarly research in the field. Journals such as *Teacher Librarian, Knowledge Quest,* and *School Library Monthly* (formerly *School Library Media Activities Monthly*) explore critical themes that delve into the complex issues facing today's library media professionals and include useful research-based features on various aspects of 21st-century learning. In addition, *SCAN,* an Australian journal, and *School Libraries Worldwide,* edited by the International Association of School Librarianship, regularly publish research on the impact of school library programs. These timely sources provide a rich compendium of information that can help library media specialists develop research-based practices.

WHAT IS THE LIBRARY MEDIA SPECIALIST'S ROLE?

While national and international studies regarding the impact of libraries on student achievement are important to the field, the *real evidence is often at the local level.* Todd (2003) maintains that principals and parents "want to hear of local successes...they want to know how their students in particular are benefiting" (14). This requires that library media specialists actively participate in collecting this evidence.

The *AASL Standards for the 21st-Century Learner* (American Association for School Librarians [AASL] 2007) reflects the increasingly complex demands that society places on today's learners. Allison Zmuda and Violet Harada (2008) elaborate: "They focus not only on skills that students need to manage and use information but also emphasize the merging of multiple literacies required for learning in today's media-intense and information-rich landscape" (86).

These standards go beyond the acquisition of discrete skills to a more comprehensive definition of the traits characterizing successful learners. They focus on the learner as a self-regulating and self-monitoring individual. Importantly, Zmuda and Harada (2008) state: "The standards support a culture of inquiry that fosters the development of the dispositions or habits of mind characterizing lifelong learners, who question, struggle with possibilities, and create personal meaning from sharing knowledge and learning with others" (86).

The current AASL standards envision library media centers transitioning from a concentration on providing resources to an emphasis on creating communities that question and inquire about issues, problems, and ideas. This transition challenges library media specialists to view their curriculum as extending beyond the traditional location and retrieval skills to skills in evaluating, synthesizing, and interpreting information and ideas. The paradigm shift requires that a focus on completion of products be tempered with an equal emphasis on the process of learning. It requires that library media specialists expand their data collection beyond the tabulation of quantitative statistics on collection size and circulation to measures of actual student learning. In short, it means shifting *mind-sets* from a concentration on *things* to a focus on *students*. Assessment becomes a shared responsibility with the classroom teacher. Figure 2.3 summarizes the paradigm shift involved.

Figure 2.3
Moving from a focus on resources to a focus on student learning.

Focus on providing resources	*Focus on student learning*
Teach skills that involve location and retrieval of library resources.	Teach skills that involve evaluation, synthesis, and interpretation of information.
Emphasize product.	Emphasize process as well as product.
Measure effectiveness through data on library's collection size, circulation, etc.	Measure effectiveness through how well students meet learning objectives.
View assessment as evaluating products, giving final grades.	View assessment as an ongoing examination of learning.
Believe that assessment is solely the responsibility of the teacher.	Believe that assessment is a shared responsibility with the teacher.

Benefits of Assessment

Students grow as learners when they participate in the assessment process. They become aware that the library media center and the classroom are part of the larger learning community with mutual targets and expectations. Students gain the following benefits:

- They are clearer about learning targets because the library media specialist is communicating learning expectations up front.
- They are more keenly motivated to learn because they know what is expected and how they can participate in the assessment of their own learning.

There are equally important benefits for the teacher and the library media specialist that are borne out by the research:

- Both instructors have a *map* for planning curriculum and instructional activities. They know more specifically what they hope to accomplish and have criteria to describe the outcomes expected. Thus assessment itself becomes an instructional activity (Asp 1998).
- When instructors assess for learning, positive changes happen. They include more opportunities for peer learning and collaboration, more choices for students in the learning environment, more integrated and interdisciplinary teaching, and increased use of learning contexts that stretch beyond the walls of the school (Falk 2000).
- Library media specialists, who are active in curriculum planning and instruction, provide support in specific areas of higher-order thinking that include the skills and processes students need to access resources and information, think about ideas, and create their own approaches to information-related problems (Tallman 1995).
- For the library media specialists, documentation of the assessment results provides a compelling case for the value of the library program. When issues of funding accountability arise and decision makers identify priorities for staffs and budgets based on programs that *show student improvement,* library media specialists can produce student-focused data to support their requests.

Essential Questions for the Library Media Specialist

The following questions are critical ones for library media specialists seeking to assess for learning that occurs in their programs.

- What difference does my library media program make to students and their learning?
- What does this learning look like?
- What is the student able to do? What does the student know?
- How do my students and I assess for this learning?
- How do I organize and communicate this assessment data?

In the ensuing chapters, we tackle the preceding questions, which are essential for assessing a dynamic program for learning.

CONCLUSION

No one can provide a one size fits all formula for designing and implementing assessments that can be used for all curricula and all students. The individual school community must craft assessment tools and strategies for students' mastery of information literacy tailored to the needs of its own school setting (Neuman 2000). As members of the school community, library media specialists have an opportunity to join the action and provide evidence of best practices that contribute to high-quality learning in their schools.

Todd (2002) supports the importance of assessment as the key to evidence-based practice thusly:

> The hallmark of a school library in the 21st century is not the teacher-librarian, nor its collections, systems, technology, staffing, or buildings (although we would all acknowledge that these, however, are critical). It is *actions* and *evidences* that show what makes a real difference to student learning, and that the teacher-librarian contributes in tangible and significant ways to the development of human understanding, meaning making, and constructing knowledge. (35)

Finally, assessment is built on the assumption that each student brings strengths to his or her work. It becomes the collective job of all adult mentors, including library media specialists, to bring these strengths to the surface so that all can benefit (Tomlinson 2008b).

CHAPTER 3

Tools for Assessment: Checklists, Rubrics, and Rating Scales

In this chapter, we look more closely at checklists, rubrics, and rating scales as tools for assessing student performance. The discussion for each tool is organized around the following key questions:

- What is it?
- When might we use this tool?
- How do we construct this tool?
- How do we use it to assess for information literacy?

To be used effectively, each of these tools requires that

- Criteria have been established to assess the quality of work in progress.
- Students are engaged in continuous use of the tools to gauge their own progress.
- Teachers and library media specialists examine the results to inform their own instruction.

Assessment tools and strategies are as varied as the goals of learning and the students themselves. Because learning goals differ in fundamental ways, instructors have developed a wide range of options to collect evidence of learning. We have found the following procedure to be useful in creating tools that assess a variety of learning goals:

- Start by identifying the specific learning goals to be achieved through the lesson.
- Determine the criteria for a successful performance.
- Design the tool to facilitate instruction and support independent learning.
- Encourage ownership on the part of learners by using the language of students.
- When appropriate, include a scoring system that is tied to the tool itself.

A few simple questions might help us to improve the assessment tools we are already using. For example, in reviewing existing tools we might ask ourselves:

- Is the goal of the lesson stated?
- Are criteria for a successful performance clearly indicated?
- Does the tool offer a structure that facilitates and guides the learning?
- Does the language used in the tool reflect the language of students?
- Will the tool be easily understood and used by students?
- Is there a system for analyzing and rating performance (e.g., a scoring guide or rating scale)?

CHECKLISTS

What Is a Checklist?

A checklist is a list of dimensions, characteristics, or behaviors needed for successful completion of the task. It can include criteria for both process and product. "Checklists are usually scored as 'yes-no' ratings. They do not tell you the *extent* to which behaviors are observed or the *quality* of the performance. They tell you only that a specified behavior was displayed" (Herman, Aschbacker, and Winters 1992, 64–65).

When it is given at the beginning of the assignment, the checklist may guide students through the research process (Donham 1998). Teachers and library media specialists use checklists to focus their observations on critical aspects of the process.

When Might We Use a Checklist?

The checklist is especially useful as a tool for observing students as they work on projects involving several layers of learning. It is one way to lessen the subjectivity that often plagues more casual observations. Feedback and observation checklists are particularly helpful during cooperative learning projects, group presentations, and class discussions (Strickland and Strickland 2000). Checklists are also useful in conferencing with students because teachers can glance over the lists and quickly pick up where they left off at the last conference.

The checklist helps students as well as the teacher and library media specialist by focusing attention on important aspects of the task. For example:

- Students use the checklist at the outset to assess their abilities in terms of the requirements of the assignment and to get an overview of the entire process. At the completion of the task the same checklist is used to reflect on the learning process.
- Teachers and the library media specialist use the checklist as an instructional tool to focus attention on the requirements for a particular performance. The same checklist is used to provide feedback as students are working on the task and as a final assessment indicating whether criteria have been met.

In short, checklists keep instructors and students focused on what is important, and they provide a record of student progress.

How Do We Construct a Checklist?

Checklists must be tailored to the requirements of the specific assignment. Figure 3.1 suggests questions that might be used to develop an observation checklist.

A well-constructed checklist has the following characteristics:

- It identifies behaviors that relate to the standards and the instructional goals.
- It focuses the observation on critical aspects of the task.
- It provides evidence linking student achievement with instructional goals.
- It serves as an assessment tool for both students and instructors.

Figure 3.1
Questions used to create an observation checklist.

- What standards do we need to assess?

- What are our instructional goals?

- How will students demonstrate their proficiency in meeting a standard?

- What are the observable or measurable indicators of success?

How Do We Use a Checklist to Assess for Information Literacy?

GRADE 2 SCENARIO

Second graders are involved in a unit study about animal adaptation. The unit engages students in an inquiry cycle that begins with the selection of an animal from a particular habitat. The student asks questions related to the theme of adaptation and identifies resources that might answer those questions. The final task will be to create a riddle book that includes clues about the animal and a picture of the animal adapting to its habitat. After students share their riddle books with research buddies, the books will be placed on display in the library media center so that other children can enjoy and respond to them.

The unit addresses content standards for reading, writing, oral communication, science, and visual arts. Evidence of learning is gathered through observation, conferencing, and the examination of student work. The library media specialist sees the project as an opportunity to teach and assess student achievement related to the first standard for 21st-century learning—inquire, think critically, and gain knowledge (American Association of School Librarians [AASL] 2007). She works closely with the teachers to design instruction that targets an important second grade benchmark: Follow a modeled inquiry process during each visit to the library to do research (AASL 2007, Standard 1.1.1). With input from teachers, she develops a checklist (Figure 3.2) to assess the skill of accessing information in a variety of formats and sources. Students also use the checklist to record their perceptions about how they are learning.

RUBRICS

What Is a Rubric?

A rubric is an instrument that employs a grid design to define components of a task as well as gradations of quality (Strickland and Strickland 2000). It identifies criteria for successful work and describes different levels or ranges of performance (Todd 2003; Callison 2003). Rubrics differ from other scoring guides in that they describe in detail the qualities that make a performance strong, adequate, or weak.

Figure 3.2
Checklist for assessing access to information in various sources.

Goal for this lesson: I will locate information about my topic in at least three resources.			
My tasks *I can . . .*	*Yes, I can do it.*	*No, I can't do it yet. I need help with:*	*Comments from me or my teachers*
Choose search words.			
Find a book in the online catalog.			
Use the call number to locate a book.			
Use the table of contents to find my topic.			
Use the index to find the page.			
Find my topic in the online encyclopedia.			
Find my topic in a print encyclopedia.			
Find my topic on a Web site that I can read.			

Scoring guide:
- I **exceed** the goal by completing six to eight tasks. For the tasks that I do not complete, I say what I need help with.
- I **meet** the goal by completing four or five tasks. For at least two of the tasks I don't complete, I say what I need help with.
- I am **getting started** on the goal if I complete one or two tasks. I am not too sure what I need help with.

A well-designed rubric is both a tool for assessment and a powerful teaching strategy. Although rubrics can take different formats, they have two characteristics in common:

- A list of criteria for a successful performance
- A description of varying levels of performance (Andrade 2000)

When Might We Use a Rubric?

Rubrics are best used to assess complex tasks, such as written compositions, projects and exhibits, and research assignments (Andrade 2000).

Assessment of the information literacy standards engages students in authentic tasks that challenge them to think, problem solve, communicate, and demonstrate various skills ranging in complexity from asking questions that focus an inquiry to producing a product that demonstrates rigor, relevance, and creativity. Students might demonstrate their growing personal knowledge of the information literacy standards in the following ways:

- They employ an inquiry process to build personal knowledge about a subject.
- They access, evaluate, and use information from a variety of sources.
- They read and enjoy a range of literary genres including fiction, informational pieces, poetry, and traditional stories.
- They collaborate with others to create products and exhibitions that are useful to members of the community.

Rick Stiggins (1997) has identified knowledge, reasoning, skills, products, and dispositions as instructional targets for which performance assessments would be appropriate. Clearly, all of these instructional goals are embedded in the *Standards for the 21st-Century Learner* (American Association of School Librarians [AASL] 2007). The challenge is to define our instructional targets and to design a performance task through which each target can be assessed.

Since performance tasks require students to work independently and to monitor their own progress, the rubric can be used as a tool for instruction as well as assessment. By describing the elements of a successful performance, the rubric takes the guesswork out of learning. Students learn to use the rubric to self-assess as they work on different phases of the project.

How Do We Construct an Instructional Rubric?

Rubrics serve more than one purpose. Some rubrics are designed by teachers as tools for evaluation. These rubrics may use technical language not easily understood by students. This is in contrast to what Heidi Goodrich Andrade (2000) calls an *instructional rubric*—one that is used for instruction as well as assessment. Since we believe that, to the extent possible, students should have a voice in deciding how their work will be assessed, we share the experiences we have had creating instructional rubrics with our students.

Designing and using instructional rubrics begins with involving students in a discussion of work samples that focus on the question

"What makes good work?" The process includes brainstorming, discussion, and decision making—all of which have the effect of engaging students in a serious conversation about quality. To create rubrics for our own projects, we have drawn from an instructional model developed by Andrade (2000). Although there may be variations, the model generally includes the steps outlined in Figure 3.3.

Figure 3.3
Steps in creating a rubric.

Steps in creating a rubric	What is involved
Present models of student work.	Models may be anonymous samples of student work, videotapes of students working on a similar task, etc.
Discuss "What makes good work?"	In small groups, students discuss which models represent the best work or the best performance and the qualities that make it best. Responses are noted on chart paper.
Explain the assignment and need for assessment criteria.	The teacher or library media specialist explains what students will be doing. The discussion of quality is related to the requirements of the assignment.
Discuss and select criteria for assessment.	Students review all of the charts and select no more than six criteria critical to successful performance in terms of the current assignment. (Limiting the number forces students to focus on what is most important.)
Draft a rubric.	The teacher and library media specialist draw upon the classroom discussion to create a rubric that identifies assessment criteria and describes different levels of performance.
Practice using the rubric.	Students practice using the rubric to assess work samples. Following the practice session, the rubric itself is assessed.
Revise the rubric.	Teachers and library media specialists draw upon students' comments and experience to revise the rubric.
Use the rubric to instruct, guide, and assess.	A revised copy of the rubric is given to each student. Students use it to self-assess, and instructors use it to monitor progress.

How Do We Use Rubrics to Assess for Information Literacy?

GRADE 8 SCENARIO

Eighth-grade students have identified "freedom" as a theme that runs throughout American history. They have learned how the desire for freedom from poverty, oppression, and other forms of injustice fueled colonization of America. They are impressed with stories of the pioneers who crossed the continent at great personal risk to exercise their freedom of self-determination. They commiserate with the plight of black slaves, Native Americans, and new immigrants who had to fight for freedom despite the rights promised by the U.S. Constitution. Now they are about to learn how the First Amendment to the Bill of Rights guarantees that every American will continue to live in freedom.

Teachers introduce the new unit by asking students to discuss what is meant by freedom of speech, religion, and press. They record responses to these questions on chart paper that is posted for discussion and review. Over the course of two weeks, students scour the news media for current events depicting one of these freedoms being challenged. Students also begin generating a list of questions about the First Amendment that can be used to reinforce the essential question: "How does the First Amendment protect our freedom?"

The library media specialist works with the teachers to design a performance task that uses the inquiry process to build knowledge and understanding. The following assignment is made.

GRADE 8 ASSIGNMENT

We will be holding a constitutional convention that focuses on the Bill of Rights. As delegates to the convention, we will each make a speech in which we address a current situation that challenges one of the freedoms protected by the First Amendment. In our presentations we should include some historical background and explain how an attack on this freedom affects our own lives and the larger society in which we live. Finally, we should suggest what can and should be done to protect the rights guaranteed by the Constitution.

Figure 3.4
Rubric for note taking.

Goal for the lesson: I will take notes that answer my questions and help me prepare my presentation.			
Criteria *My notes should be*	*Advanced*	*Proficient*	*Basic*
Accurate and complete	<u>All</u> information is accurate.	My information is accurate but may not be complete.	Some facts are not accurate.
	My notes include both historical facts and ideas related to freedom.	My notes include some historical facts (names, dates, places, etc.).	No examples from history are given.
	My notes have enough details to support main ideas. My information comes from reliable sources.	My sources are given.	My sources are not listed.
Related to my topic and research questions	All notes are about freedom and the First Amendment.	My notes are about freedom, but some don't connect to the First Amendment.	It is not clear how my notes relate to freedom.
	My notes answer all my research questions.	The notes answer most of my research questions.	Some notes do not directly answer my research questions.
Meaningful to me	All the notes are in my own words.	**Some** of my notes are copied from the source. They are not meaningful to me.	All of my notes are copied directly from the sources.
	I know the meaning of every word I use.	I understand the meaning of **most** words in my notes.	My notes don't make sense to me.

(continued)

Figure 3.4 *(Continued)*

Criteria *My notes should be*	*Advanced*	*Proficient*	*Basic*
Well organized	All the notes that answer a question are grouped together.	My notes are grouped by the questions they answer.	There is no organization to my notes.
	Bullets are used to separate notes.	It is hard to tell where one note ends and the next begins.	My notes are just a list of facts about freedom.

Directions for self-assessment: *Use the rubric to assess your notes and make needed improvements. Then check and complete the statement that best describes your work.*

My notes show that
☐ I can take notes that answer my questions accurately and completely. My next step is

_____

☐ I have some notes that help answer my questions, but here is something I can do to improve them:

_____

☐ My notes do not answer my questions. Here are some changes I will work on:

_____

_____

The task involved students in an inquiry process that began with selecting a topic, generating questions, and gathering information from a variety of resources. Through observation, three things became apparent to the instructors:

- Students were quite proficient at accessing information in both print and electronic resources.
- The information being gathered was general in nature and did little to address the specific research questions.
- Students did not know how to extract information that was critical to their research questions.

The library media specialist identified note taking as a skill that needed to be developed and offered to take the lead in teaching this part of the process. Following the procedures outlined earlier in Figure 3.3, she involved students in designing a rubric for the note-taking process. Figure 3.4 displays the rubric created by instructors with help from students.

RATING SCALES

What Is a Rating Scale?

A rating scale is similar to a rubric in that it identifies the criteria for successful performance. The critical difference is that the rating scale does not describe varying levels of achievement. Instead, it provides a scale ranging from the highest to the lowest performance levels.

When Might We Use a Rating Scale?

A rating scale is used when the task involves multiple performance targets that need to be assessed. It is used to focus the assessment on specified targets, thereby eliminating some of the subjectivity associated with observation of complex tasks. The rating scale is used effectively in situations where performance can be placed along a continuum ranging from the lowest to the highest level of achievement.

Rating scales can be numerical or qualitative. A *numerical scale* uses numbers or assigns points to a continuum of performance levels. The number of scale points can vary. A *qualitative scale* uses adjectives rather than numbers to characterize and label student performance (Herman, Aschbacker, and Winters 1992).

How Do We Construct a Rating Scale?

The first step in constructing any assessment tool is to identify the instructional targets. We approach the construction of the rating scale in much the same way that we develop the rubric—by discussing the components of good work. This discussion leads to the identification of criteria that need to be assessed. In Figure 3.5 we look at four instructional targets identified for the Bill of Rights project and consider what might be accepted as evidence that the goals have been met.

Figure 3.5
Evidence to assess instructional targets for Bill of Rights unit.

Instructional target	Evidence of learning
Knowledge/understanding	Shows knowledge of the Bill of Rights. Demonstrates understanding of the rights protected by the First Amendment. Explains the concept of freedom and how it affects his or her own life.
Thinking	Interprets historical events in relation to the First Amendment. Connects current events with history. Expresses a personal point of view about the importance of freedom.
Inquiry and independent learning skills	Poses questions to focus research. Accesses and evaluates information sources. Collects and organizes information. Prepares and presents findings. Assesses process and product.
Presentation	Includes both facts and ideas. Uses facts and information to support a point of view. States what should be done to protect freedom. Speaks clearly and effectively.

How Do We Use a Rating Scale to Assess for Information Literacy?

We continue with the grade 8 scenario to demonstrate how a rating scale might be incorporated into this unit. As students worked on different phases of the project, the library media specialist saw a need to focus assessment on those aspects of the project that involved inquiry and independent learning. She designed the rating scale presented in Figure 3.6 to focus her observations and rate each student's performance along a continuum. In this example, a numerical scale is used to indicate an assessment at a particular point in time. Four points would indicate the highest level of achievement, and one point would be the lowest. Assessments taken at different points in the process are dated and compared to

Figure 3.6
Rating scale for assessing targeted aspects of the inquiry process.

Instructors Rating Scale for Bill of Rights Research Project			
1. Are meaningful questions asked about the Bill of Rights, the First Amendment, and the importance of freedom in American life?			
1	2	3	4
2. Is the student using a variety of sources to answer questions?			
1	2	3	4
3. Is the student evaluating sources for accuracy and relevance?			
1	2	3	4
4. Do notes answer the research questions accurately and completely?			
1	2	3	4
5. Does the presentation link the First Amendment to what is happening today?			
1	2	3	4
6. Does the final presentation show that the First Amendment has personal meaning for this student?			
1	2	3	4
Overall assessment of student's progress: _____			
Date: _____			

indicate whether progress is being made. Periodically, rating scales are shared with teachers to compare assessment data and to plan appropriate interventions.

A similar rating scale (Figure 3.7) is designed for use by students as they self-assess their final presentations. In this example, students use a qualitative scale to rate how well they performed.

CONCLUSION

The tools described in this chapter are critical front-end instruments that require instructors and students to define criteria for assessment. Precise criteria make it possible to give meaningful feedback, not just "I like it" or "This is well done" but *why* and *how*. They allow instructors to identify deficiencies in a timely manner. At the same time, students

Figure 3.7
Rating scale for self-assessing Bill of Rights presentation.

Self-Assessment of My Presentation
Goal of my presentation: I will show why the First Amendment is important in my life and in the lives of all Americans.

In my presentation I will…

Identify a situation in which a basic freedom is under attack today.

> *I do this very well.*   *I'm getting there.*   *I'm not there yet.*

Show how the current problem affects my own life.

> *I do this very well.*   *I'm getting there.*   *I'm not there yet.*

Provide some historical background about the freedom that is under attack.

> *I do this very well.*   *I'm getting there.*   *I'm not there yet.*

Explain how the denial of this freedom is an attack on the First Amendment.

> *I do this very well.*   *I'm getting there.*   *I'm not there yet.*

Suggest something that can be done to protect the rights guaranteed by the First Amendment.

> *I do this very well.*   *I'm getting there.*   *I'm not there yet.*

My overall assessment

Something I did very well:

_____

_____

Something I can improve on:

_____

_____

Something I need help with:

_____

_____

can immediately see what is expected for an assignment (Strickland and Strickland 2000). Involving students in creating and using these tools strengthens their confidence in analyzing their own work (Harada and Yoshina 1997). Such assessment empowers everyone involved in the learning process.

CHAPTER 4

Tools for Assessment: Conferences, Logs, Personal Correspondence, and Exit Passes

In this chapter, we look more closely at assessment tools that invite interaction and communication. The tools highlighted are conferences, logs, personal correspondence, and exit passes. As in Chapter 3, discussions are organized around the following key questions:

- What is it?
- When might we use this tool?
- How might we construct this tool?
- How might we use it to assess for information literacy?

CONFERENCES

What Is a Conference?

An assessment conference is any conversation between instructors and students for the purpose of gathering information related to important aspects of a particular learning situation. According to Rick Stiggins (1997) the most natural way to gather achievement data is to talk to the students. The communication may take the form of a casual conversation, a simple question to check for understanding, or a formal interview with specific goals.

When Might We Use Conferences to Assess Learning?

Conferences, which may be formal or informal, take place throughout the day whenever there is a need for information related to learning. Informal conferences occur when the instructor asks a question or engages the student in an on-the-spot conversation to clarify thinking or check for understanding. Librarians often gather needed information by asking questions like:

- Why did you select this resource? Are there any other resources that might be helpful?
- What keywords did you use? Can you think of other terms to search?
- How can you narrow your topic? What aspects of the topic are most interesting to you?
- What else do you want to find out about the topic?

This kind of natural exchange has a flexibility not associated with more structured assessment strategies. Informal conferences such as these are best used when there is an immediate need for information to guide the learning.

The formal conference, on the other hand, is more like an interview. Formal conferences may be held at specific points in the process so that instructors can monitor progress. For example, conferences held early in the process may focus on topic selection, research questions, or search strategies. Later, students may sign up for conferences to review their notes with the teacher before they work on their presentations. Other conferences are held after the presentation to assess both the process and product. Often the conference schedule is determined in advance and included in each student's action plan.

The library media specialist can play an important role in these conferences. If the goal is for students to become independent users of information, instruction will more than likely follow an information search model. Students will be expected to demonstrate skill in areas like selecting topics and issues; questioning; and accessing, evaluating, organizing, and using information. Scheduling a quick conference early in the process provides an opportunity to identify students who are struggling so that adjustments can be made in a timely manner.

While conferences can be highly effective instructional tools, it is important to note that the formal conference, in particular, is labor intensive. We suggest several ways of managing the task:

- Hold group interviews whenever possible. This works best when students are engaged in team projects.
- Divide up the work. The teacher may briefly confer with students about their topic selection and research questions. The library media specialist may follow up by reviewing search strategies and suggesting additional resources.

- Hold conferences on a selective basis. Use work samples and observations to determine which students need more guidance. Schedule conferences with these students, but insist that every student present evidence of achievement before proceeding.

The time spent talking to students about their research questions, search strategies, and possible resources pays big dividends in terms of the overall success of the project.

How Do We Structure the Conference?

The formal conference, in particular, needs to be planned to ensure success. Questions like the following help us plan for upcoming conferences:

- Which of the instructional targets are best assessed through conferences or interviews?
- What information do we want to gather through the conference?
- What questions will help to elicit the desired information?
- How can we use the interview to guide the student through the process?

Once the conference targets have been clearly identified, instructors develop a list of questions to guide the interview toward evidence collection. Figure 4.1 includes several instructional targets and related interview questions that might be used to shape a conference.

Figure 4.1
Linking conferencing questions with instructional targets.

Instructional targets	Interview questions
Knowledge and understanding	What is the most important thing you learned about your topic? How does this relate to your own life?
Research questions	What else would you like to find out about your topic? Which questions will lead to a deeper understanding of the issues?
Notes	How do these notes help answer your research question? Can you think of any examples to make this point clear?
Product	Who will be your audience? How can you best share your knowledge with them?

How Do We Use Conferences to Assess
for Information Literacy?

Conferencing is a potent tool for developing and assessing information literacy. Many of the exchanges that are so natural to the
instructional setting provide valuable information about achievement
in terms of information literacy skills. As students work on their projects, teachers and library media specialists often ask questions that
focus on elements of the research process or product. Those casual
conversations that go beyond a simple "How are you doing?" often
provide valuable insight into how students are approaching the task.
Picture the following scenario.

GRADE 6 SCENARIO

Sixth graders are exploring the theme of civilization. They wrestle
with two overarching questions:

- How can we identify an ancient civilization?
- What aspects of this civilization are still alive in our world
  today?

Students work in teams to investigate the origin of specific
civilizations, summarize their defining features, and identify
aspects of these civilizations that still influence our lives today.
They use an inquiry process that involves posing questions to
drive the research, identifying appropriate resources, reading
and evaluating information, taking notes, and creating a product or performance. As a final presentation, all of the sixth-grade
classes work on a museum of ancient history where they display
their products, give performances, and hold competitions (e.g.,
the Olympics). The entire school community is invited to participate in the activities.

Throughout the project, a class matrix keeps students focused
on the essential questions surrounding the characteristics of civi-
lized societies. Students use the matrix to record their findings
and to make generalizations about the civilizations being inves-
tigated by various search teams.

For the project described in the scenario, conferencing was included
in the plan from the beginning. Students were instructed at the outset

to conference with either the teacher or the library media specialist before they began working on their final presentations. They were asked to bring to the conference their research questions, notes, and ideas about how best to share their findings. These items became the focus for the final conference.

Throughout the project, the instructors regularly engaged students in conversation as they worked on the process and the product. In the following example, the library media specialist (LMS) and a student are discussing the merits of using the Internet to find information about pyramids.

Excerpt from a conference:

LMS: "Who was the author of this Web page?"
Student: "It was part of a class project so I guess it was done by a student."
LMS: "Do you think it's a reliable source?"
Student: "I don't know. Maybe I can check out her sources. Some of them are on the Internet so they should be easy to find."
LMS: "Where else could you look for information comparing Egyptian pyramids with those built in the New World?"
Student: "Well, the Internet is really a great resource, but I guess I could check out some of the books the library has on ancient Egypt."

Informal exchanges, like the one just described, helped students to think about the task in different ways. In this situation, the library media specialist prodded the student to think more critically about information found on the Internet. Similar conversations provided guidance and directions as students worked on the different phases of the information search process.

As data were acquired through various assessment strategies, the instructors began to identify students in need of more guidance and support. For these students, more structured conferences were scheduled to pinpoint problems and provide necessary direction. The classroom teacher usually initiated these conferences. However, in many instances the library media specialist was asked to follow up when students needed help with search strategies, alternative resources, or other areas specific to the information search process.

LOGS

What Is a Log?

The log is a valuable tool for self-assessment and reflection that can be used by students to monitor their own learning. Students use logs to reflect on what they are learning, how they are learning, and how they feel about the process. Keeping logs encourages students to express their feelings, to reflect on different aspects of the topic, to articulate problems they are having, and to put out a call for help.

Logs have many uses in both classroom and library settings. Students use them to clarify questions, identify themes, summarize ideas, review discussions, plan future applications, and pose solutions to problems. They are especially powerful tools when students use them to share ideas and interact with teachers and peers. Importantly, instructors often use logs to assess the effectiveness of their teaching and identify valuable clues to student needs and insights (Harada 2002). They allow instructors to get inside the minds of all students and not just those who are highly verbal.

The key to using logs as an assessment tool lies with the prompt. It is critical to design prompts that target specific goals. If, for example, one of the objectives is for students to pursue information that satisfies their own personal interests, the prompt might be: "What aspects of the general topic are you most interested in? How does this topic relate to your own life?"

When Might We Use Logs as Assessment Tools?

Although the primary purpose of the log is to encourage students to think more deeply about their work, teachers and librarians sometimes assess learning by reading and evaluating students' responses to specific prompts. The log becomes an assessment tool when three components are present:

- A learning goal that focuses on standards or benchmarks
- A prompt that clearly targets the learning goal
- Assessment criteria that describe expectations for an acceptable response

Figure 4.2 presents examples of journal prompts that might be used to assess different learning goals, including: skills, dispositions, and

Figure 4.2
Matching journal prompts with AASL *Standards for*
the 21st-Century Learner.

Assessment targets	Learning goals	Prompts	Assessment criteria
Skill	Use prior and background knowledge as a context for new learning (AASL Standard 1.1.2).	What do I know about the topic? How do I know this?	I state three things I know about the topic. I explain how I came to know this.
		Where can I look for more background information?	I state one or more places to look for more background information.
Disposition	Display initiative by posing questions and investigating the answers beyond the collection of superficial facts (AASL Standard 1.2.1).	What questions do I have related to the essential question?	All of my questions relate to the essential question.
		Which of my questions target basic facts about the topic?	I have questions that ask who, what, when, and where.
		Which questions will lead to deeper understanding?	I have questions that ask how, why, or what if.
Responsibility	Contribute to the exchange of ideas within the learning community (AASL Standard 1.3.4).	What did I contribute to today's discussion?	I state at least one thing that I contributed to the discussion.
		Did others appreciate my contributions? How do I know this?	I reflect on how my contributions were received.
		What did I learn by listening to others?	I write at least one thing that I learned by listening to others.

responsibilities. Because self-assessment and reflection are vital to the inquiry process, students help to determine criteria that they use to craft responses and to self-assess their work.

The value of logging is not limited to the information search process. This strategy can be used to assess feelings and attitudes as well as skills and knowledge. When students are asked to respond honestly to a piece of literature by telling how it relates to their own lives, they are encouraged to think more deeply and to make connections they may have overlooked during the initial reading. The resulting entry may provide teachers and library media specialists with a valuable window into the student's thoughts and feelings.

As an example, after fifth graders read the opening chapters of *The Island of the Blue Dolphins*, they were given the following prompts: "Have you ever felt alone or abandoned? How do you think Karana felt when the ship left without her and her brother? What do you think will happen to them?" Note the empathy expressed in one student's response.

EXAMPLE OF A STUDENT LOG

Karana must have really felt abandoned. Her father was killed, and now the boat left with everyone on board but her brother and her. They were all alone on the island except for the wild dogs. She must have been scared stiff, but she had to act brave for her brother's sake. She is very strong on the inside.

I don't think I could have been so tough. What would I do if something happened to my parents and I was left in charge? I wouldn't know how to find food for my sisters and me. And even though I like dogs, I wouldn't know how to protect my sisters from the wild ones that lived on the island.

I think the boat will come back to get them, or maybe they will send a rescue team. Karana can send up smoke signals to let them know where they are. But in the meantime, they will have to live by eating plants and berries and stuff like that. If I were Karana, I would feel very lonely and scared. I hope someone comes for them soon.

To assess journal entries, students are referred back to the initial prompt. The following questions are intended to encourage self-assessment and reflective analysis:

- Did I address the prompt clearly and directly? (Draw a box around the main idea expressed in your response.)
- Did I refer to the literature to make my point? (Underline an example from your response.)
- Did I express how I would have felt in a similar situation? (Circle the word that best expresses your feelings.)

Log keeping is often used in conjunction with other assessment methods. For example, after students have worked on creating a rubric, we might ask them to respond to a question like "Which criteria do you think are most important for a successful project? Why do you think this?" After a conference, we might ask students to reflect on what happened at the conference and if it was helpful. Whether we use it alone to assess students' reactions to a literary experience or as a tool for reflection during a complex project, the journal is an invaluable component of the assessment toolbox.

Figure 4.3
Learning log for primary research projects.

My Research Log

Today I worked on _____

I learned that _____

Here are some problems that I had _____

Tomorrow I am going to _____

This is how I feel about myself as a researcher: (Write your name by the one that is you.)

SAD   HAPPY   CONFUSED

How Do We Facilitate the Use of Logs?

The log may be structured to assess learning targets over time. When this is the intent, students respond to a few prompts on a regular basis so that progress can be measured throughout the process. Figure 4.3 is an example of a log developed to help primary students reflect on their progress as independent learners (see p. 41).

Logs may take many other forms depending on the intended learning goals (S.C.O.R.E. Language Arts n.d.). Here are several examples. Figure 4.4 is an example of a log that requires students to summarize their various learning activities in a project and consider application of that learning.

Figure 4.5 is an example of a log that invites students to share affective as well as cognitive responses.

Figure 4.6 is an example of a log that encourages student response to a literary piece.

Figure 4.4
Example of synthesis log A.

What I did
What I learned
How I can use it

Figure 4.5
Example of synthesis log B.

What happened?	How do I feel about it?	What did I learn as a result?

Figure 4.6
Example of literary response log.

Which of the characters seemed more real to you? Why was this?	
Were you able to make connections between events in the story and your own experiences? How so?	
Were there any striking phrases and images in the story? Why do you think they were chosen? How do they add to the story?	

How Do We Use Logs to Assess for Information Literacy?

GRADE 10 SCENARIO

A high school biology class is investigating the complex relationship between science and ethics. An important goal of the science curriculum is to provide students with a means for understanding how scientific decisions may be influenced by the ethics and values of various groups within the community. With this in mind, biology teachers have designed a unit focusing on recent developments in bioethics. The study is framed by the essential question: "How do values and ethics influence scientific thought?"

Students form search teams to investigate topics like evolution, stem cell research, organ transplants, cloning, and the use of human and animal subjects in scientific experiments. They use various print, electronic, and personal resources to develop an overview of their topics and to identify different points of view related to the issue. The culminating activity is a series of panel discussions focusing on the research topics. Each student on the team expresses the point of view of one of the key parties who might be affected by the research. Class members who are not participating in a particular discussion direct questions at the panel to clarify the issues. Each panel discussion ends with a peer evaluation and a discussion of the values and ethics raised by the team members.

The library media specialist contributes to the process by:

- Helping teachers identify issues for students to investigate
- Providing short articles to introduce the issues
- Helping teachers to keep the discussion focused on values and ethics and their impact on scientific decisions
- Developing mini-lessons on selected phases of the information search process, namely, asking questions to frame the search, identifying potential sources of information, and taking notes to support a particular point of view

Throughout the unit, students use their logs to reflect on what they are learning and how it relates to the essential question. The prompts are carefully chosen to keep students focused on the ethical dimensions of scientific reasoning. For example:

- Why is this research important?
- What arguments are given for and against the research?
- How do you think this research will benefit or harm humanity?
- Who has an interest in supporting or stopping this research? Why?
- Do you think this research might have unintended side effects? What might they be?
- Who should pay for this research? Should it be publicly or privately funded?
- How costly will this research be in terms of both money and unintended consequences? Is the benefit worth the cost?

When the purpose is to assess proficiency in terms of the information literacy standards, the questions may be quite different. Figure 4.7 displays some prompts that are used to gather information needed to assess aspects of information literacy.

This is what one student had to say in response to the question about choice of topic.

EXAMPLE OF A STUDENT LOG

I think I am most interested in stem cell research. I don't know a lot about it, but the article we read says that scientists are using stem cells to cure diseases like Parkinson's and Alzheimer's. My grandfather is in the early stages of Alzheimer's disease. The doctor said that even if he takes his

(continued)

---

medicine, there is no cure for this condition. I saw on TV that some people get so sick that they don't even recognize their own children and grandchildren. I hope this doesn't happen to my grandpa.

Stem cell research may help people with other diseases, too. Scientists don't really know yet where the research will lead, but I think a lot of people will be able to live better lives if the government would support stem cell research. On the other hand, if the research doesn't get funded, more and more people will die from incurable diseases.

Figure 4.7
Prompts for assessing aspects of information literacy.

Purpose of assessment	Example of prompt
Choice of topic	Which scientific developments have the greatest potential for good? For harm? Which research are you most interested in? Why?
Research questions	What do you already know about your choice of topic? What would you need to find out in order to support it or oppose it?
Selecting and evaluating information sources	What criteria did you use to select resources? Which sources did you find most helpful? Which were of little or no help? Give reasons for your response.
Using information to make a persuasive argument	Whose point of view will you represent on the panel? Will you be supporting or opposing continuation of the research? What reasons will you give for your position? How will you validate your information?
Working as a team to produce and communicate knowledge	Was it helpful to work as a team? Why or why not? What did you contribute to the group effort? What did you learn from the panel discussions that you could not have learned on your own?

A reflection like this tells the instructors several things about the writer. Importantly, the student has chosen a topic that is personally meaningful to her. She knows enough about the topic to identify it as an important area for scientific study. She recognizes the value of the research and has some sense of its potential benefits. However, the student does not seem to be aware of the controversy surrounding the topic. The library media specialist suggests that she include a research question focusing on the arguments offered by opponents of stem cell research.

Log keeping is an open-ended process that provides valuable insight into aspects of information literacy that are often difficult to pin down. These include skills and attitudes related to independent learning and social responsibility as well as information literacy. Because collaboration and teamwork were goals of this project, students were asked to express their feelings about the group experience by responding to these questions:

- How did you feel about working with a team on this project?
- How would you rate your contributions to the group?
- Do you think the panel discussion was an effective way of dealing with issues of values and ethics in science?
- What contributed to the success or failure of the project?

The student who selected stem cell research as her project wrote the following in her response.

This reflection clearly indicates that the student sees the benefits of collaboration and understands her role on the team. Log entries from

---

EXAMPLE OF A STUDENT LOG

Being part of a panel discussion was a good experience for me. Because we all represented different parties in the dispute, I got to see how stem cell research was viewed by doctors, patients, and religious groups. I found out that the cost of the research was very high so it was important to convince politicians that it was worthwhile.

One of the first things my group did was to decide who would represent which point of view on the panel. I said I wanted to speak for the families of people with Alzheimer's. Other kids took the parts of a patient, a doctor, a taxpayer, and a senator whose committee decided which health-related projects to fund.

(continued)

> Everyone agreed that we needed to begin the research by find-ing out what the pros and cons were for experimenting with stem cells. We also wanted to get information about the other diseases that might be cured through stem cell research; and our teacher said that we should learn more about how stem cells work. After we wrote our questions, we made a list of all the resources we could use. Then we divided up the work.
>
> Even though we worked well together, we didn't always agree about things like funding and whether the benefits were worth the cost. So there were some arguments, and sometimes we chal-lenged each other to prove a point. The disagreements turned out to be good practice for the panel discussion. The best thing about my group was that we all learned from each other. That's a good thing.

various students gave instructors a better understanding of the role of group dynamics in student projects. In general the logs showed that

- Students prefer working in groups to working independently.
- Some structure is needed for groups to work effectively.
- Groups work best when each student understands his or her role and responsibilities.
- Instructors need to facilitate and guide the group interaction to-ward the stated objectives.

Before leaving the topic of learning logs, it is critical to emphasize the importance of using logs in conjunction with other assessment tools. While logs provide valuable insight into student achievement, more quantifiable methods are needed to complete the assessment picture. In the bioethics unit, for example, several assessment tools were used in addition to the learning logs. These included a checklist to monitor the steps in the information search process and a rubric for assessing questioning and note-taking skills.

PERSONAL CORRESPONDENCE

What Is Personal Correspondence?

Anne Davies and her colleagues (1992) have written extensively about the power of personal correspondence as an assessment tool. Personal correspondence includes letters and notes written by students that focus on specific learning goals and provide information important to the learning process. Letters and notes have the added advantage of providing a real audience from whom feedback may be expected.

When Might We Use Personal Correspondence to Assess Learning?

Letters of invitation, appreciation, and explanation are a natural way for students to involve others in the learning process. Children write letters to their parents in which they point out important aspects of a project or summarize key discoveries. A note to the teacher might solicit advice on specific aspects of a student's work. Similarly, students can exchange notes that provide informative feedback and serve as a vehicle for peer review. Figure 4.8 presents several instructional targets for which letters and notes may be used appropriately as an assessment tool.

How Do We Construct the Correspondence?

If the purpose of the correspondence is to assess some aspect of learning, the initial instruction needs to provide a structure for students to follow. For older students this can be accomplished by discussing sample notes and pointing out how key elements are addressed. However, more direction may be needed to achieve the desired outcomes for younger learners. Figure 4.9 represents a template we developed for upper elementary students to write personal invitations to the school's annual science fair. Notice that the student is asked to mention three things that he considers most important to his project.

Figure 4.8
Using letters and notes to assess instructional goals.

Instructional goal	Correspondence
Students will select and read books that satisfy their personal interests.	Students write notes to their parents telling about the books they are reading. They include details explaining why the book is interesting to them.
Students will use the information search process to create personal knowledge.	Students write letters to the editor explaining their personal viewpoint on an issue and giving reasons for their stand.
Students will participate effectively in groups to pursue and generate information.	Students write notes to their peers in which they make positive comments about a product or performance.
Students will strive for excellence in information searching and knowledge generation.	Students write notes to their teachers expressing their feelings about the search process and seeking help with specific problems.

The template displayed in Figure 4.10 is provided for parents and guardians to comment on the project.

Figure 4.9
Template for invitation to a science fair.

May 10, 2010

Dear _____

    Please come to our science fair. It will be held in the school library from May 15 to May 19.

The title of my project is _____

In my project I wanted to _____

Three things I would like to point out about my project are:

_____

_____

_____

Sincerely

_____

Figure 4.10
Template for guardians' response.

May 15, 2010

Dear _____

    Thank you for sharing your project with us. It showed us that you have

learned _____ .

We especially liked _____

One question we have is _____

Love,

_____

How Do We Use Personal Correspondence to Assess for Information Literacy?

GRADE 7 SCENARIO

A seventh-grade health class is engaged in a problem-based unit on wellness. Students have used the Internet to search for health-related problems of particular interest to adolescents. One group has decided to focus on the problem of obesity. Their task will be to research the causes and effects of the problem, to find out what can be done to counteract the problem, and to initiate a public relations campaign to educate the community about the consequences of childhood obesity. Students use an inquiry-based model to guide them through the process of asking questions; accessing resources; collecting, evaluating, and organizing information; and planning an effective presentation.

In Figure 4.11 we take a look at some of the notes and letters produced during the wellness unit.

Figure 4.11
Notes and letters used to assess the information literacy process.

Description of the correspondence	Writing sample

A note to teachers explaining the choice of topic and some of the questions they have about it	*Dear Mrs. Brown,*
	    Our group decided to research obesity because we found out that one out of every five kids is seriously overweight and that this condition leads to many other health problems like diabetes, heart problems, and some kinds of cancer.
	    Some questions we want to answer are:
	• *How do you know if you are obese?*
	• *What are the causes of obesity?*
	• *How can obesity be cured or controlled?*

A note written to provide informative feedback on the products and performances of other students	*Dear Emily, Jon, and Ethan,*
	    I really like your video about the importance of exercise. The part I liked best was when you showed the kinds of exercises kids can do to stay fit.
	    One thing I didn't understand was why some people exercised but didn't lose weight. Can you explain that?

Figure 4.11 *(Continued)*

A note to parents explaining the final product and what was learned through the process	*Dear Mom and Dad,*
	I hope you will read the brochure my group made about obesity. We wanted to tell kids and their parents about the causes and effects of obesity and to show what can be done about it. We found most of the information on the Internet and by talking to people from the Department of Health. We collected some of the information by having kids keep a record of what they ate and then we made a graph to show the results. We also made a survey to find out how often kids exercised.
	We found out that the main causes of obesity are a poor diet and lack of regular exercise. We think the way to solve the problem is through education. That's why we made the brochure.

As with logs, letters and notes become assessment tools when two conditions are met:

- A purpose for the correspondence is clearly expressed and understood by students.
- The assessment criteria are agreed upon at the outset.

EXIT PASS

What Is an Exit Pass?

An exit pass is a tool for assessing student learning at the end of the lesson. Typically, instructors provide a question or a prompt to focus attention on important elements of the lesson. Students are instructed to write a response that clearly and concisely answers the question. Effective prompts may ask students to respond to an essential question, to summarize what was learned, or to elaborate on ideas that have been presented. Prompts may address content knowledge or target the skills developed through the lesson. Some instructors use exit passes to engage students in reflection or self-assessment. Here are some examples of each kind of prompt:

- What are the three most important things you learned about the topic that you didn't know before?
- What is the best resource you found on your topic? Why do you think this?

- What is one thing that went well during this activity? What is one area that you need to improve on?

When Might We Use an Exit Pass?

As the term implies, students work on the exit pass at the end of the lesson and use it as a ticket permitting them to leave the classroom or library. Many instructors have found that this strategy works best for lessons that present so much information that students may be overwhelmed. Exit passes encourage learners to analyze the information that has been presented, to determine what is important and what may be irrelevant, and to synthesize their thoughts around key ideas that represent important learning goals.

How Do We Construct an Exit Pass?

The form of the exit pass depends on the age of the students and the goal of the lesson. For older students who have some experience with writing, instructors may provide students with index cards where they respond to a prompt or question. Teachers of younger children often prepare handouts consisting of a template that guides students as they compose their responses. In either case, the design of the exit pass begins with the learning goals for the lesson. Instructors ask themselves: *What do we want students to know and be able to do at the end of the lesson?* The answer to this question determines the task presented on the exit pass. Figure 4.12 provides examples of prompts that were used on exit passes to assess different learning goals during a unit on space travel.

Figure 4.12
Prompts used on exit passes.

Goal of the lesson	Question or prompt for exit pass
Students will design and implement a search strategy to find resources on their topics.	What key words did you use to search? How do you plan to locate resources that will be useful for your project?
Students will work in groups to create an idea web addressing the essential question: *What were the key events in the history of space travel?* Each group member will select one idea from the web as a topic for inquiry.	What ideas did you contribute to the idea web created by your group? Which event in the history of space travel are you most interested in learning about? What sparked your interest?
Students will identify at least three sources that help answer the essential question.	Which source is most likely to help you answer the essential question? How did you decide this?

How Do We Use an Exit Pass to Assess for Information Literacy?

MIDDLE SCHOOL SCENARIO

National Drug Prevention Week is an annual event that encourages schools across the country to focus on drug education and prevention. At one middle school, the librarian decides to hold an interactive read-in activity with the goal of exposing students to a wide range of resources on the topic of substance abuse and addiction. An invitation is issued to any class that wishes to participate. Tables are set up with a variety of print resources including books, pamphlets, magazines, newspapers, and print-outs from various Web sites. Index cards and pencils are provided for students to use. The goal of the activity and directions for the read-in are presented in Figure 4.13.

Figure 4.13
Directions for read-in activity.

Goal of today's read-in: We will learn more about the topic of substance abuse and addiction by surveying and discussing print resources available in our media center.

Directions for the Read-In

1. **Select** something to read.
2. **Read** for 5 minutes.
3. **Write** on an index card something new and interesting you read about.
4. **Share** something you learned from the resource with others at your table. (Allow time for students to exchange comments and questions.)
5. **Begin again.** (Go to another table with new resources and different students).

After three rounds of reading and sharing resources, students fill out the exit pass presented in Figure 4.14.

The primary goal of the read-in activity is to provide an opportunity for students to survey a wide range of resources on the issue of substance abuse. A secondary, but perhaps no less important, purpose is to engage students in a discussion of the content provided by the resources. The exit pass encourages students to think about the resources they reviewed and to reflect on the activity itself. For the librarian, the exit pass is both a tool for assessing how well the goal was achieved and a way to bring closure to the activity.

Busy librarians, constrained by a tight schedule, may find many different uses for exit passes. As an assessment tool, they are quick, targeted, and easy to administer. We have found it helpful to prepare exit passes to track progress during the independent practice phase of inquiry. One such pass is presented in Figure 4.15.

Figure 4.14
Exit pass for read-in activity.

Exit Pass for Read-In

The most interesting resource I read was _____

A resource I would like more time to read is _____

The most important thing that I learned about substance abuse and addiction

is _____

One idea for improving the read-in is _____

Figure 4.15
Exit pass for inquiry process.

Exit Pass for Inquiry Process

Name: _____   Date: _____

Today I worked on _____

I learned that _____

One problem I had was _____

Tomorrow I am going to _____

CONCLUSION

Conferences, logs, letters, notes, and exit passes add another dimension to the assessment picture provided by the more structured strategies described in Chapter 3. The open-ended nature of these assessment methods creates a window into students' thoughts and feelings that might otherwise remain closed to inspection. They allow instructors to see not only what a student knows but also how he or she has come to acquire the knowledge. These methods cast a light on aspects of learning that are difficult to measure using criterion-based assessments.

As students talk and write about what they are learning, they become more engaged in the process. Honest reflection leads to deeper levels of understanding about both the learning process and the student as a learner. Prompts and questions that are meaningful and purposeful can be the catalyst for change and growth (Martin-Kniep 2000). Students who are engaged in talking and writing about what they are thinking and how they are learning are well on their way to a lifetime of learning.

CHAPTER 5

Tools for Assessment: Graphic Organizers

In this chapter, we examine several types of graphic organizers that are frequently used in schools. These include concept maps, webs, K-W-L (know, wonder, learn) charts, and matrices. The discussion for each tool is organized around the following key questions:

- What is it?
- When might we use the tool?
- How do we construct this tool?
- How do we use it to assess for information literacy?

WHAT ARE GRAPHIC ORGANIZERS?

Graphic organizers are visual representations of thinking. They contribute to learning by providing a structure that supports critical thinking and problem solving. Daniel Callison (2003) defines organizers as:

> tools or techniques that provide identification and classification along with possible relationships or connections among ideas, concepts, and issues. Organizers are useful to the learner when given in advance of instruction and often serve as clues to ideas that the instructor plans to introduce. (251)

Organizers are not a new concept. David Ausubel's (1967) research with advance organizers in the 1960s has provided the foundation for effective teaching based on visual mapping of concepts and ideas. According to Marjorie Pappas (1997), a range of organizers have been used in various disciplines. As she explains:

> The math discipline uses Venn diagrams to examine numerical relationships. Flow charts are used to illustrate a decision-making process in math and computer science. The language arts teachers have been using webs to explore relationships of characters and plot in fiction stories. (30)

Graphic organizers can be designed for specific learning objectives (Ekhaml 1998), including:

- Seeing connections and patterns
- Outlining ideas
- Comparing and contrasting ideas
- Showing cause and effect
- Developing a global view of a topic or an issue
- Preparing summaries and conclusions
- Facilitating the retention of key ideas
- Recalling or retelling of literature
- Organizing the research process

Organizers must be broad and conceptual in nature so that they "provide a large umbrella under which many more specific items can be identified, discussed, and related" (Callison 2003, 252). Figure 5.1 provides examples of organizers that might be devised for different learning objectives.

The same organizer that is used as an instructional tool can be used to assess various aspects of information literacy. In this chapter we present four basic graphic organizers—concept maps, webs, K-W-L charts, and matrices—that are well suited for use in assessing a range of information literacy skills.

CONCEPT MAPS

What Is a Concept Map?

A concept map is a visual diagram that is used to show the links among important related concepts. The technique of concept mapping as a tool for learning originated in the 1970s with Joseph Novak (1977) of Cornell University, who believed that the process helped students to integrate new information with prior knowledge. Concept maps use a hierarchical structure to show the relative importance of ideas. The process involves identifying important concepts, creating spaces and labels for each concept, and constructing links to show relationships. It helps learners clarify what they have read or heard. It affords a visual sketch of key terms around a central idea or concept (Callison 2003).

When Might We Use a Concept Map?

Meaningful learning involves the assimilation of new concepts and propositions into existing cognitive structures. Simply put, concept

Figure 5.1
Examples of organizers for different learning objectives.

Learning objectives	Graphic organizers	Example
To explore aspects of the topic or theme	Idea web	Idea A, Idea B, Idea C, Topic, Idea E, Idea D
To compare and contrast	Compare/contrast matrix	Item 1, Item 2 — Attribute A, Attribute B, Attribute C
To examine cause and effect	Fishbone map	(causes) Effect (causes)
To provide a framework for solving problems	Problem-solving model	Problem: / Solutions — Consequences / A / B / C / Preferred solution:
To categorize or show relationships of parts to whole	Tree map	Big Idea — Category A, Category B, Category C
To connect new learning to prior knowledge	K-W-L chart	I know, I wonder, I learned
To plan a video, a multimedia presentation or a Web page	Storyboard	Visual, Text, Production notes

mapping provides a structure for organizing existing knowledge and connecting newly acquired ideas to it. According to Callison (2003), "because the process involves choices and a focus, along with some organization of terms, the learner becomes engaged with the content" (139). Concept maps might be used to:

- Organize a unit of study around major concepts
- Show the relative importance of ideas
- Promote deeper levels of understanding
- Increase retention of important concepts
- Assess convergent thinking and problem solving
- Recognize patterns and relationships

How Do We Construct a Concept Map?

The design of a concept map should reflect the relationships among the ideas being represented. Because concept maps are created for

Figure 5.2
Steps in constructing a concept map.

Step in the process	Questions to guide the process
1. Clarify instructional targets.	What are your instructional goals? What do you want your students to know and be able to do?
2. Identify the most important concepts.	What are the most important ideas you want students to take from the study? How will you involve students in identifying important concepts?
3. Tap into students' prior knowledge.	What do students know about the topic? How do they know this? Which of these ideas is most important?
4. Design a graph that shows relationships among major concepts.	How can students graphically represent the major concept? How can they show related concepts?
5. Create links to connect concepts.	How are these concepts connected? What is the relationship between major and subordinate concepts?
6. Provide a system for expanding the map.	How can students add new information to the map? How will they differentiate between new and prior knowledge?
7. Use the map for assessment.	What information did students have at the beginning of the study? Was it accurate? What did they add during the study? How is it connected to what they already knew?

different purposes, no two are exactly alike. The final design of the map is determined by factors like:

- Instructional goals underlying the construction of the map
- Complexity of the ideas being studied
- Intrinsic structure of the area of knowledge being represented
- Ability of students to identify major concepts and to show how they relate

Figure 5.2 outlines key steps involved in creating a concept map for instruction and assessment purposes.

How Do We Use a Concept Map to Assess for Information Literacy?

GRADE 3 SCENARIO

A third-grade class is learning about the rain forest. Two essential questions are used to focus learning around important concepts:

- How are the plants and animals in the rain forest dependent on each other?
- Why is it important to save the rain forest?

Each student will be responsible for:

- Researching a rain forest plant or animal
- Creating a visual representation of the plant or animal
- Preparing a sign to identify the plant or animal and provide important information relevant to the research questions
- Working with a group to create a poster promoting actions that will save the rain forest

Students will work in teams to create a simulated rain forest environment in the classroom. The design will start with the four layers of life and include visuals to represent the plants and animals that live in each zone. Students will post signs with important information about the different organisms. As visitors walk through the rain forest, they will hear ambient sounds created with musical instruments. The third graders will serve as guides and explain the exhibit to parents and other guests. They will also help the younger students with reading and interpretation.

The primary goal for this unit was to develop an understanding of the rain forest as a system of interconnected parts. To reinforce this concept, the instructors worked with students to create a concept map. That map, illustrated in Figure 5.3, shows the complex relationships that exist in the rain forest ecosystem.

The study of the rain forest began with a visit to Enchanted Learning's *Zoom Rainforests* Web page (Col 2010). Here students found out that the rain forest is a living environment that is home to millions of different plants and animals. They examined a visual representation of the rain forest that clearly illustrated and labeled the four vegetative zones. They learned about human activities that affect the health of the rain forest. Finally, they used the Web site to find the names of plants and animals living in each of the layers. These names were added to the concept map (Figure 5.3) and used as a point of reference throughout the unit study.

The map provided a framework for the research. Teams were formed to investigate the four layers of life represented in Figure 5.3. Each student in the group chose one plant or animal as a research topic. They used a variety of print and electronic resources to collect information related to their research questions. Throughout the process, teachers asked questions like the following to help students understand the rain forest as a system of interdependent organisms:

- What conditions make some animals prefer the forest floor, some the understory, and still others the canopy?
- How do rain forest animals depend on each other? How do they depend on the plants?
- What are the dangers facing the rain forest and the animals that live there?
- How does the fate of one organism affect others in the ecosystem?

The instructors helped third graders to design concept maps to organize the inquiry. After a discussion of the learning goals, students helped decide which categories to include on their maps. As they worked through the various stages of inquiry, they relied on their concept maps to guide them through the process of collecting, organizing, and expressing what they learned about their topics. One student's map is illustrated in Figure 5.4.

The librarian saw this activity as an opportunity to assess students' ability to take notes that made sense and to use their notes to write

Figure 5.3
Concept map for the rain forest ecosystem.

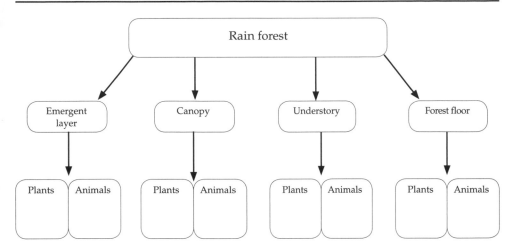

coherent sentences. With this in mind, she asked the third graders to use their logs to respond to the following questions:

- Did I fill in the spaces with facts that made sense to me? How did I decide what notes to take?
- Where did I find the information needed to fill in my concept map? Which resource was most helpful? What made it so?
- Did I write sentences that clearly expressed what I learned about my topic? Did I use notes from my concept map to add rich details to my writing?

The librarian reviewed students' responses to the prompts as she examined their concept maps. Her comments and questions provided valuable feedback that, in many cases, prompted the student to make improvements to the original piece of work. Following this activity, students used sticky notes to post information about their animals on the class concept map. Instructors helped them to synthesize their findings and to make generalizations about life in the rain forest that addressed the essential questions for the unit.

Figure 5.4
Concept map for howler monkey.

Learning goals: I will create a concept map to help me organize information about my topic. I will use my concept map to write sentences that show what I have learned.

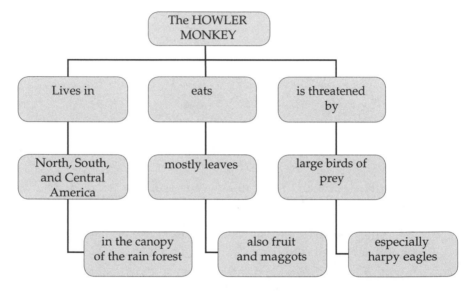

What I learned about the howler monkey

Howler monkeys live in the rain forest canopies of North, South, and Central America.

They eat leaves, fruit and maggots that they find in the rain forest trees.

Their natural enemies are large birds of prey that also live in the rain forest. One of them is called the harpy eagle.

Some questions I still have about the howler monkey

How does the howler monkey get food?

Why does it have such long arms?

What does it use its tail for?

How did it get its name?

WEBS

What Is a Web?

A web is a graphic organizer that clusters key words around a central topic or main idea. It provides a structure that allows students to show how facts and ideas are related to each other and to the main topic. The web is a flexible tool for students to use as they brainstorm ideas and generate questions.

When Might We Use a Web?

The web is an effective means of assessing divergent thinking. It provides a graphic representation of internal thought processes and gives students a framework that encourages adventurous thinking. Kay Vandergrift (1994) indicates that webbing allows for ideas to be expressed and captured without the constraints of an ordered progression. Because it is characterized by a free flow of thinking, webbing is an effective strategy for:

- Generating ideas and questions
- Brainstorming prior knowledge about the topic
- Expanding thinking about the topic
- Displaying the range of subtopics related to a theme or topic

Webbing is also an effective way to engage students in the appreciation and interpretation of literature. This type of web is easily created by writing the name of a literary piece in the center of the paper and brainstorming related ideas around it. These ideas may include:

- Narrative elements—setting, characters, plot, theme, resolution
- Related pieces of literature—books or poems with a similar theme
- Research topics suggested by the literature
- Other works by the author

Teachers and library media specialists have found webbing to be an effective way to facilitate small group work. When the task calls for students to cooperate on the construction of a web, they learn the importance of incorporating the contributions of each group member. As an added bonus, students can use their webs to focus on different aspects of a collaborative research project.

How Do We Construct a Web?

Webbing is a dynamic process. It begins with a question, a theme, or an issue and grows to reflect a wide range of thinking about the concept. To construct a web we begin by writing the main topic or essential question in the center of the work space and drawing a circle around it. Next we engage students in a list-group-label strategy commonly used to promote reading comprehension. This process involves the following three steps:

- List ideas related to the main topic or the essential question.
- Group ideas that have similar characteristics.
- Label the categories.

Following the list-group-label activity, instructors walk students through the following steps to complete their webs:

- Draw smaller circles (one for each category) around the main circle.
- Label each category circle.
- Write ideas belonging to the category outside the circle.
- Draw lines to show how ideas connect.

Finally, the teacher or librarian models the process of extending the web as the inquiry process uncovers new information or fresh insights.

How Do We Use a Web to Assess for Information Literacy?

GRADE 5 SCENARIO

The fifth grade is planning a colonial fair. They will be preparing booths, exhibits, and activities to simulate life in colonial times. Two essential questions will provide a focus for the event:

- How did the colonists live?
- How did individuals contribute to the welfare of the colony?

Students are divided into two teams with each group addressing one of the overarching questions. Group meetings are held to plan the research and the presentation. During these sessions students work collaboratively to:

- Outline the information to be presented
- Brainstorm how to present information
- Decide *who* will be responsible for *what*

The group addressing the question "How did the colonists live?" began by creating a web with the question at the center. Their web is illustrated in Figure 5.5.

Figure 5.5
Web for "How did the colonists live?"

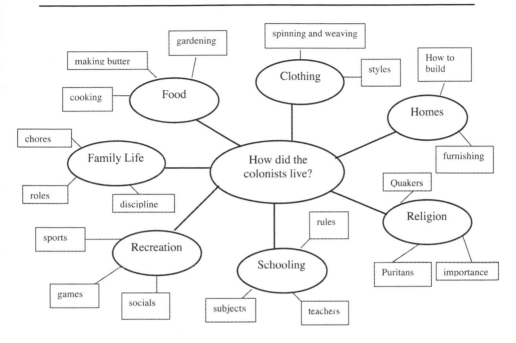

The group responsible for addressing the question "How did indivi-duals contribute to the welfare of the colony?" decided to focus on the trades and to show how they contributed to colonial life. Their web is illustrated in Figure 5.6.

Although the creation of the web was a group activity, students were asked to self-assess their contributions by filling in an exit pass that asked: *What ideas did you contribute to the web created by your group?* As they reviewed the exit passes, the instructors added com-ments and questions for students to respond to the following day. In some cases, these comments led to an improvement in the web.

Once created, the web served as a conceptual framework for the entire project. It kept students focused on the essential question, and it enabled instructors to see at a glance how students were building knowledge by adding new ideas and concepts to the original web.

The colonial fair was an event to remember. Students dressed in breeches, vests, aprons, and caps and treated their peers to johnnycakes and homemade butter. They learned to read with a hornbook and demonstrated the arts of quilting, weaving, and candle making. They organized foot races and games of hopscotch and hide-and-seek. In

Figure 5.6
Web showing contributions made by colonial tradespeople.

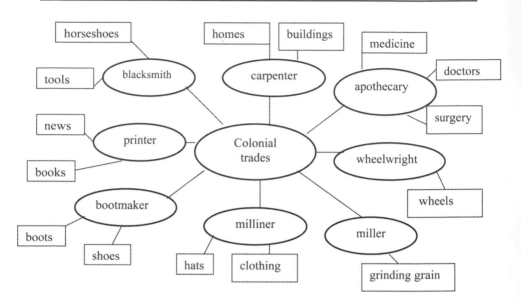

improvised workshops, they explained the work of carpenters, black-smiths, and wheelwrights. Visitors to the fair were given colonial currency to purchase goods and services at the apothecary, the print shop, the millinery, and the general store. In the end, the children all agreed that the colonists led difficult but busy lives and that every member of the community, including the children, contributed to the colony's success.

K-W-L CHARTS

What Is a K-W-L Chart?

The K-W-L chart, originally created by Donna Ogle (1986) and illustrated by James Bellanca (1992), is a tool commonly used to help students plan and assess their research projects. The chart usually consists of three columns:

K—Students use this column to write what they *know* about the topic.
W—In this column students write what they *wonder* about the topic.
L—Students write here what they *learned* through their reading and research.

Teachers and library media specialists have adapted the basic structure of the K-W-L chart to serve specific purposes. For example, some
educators describe tables that add a fourth column for "How can we
learn more?"

When Might We Use a K-W-L Chart?

The K-W-L chart is one of the simplest strategies for organizing
students' thinking about a topic or an issue; therefore, it is especially
effective in work with younger children. Figure 5.7 describes how
the K-W-L chart might be used at different points in the research
process.

The K-W-L chart is often used as a group strategy to record the
collective thinking of the class about the general topic. It is also used
to guide independent learning by providing a structure for students
to reflect on prior knowledge, pose questions for further study, and
reflect on what has been learned.

How Do We Construct a K-W-L Chart?

The K-W-L chart is a three-column table that provides space for
students to record their responses. Figure 5.8 displays a basic K-W-L
chart.

When the task involves the information search process, library
media specialists may prefer to use a variation known as the K-W-H-L

Figure 5.7
Using the K-W-L chart to organize the research process.

Part of the chart	Purpose
(K) Beginning: Explore the general topic	To activate thinking about what is already known about the topic and to pose questions to guide the search.
(W) Middle: Pose questions Evaluate and collect information	To record new information and insights as they are uncovered.
(L) End: Organize and present information Assess process and product	To reflect on what has been learned through the research; to make connections.

Figure 5.8
Basic K-W-L chart.

Topic:		
This is what I know	*This is what I wonder*	*This is what I learned*

Figure 5.9
K-W-H-L chart.

Topic:			
What I know	*What I wonder*	*How I will find out*	*What I learned*

strategy. In this case, the table might look more like the one in Figure 5.9. In this example, the *how* column is used to consider possible resources and strategies for finding information.

How Do We Use a K-W-L (or K-W-H-L) Chart to Assess for Information Literacy?

GRADE 1 SCENARIO

A first-grade class wants to select a pet for the classroom. Students brainstorm criteria to assess the characteristics of an appropriate pet and speculate about animals that might meet the criteria. In pairs, students select different pets to research. They also have opportunities to interview a veterinarian and take a field trip to a local pet shop. As a class they share their research results and vote for their class pet.

Figure 5.10
K-W-H-L chart for pet project.

We know	We wonder	How will we find out	What we learned
Pets live in your house or yard.	What animals make good pets?	Look in books about pets. Ask the vet.	Pets should not be wild animals. Pets shouldn't be too big, or you won't be able to feed them or keep them in the classroom.
Pets are tame. They won't hurt you.	How can you train a pet so it won't hurt anyone?	Look in books under "training." Ask a person who trains pets.	Treat your pet with kindness. Reward your pet for good behavior. Be patient with your pet.
Cats, dogs, fish, and birds make good pets.	How can you tell which animal will be a good pet?	Look in books. Ask people at the Humane Society.	Watch the animal in the shelter or kennel before you buy it.
You have to feed your pet and clean up after it.	What else do you have to do to take care of your pet?	Ask the person at the shelter or the Humane Society. Look in books about the kind of pet you choose. See if there is a Web site about your pet.	Feed it and change the water everyday. If it's a fish, keep the tank clean by putting in snails. If it's a bird, put clean paper in the cage. Dogs and cats need shots.

To launch the project described in this scenario, the teacher posted a large K-W-H-L chart in the front of the classroom where children recorded what they knew about pets and what they wanted to find out. The teacher scheduled time for the class to meet with the library media specialist so that they could discuss their need for information and talk about how and where the information might be found to answer their questions. The library media specialist worked closely with the teacher to help students plan a search strategy. As they developed fresh insights, the children charted what they learned with their teacher's help.

Throughout the process, group discussions focused on comparing what was known at the outset with what was being learned. Opportunities were provided for students to reflect on the *how* as well as the *what* of learning. Under the skilled direction of the teacher and library media specialist, the K-W-H-L chart provided graphic evidence of learning and self-evaluation. Figure 5.10 represents the final version of the chart.

MATRICES

What Is a Matrix?

A matrix is a grid that can be used to show similarities and differences among items with comparable characteristics (Marzano, Pollock, and Pickering 2001). The primary purpose of the matrix is to guide thinking by helping students organize their ideas and make meaningful comparisons. Because the matrix presents information in a visual format, it is a valuable tool for helping students to see the big picture even as it displays all of the parts. The process of constructing and using a matrix to analyze and synthesize information leads to deeper understanding—the ultimate goal of learning.

When Might We Use a Matrix?

A matrix is used to systematically organize and display information and to compare and contrast topics and subtopics. Often, a class matrix is constructed to model the process and to represent the collective thinking of the group. Once they know how it works, students create their own matrices to:

- Take notes
- Make comparisons

- Form generalizations based on evidence
- Synthesize findings
- Display information in a systematic manner

How Do We Construct a Matrix?

To construct a matrix, students start with three basic questions:

- What items do we want to compare?
- What characteristics can be used to make the comparison?
- How are the items alike? How are they different?

Guided by these questions, students create a grid that places the items being compared on one axis and the characteristics on the other. In the remaining cells they write how the items are alike and how they are different. To construct a comparison matrix students use a template similar to the one illustrated in Figure 5.11.

How Do We Use a Matrix to Assess for Information Literacy?

MIDDLE SCHOOL SCENARIO

Middle school students will be participating in the Kids Voting Program. They will accompany their parents to polling places and use special ballots to cast their votes for important national, state, and local offices. A speaker from the state election office visits the class to explain the process and encourage participation. One student asks, "How do we know who to vote for?" Teachers seize the opportunity to engage their classes in a discussion of issues. Two questions are used to frame the discussion and the subsequent search for information:

- What are the important issues in this election?
- Where do the different candidates stand in respect to these issues?

The library media specialist and the social studies teachers developed a unit plan around these essential questions. Their goals were to encourage thoughtful participation in the voting process and to develop informed voters who made reasoned choices based upon an analysis

Figure 5.11
Model for constructing a comparison matrix.

	First point of comparison	*Second point of comparison*	*Third point of comparison*
Item A			
Item B			
Item C			
How are the items alike?			
How are the items different?			
Conclusion or generalization			

of the issues. The inquiry process provided an instructional model steering the learning toward these goals.

The unit began with students scouring the news media for articles dealing with the candidates and the issues. These articles were discussed, analyzed, and debated as the class tried to pin down the important themes. As issues were identified, they were posted on a wall chart to be added to or modified as new information was uncovered.

The class was divided into three groups representing national, state, and local government. The library media specialist showed students how to use the Internet to find out which offices were open and who the candidates were for these positions. To keep the focus on comparing candidates' views in relation to specific issues, the instructors helped students to design a matrix (Figure 5.12) that targeted both group and personal learning goals.

Using the matrix as a framework, each student selected one open office to investigate. They read campaign literature and, in some cases, attended rallies sponsored by local political organizations. They used e-mail and the telephone to collect additional information on the candidates and the issues. As information was gathered, it was posted on the matrix for analysis by the entire group. Instruction focused on asking the right questions and keeping an accurate record of the responses. Students honed their interview skills through role playing and learned how to use the tape recorder and video camera to capture the message.

Figure 5.12
Matrix for comparing candidates and issues.

Group learning goal: We will use the matrix to compare the views of candidates for the office of			
	Candidate A	Candidate B	Candidate C
Issue 1			
Issue 2			
Issue 3			
Which issues do the candidates agree on?			
Which issues do they disagree on?			
My personal learning goal: I will support a candidate based on where he/she stands on the issues.			
Which candidate will I support? Why?			

Guide for Self-Assessment

Criteria	Yes, I did	No, I did not	I'm not sure because
Did I post accurate information about my candidate on the matrix?			
Did I contribute to the discussion of candidates and issues?			
Did I base my support for a candidate on his/her position on the issues?			

Teachers and library media specialists used the matrix to track the progress of individuals within the group and to engage students in an ongoing conversation about the issues. The matrix documented students' ability to compare and contrast, to make generalizations, and to reach conclusions based on evidence. It provided a framework for collaborative learning and kept students focused on the goals of the project. For the library media specialist, the matrix was an effective tool for gauging students' ability to gather information using a variety of less traditional sources and techniques, including e-mail, personal interviews, campaign literature, guest speakers, and political debates.

As students learned more about the candidates and their positions, they began to align themselves with particular nominees. Debates were held in which student candidates wrangled over the issues. Campaign slogans were printed on homemade buttons, and students lobbied for their favorite candidates in the classroom, the cafeteria, and the library media center.

The turnout on election day was overwhelming. Students came to the polls armed with information about the candidates. Their enthusiasm and zeal served as a reminder to the entire community that voting is a dynamic process requiring careful study and the active engagement of informed citizens. Eighth graders and their parents agreed that they had learned some valuable lessons about the importance of voting in a democratic society.

CONCLUSION

As visual representations of students' thought processes, graphic organizers have many applications related to instruction and assessment. In this chapter, we have identified just a few of the many graphic organizers that may be used to instruct and assess different aspects of information literacy. In particular, we have described organizers that may be used to document achievement of the following goals related to information literacy:

- Explore different aspects of a topic
- Develop a global view of the topic
- Pose questions related to the topic
- Organize notes around research questions
- Compare and contrast topics and ideas
- Connect isolated pieces of information to create personal knowledge

In addition to these obvious benefits, we have found graphic organizers to be an effective way to differentiate learning for special needs children as well as those with language deficits. Graphic organizers allow these students to express ideas and make connections using signs, symbols, words, and phrases in place of rather sophisticated language constructions.

CHAPTER 6

Student Portfolios

This chapter addresses the following questions:

- What is a portfolio?
- What is a digital portfolio?
- How do portfolios differ from other assessment tools?
- Why use portfolios?
- Who are the audiences for portfolios?
- How might the library media specialist use portfolios?
- What is a process folio and how is it developed?
- What might a process folio look like?

WHAT IS A PORTFOLIO?

A portfolio is a collection of selected work samples that shows a picture of achievement over time. The components of the portfolio are carefully chosen to provide evidence of growth toward identified instructional goals. The typical portfolio includes the following:

- Examples of student work
- Tools used to assess performance
- Evidence of reflection and self-examination

Taken together, these documents become the basis for meaningful communication involving students, parents, teachers, library media specialists, and other members of the instructional team. They are a valuable tool to better understand how students develop and learn (Seitz 2008).

Librarian involvement in portfolio systems is admittedly on the cutting edge. Librarians who are engaged in collaborative planning and teaching may find in portfolios a valuable tool for assessing key components of the *Standards for the 21st-Century Learner* (American Association of School Librarians [AASL] 2007). The long-term developmental goals expressed in this document are especially pronounced in the sections dealing with dispositions, responsibilities, and self-assessment strategies. A well-implemented portfolio system provides a structure for tracking the kind of learning described in the most current standards document.

The increasing emphasis on critical thinking along with a constructivist approach to building knowledge requires innovative approaches to assessment as well as instruction. Increasingly, students are required to demonstrate understanding by working on products and performances that require the integration of skills and content areas. For library media specialists who are already integrating information literacy skills with classroom assignments, a portfolio system can be a critical way to engage in positive, individual connections with students (Jaquith 2005). Although the benefits of using a portfolio system may be apparent to library media specialists, successful implementation requires that teachers are also integrating classroom student portfolios into their instructional plans.

WHAT IS A DIGITAL PORTFOLIO?

Digital or electronic portfolios allow students to digitize and store artifacts that use a range of technologies and multimedia elements. These might include images that have been scanned or produced with a digital camera, allowing for a mix of sound and video, as well as multimedia products using various authoring programs (e.g., HyperStudio, KidPix, Dreamweaver).

The advantages of electronic over print portfolios include the following (Zuger 2008; Tuttle 1997):

- Students can demonstrate more creative dimensions of learning, such as digitizing a speech or showing a movie or producing a Web page on a project.
- Students can connect various portions of their portfolios through hyperlinks.
- New work can replace older work with minimal effort.
- There is no need to wade through a voluminous folder or a box of documents.
- Electronic portfolios definitely save space.

The concept of digital portfolios continues to evolve along with developments in technology. Some educators are experimenting with Web-based portfolios that offer many of the benefits associated with the new media available online. Using the power of the Internet, students and teachers are able to store, search, organize, and share information using familiar online technologies. Web-based portfolios have the added advantage of being accessible to a community of educators who might use them as a resource for improving teaching and learning or for evaluating the effectiveness of instructional programs (Gathercoal et al. 2002).

The portability of the digital portfolio, whether in a disk or Web-based format, makes it easier for students to carry a record of their work with them as they move from grade to grade or school to school. The digital format allows students to create links, provide explanatory notes, and incorporate artifacts like video clips, artwork, or audio recordings. Perhaps the greatest appeal for older students is knowing that digital portfolios can easily be included with college and career applications.

Once a school chooses to adopt a portfolio system, the next step is to decide whether to develop a hard copy, electronic, or Web-based format. Before making the decision, educators should consider the following factors (Heath 2005):

- Computer skills of the teachers
- Computer skills of the students
- Access to computers by students and teachers
- Networking capacity in the school building and classrooms
- Budget for additional hardware and software
- Budget for staff development
- Resources for technical support
- Security and confidentiality of information stored in electronic form

HOW DO PORTFOLIOS DIFFER FROM OTHER ASSESSMENT TOOLS?

Richard Stiggins (1997) draws a clear distinction between portfolios and other assessment methods. He says that portfolios are collections of work that tell the whole story of student achievement. The purpose is to communicate "about student effort, growth, or achievement at any point in time" (Stiggins 1997, 79). Most assessment methods define the criteria for a successful performance in relation to specific learning targets. By contrast, the portfolio shows how learning grows and evolves across multiple projects and disciplines. The collection of work samples and assessment tools included in the portfolio provides a picture of learning that is authentic, integrated, and meaningful. Figure 6.1 highlights how portfolios differ from other forms of assessment.

Figure 6.1
Portfolios versus other assessment measures.

Characteristic	Portfolios	Other assessments
Purpose	Show evolution of skills and knowledge	Assess specific targets in a specific time frame
Use	Communicate a range of achievement	Inform teaching and learning
Format	Include work samples, assessment tools, and reflections	Focus on specific assessment tools, including checklists, rubrics, rating scales, and graphic organizers
Responsibility	Involve students, teachers, parents	Involve primarily teachers, with students participating

WHY USE PORTFOLIOS?

With the increased emphasis on accountability, many educators view portfolios as a way to complement data provided by standardized testing. Although standardized tests have been widely adopted as a way of tracking progress in relation to local and state standards, controversy over the exclusive use of these tests as a measure of achievement has persisted. Critics point out that typical test items focus on a narrow range of knowledge and skills that do not reflect deeper levels of understanding. In addition, many school districts have identified some learning goals that represent attitudes and abilities that are developmental in nature and extend across disciplinary lines. These broad-based learner goals include:

- The ability to read, write, and communicate effectively
- The ability to think critically and creatively
- The ability to construct knowledge and understanding related to core areas of the curriculum
- The ability to work with others to make decisions and solve problems
- The ability to produce products and performances and to assess their quality

The outcome-based approach supports overarching goals like these by requiring students to demonstrate knowledge by working on tasks that involve decision making, problem solving, and a range of skills and aptitudes (Mundell and DeLario 1994). For teachers and librarians, portfolios represent an approach to assessment that is more in line with the emerging emphasis on process and authenticity in learning.

WHO ARE THE AUDIENCES FOR PORTFOLIOS?

Schools that use a process approach to instruction have found portfolios to be a valuable tool for communication as well as assessment. Ideally, teachers, parents, and students use portfolios to engage in conversations about the *how* as well as the *what* of learning.

Different audiences review portfolios for different purposes. Figure 6.2 identifies how various members of the school community might use the information provided by portfolios.

The most important audience, of course, is the learner himself. According to the *Standards for the 21st-Century Learner* (American

Figure 6.2
Use of portfolios by different audiences.

Audience	How portfolio is used
Students	To self-examine growth as learners To communicate with others by displaying evidence of learning To value themselves as learners To provide a mechanism for sharing their products and experiences
Instructors	To monitor progress toward standards To plan interventions To modify teaching and learning
Parents	To monitor achievement To assess child's strengths and areas needing improvement To support the school's instructional program
Policy makers and other stakeholders	To supplement test data with qualitative measures of achievement To provide information needed to evaluate programs To make budgetary decisions To set policies and make decisions based on student achievement

Association of School Librarians [AASL] 2007), students need to take charge of their own learning in order to make sense of the overwhelming amount of available information and use the information to fulfill personal and academic needs. A well-designed portfolio system involves students in critical decisions about both the content and the process of learning. Students who plan, implement, and share portfolios engage in activities like the following:

- They set personal and academic goals.
- They plan products and performances to demonstrate achievement of their goals.
- They select work samples and artifacts to include in their portfolios.
- They self-assess their products and performances.
- They reflect on learning at critical points in the process.

In some schools, students are trained to lead conferences with their parents and teachers by displaying their work samples, along with the tools used to assess them, and explaining the significance of each piece of evidence. Ideally, students will see planning, maintaining, and sharing a learning portfolio as a personal achievement rather than simply a task to be completed. With this in mind, it is critical that students determine the artifacts to include in their portfolios and for instructors to resist "formulaic approaches that require students to furnish three examples of this and four examples of that" (Fisher and Frey 2007, 85). The portfolio becomes the student's own story about learning. Therefore, it's tricky but important to find the appropriate balance between requirements and student ownership of the portfolio's contents. While some direct instruction about the kinds of artifacts to include is necessary, teachers and librarians will need to avoid heavily prescriptive demands (Fisher and Frey 2007).

HOW MIGHT THE LIBRARY MEDIA SPECIALIST USE PORTFOLIOS?

With the publication of the *Standards for the 21st-Century Learner* (American Association of School Librarians [AASL] 2007), library media specialists are faced with the challenge of assessing learning goals that extend beyond the skills traditionally associated with information literacy. The learning behaviors described in the dispositions, responsibilities, and self-assessment strategies point to the importance of collaboration between the library media specialist and other interested parties. Portfolios can be an effective way to open up conversations between the library media specialist and students, teachers, and parents.

Although a student may demonstrate a desired behavior at any point in the learning process, competence often develops incrementally through engagement in a variety of challenging experiences. Dispositions, responsibilities, and self-assessment strategies represent long-term learning goals that are developmental in nature. For teachers and librarians, the challenge is to devise a system that tracks these behaviors over time so that a pattern of growth can be determined.

Some educators have been experimenting with portfolios as a way to assess attitudes and behavioral patterns that span grade levels and extend across disciplinary lines. In one school, the librarian works with teachers to choose a disposition as a focus for the entire year. Together they plan learning experiences that require students to demonstrate that attitude or behavior, and they involve students in setting criteria to assess their work. Products and performances that exemplify the disposition are assessed, dated, and filed by the student. At the end of the year, the students review their work samples and choose the one that best meets the criteria for the disposition in question. They write brief reflections giving their reasons for choosing the piece and explaining how it demonstrates the disposition. During a portfolio night, they share the selected piece with their parents along with assessment records and personal reflections. The instructional team intends to carry on the process by focusing on a new disposition or responsibility each year. They are also working on a developmental continuum to monitor students' growth in areas already targeted.

WHAT IS A PROCESS FOLIO AND HOW IS IT DEVELOPED?

A form of portfolio that is particularly useful for the library media specialist is the *process folio*. The process folio is a collection of student work that documents different phases of the learning process. Typically, it includes the notes and drafts leading up to a final product or performance along with the tools used to assess the learning. Importantly, process folios also include reflections by students on how they are learning, problems they are having, connections they are making, and their feelings about the entire process.

Because process folios focus on *how* students learn, they can effectively document complex tasks that involve a range of skills and aptitudes. By addressing all phases of the information search (Kuhlthau 2004), the process folio provides an excellent way to assess students' ability to access, manage, and use information. The best process folios are the result of close collaboration between the library media specialist and the classroom teacher. We find the following questions to be helpful as we begin to plan with teachers:

- Which standards will be the focus for instruction and assessment?
- What skills, dispositions, and responsibilities will be addressed?
- How will students demonstrate achievement in terms of each of the learning goals?
- What tools and strategies are needed to encourage self-assessment?
- What kind of a rating system can be designed and used with multiple assessment tools?
- What work samples will be collected to document achievement of learning goals?
- Where in the process can student reflections be most effective, and what prompts might guide the writing?
- How can we design a summary sheet to serve as an overview and help make sense of the materials contained in the process folio?

WHAT MIGHT A PROCESS FOLIO LOOK LIKE?

On the following pages, we describe the contents of a process folio developed by a student for the wetlands unit detailed in Chapter 10. In this unit, third graders use an inquiry process to investigate topics related to the wetlands. They brainstorm questions to be addressed throughout the inquiry and use field trips and a full range of resources to build knowledge and understanding of the wetlands as an ecosystem. Students ultimately author books on their findings. During the project, the teacher uses the process folio to collect achievement data for language arts and science, while the library media specialist focuses on the information search process.

The classroom teacher maintains the process folios for the duration of the third-grade year. When students work in the library setting, they bring along their process folios so that work samples, assessments, and reflections are properly filed and available to both the teacher and the library media specialist. Importantly, responsibility for maintaining the process folios is shared by the instructors and the students.

With guidance from their teachers and the librarian, the third graders are able to:

- Participate in setting criteria for quality work
- Select appropriate artifacts to demonstrate what they are learning and provide reasons for their selections
- Assess personal learning
- Reflect upon what they were learning and how they were learning

The teacher is responsible for:

- Setting up and maintaining the process folios
- Guiding the selection of items to be included
- Developing strategies and tools for assessing work samples
- Providing time for reflection and self-assessment
- Using the portfolio to communicate with parents

Throughout the wetlands project, the library media specialist works closely with the teacher to help students select artifacts and to create tools and strategies for assessment. The following steps are taken to develop the process folio:

Step 1: Determine Standards for Instruction and Assessment and Agree upon Skills, Dispositions, and Responsibilities to Address.

The library media specialist uses the first of the *Standards for the 21st-Century Learner* (American Association of School Librarians [AASL] 2007) as a focal point for instruction and assessment. In addition to the long-term goals reflected in the standard, her targets include the skills, dispositions, and self-assessment strategies needed to accomplish the goal. Accordingly, instruction and assessment for the wetlands unit are designed to focus on the following:

- Standard 1: Inquire, think critically, and gain knowledge.
  - Skill 1.1.2: Use prior and background knowledge as context for new learning.
  - Skill 1.1.4: Find, evaluate, and select appropriate sources to answer questions.
  - Skill 1.1.5: Evaluate information found in selected sources on the basis of accuracy, validity, appropriateness for needs, importance, and social and cultural context.

- Disposition 1.2.3: Demonstrate creativity by using multiple resources and formats.
- Responsibility 1.3.4: Contribute to the exchange of ideas within the learning community.
- Self-assessment 1.4.1: Monitor own information-seeking processes for effectiveness and progress, and adapt as necessary.

Step 2: Develop Tools and Strategies to Assess Achievement of the Standard

The library media specialist creates the following tools and strategies to assess achievement in relation to the standard for the wetlands unit (Figure 6.3).

Figure 6.3
Standards and assessment measures for wetlands unit.

Standard	Assessment measure
Standard 1: Inquire, think critically, and gain knowledge.	
Skill 1.1.2: Use prior and background knowledge as context for new learning.	Reflection log prompts: What do I already know about this? How do I know this?
Skill 1.1.4: Find, evaluate, and select appropriate sources to answer questions.	Matrix for identifying resources
Skill 1.1.5: Evaluate information found in selected sources on the basis of accuracy, validity, appropriateness for needs, importance, and social and cultural context.	Checklist for evaluating resources
Disposition 1.2.3: Demonstrate creativity by using multiple resources and formats.	Tracking sheet to note resources used
Responsibility 1.3.4: Contribute to the exchange of ideas within the learning community.	Reflection log prompts: What suggestions did I make? What contributions did I make in solving our problem?
Self-assessment 1.4.1: Monitor own information-seeking processes for effectiveness and progress, and adapt as necessary.	Checklist for bookmaking activity

Step 3: Devise a Consistent Rating System for Assessment Tools Used

As shown in Figure 6.3, the library media specialist used several tools to assess student learning in this unit. To organize and make sense of the assessment data collected, it was important for her to devise a rating system that could be applied to different assessment tools, such as matrices and checklists.

For this unit, the library media specialist devised a four-level rating system (i.e., exceeds, meets, approaches, and does not meet standards) that she used for the following assessment tools: (1) the matrix for identifying resources and (2) the checklist for bookmaking.

Example A: Matrix for Identifying Resources. Figure 6.4 displays the matrix and Figure 6.5 shows the rating system as applied to the matrix.

Figure 6.4
Matrix for identifying resources.

Link to the standards: In this lesson I will show that I can find information about my topic in different kinds of print and electronic resources.

Resource Matrix

The topic of my book is _____.

My research questions are

_____

_____

_____

The keywords I will use to search are _____.

Source of information (title)	Type of information (format)	One important thing I learned from the source

The best source that I found was _____

The reason I think this is _____

Figure 6.5
Rating system for matrix.

Number of resources used	
Not met	I found only one resource for my topic.
Approaches	I found two resources for my topic.
Meets	I found three resources for my topic.
Exceeds	I found at least four resources for my topic.
Range of resources used	
Not met	I found only a print or an electronic resource.
Approaches	I found one print and one electronic resource.
Meets	I found more than one print and electronic resource.
Exceeds	I found print, electronic, and people resources.
Information found	
Not met	I didn't find anything to report.
Approaches	I reported something I learned from at least one resource.
Meets	I reported something I learned from each resource.
Exceeds	I reported something I learned from each resource. I also selected the best resource and told why I chose it.

Because significant value was placed on student involvement in the assessment process, the rating system was written from a student's perspective. Students used the rating system to assess their own resource matrices. Instructors reviewed each student's self-assessment and added their own comments. If there was a discrepancy between the student's evaluation and that of the teacher or library media specialist, a brief conference usually resulted in agreement.

Example B: Checklist for Bookmaking. Figure 6.6 displays the checklist and Figure 6.7 shows how the rating system was applied to this assessment tool.

Step 4: Identify Samples of Student Work to Include for Each Standard

The students included samples of their completed matrices and checklists in their process folios to document their learning throughout the wetlands unit.

Figure 6.6
Checklist for assessing wetlands books.

Link to the standards: In this lesson I will learn how to improve my work by using a checklist to assess my writing, my art, and my book as a whole.

Title of the book: _____

Author/Illustrator: _____

Assessing My Wetlands Book

Criteria—what's important?	Yes	No	Comments
Writing			
Do I provide important information about the wetlands?			
Do I have a beginning, middle, and end to my book?			
Do I use my own words?			
Do I carefully choose my words to describe the sights and sounds of the wetlands?			
Do I carefully check my spelling, grammar, and punctuation?			
Art work			
Do I accurately show the wetlands in my pictures?			
Do my pictures and text go together?			
Do I use color, design, and composition creatively?			
Overall presentation			
Do my words and pictures present the wetlands in an interesting way?			
Does my book have an attractive cover?			
Does my title page have the title, names of author and publisher, and place of publication?			
Do I have four or more pages with text and pictures?			
Do I list the resources I used to find information?			
Do I include a section about myself as the author?			

Figure 6.7
Rating system for checklist.

Writing	
Not met	My writing meets fewer than two of the criteria.
Approaches	My writing meets two or three criteria.
Meets	My writing meets four of five criteria.
Exceeds	My writing meets all five criteria.
Artwork	
Not met	My artwork does not meet any of the criteria.
Approaches	My artwork meets one of the criteria.
Meets	My artwork meets two of the criteria.
Exceeds	My artwork meets all three criteria.
Overall presentation	
Not met	My overall presentation meets only one of the criteria.
Approaches	My overall presentation meets two or three criteria.
Meets	My overall presentation meets four or five criteria.
Exceeds	My overall presentation meets all six criteria.

Sample Work A: Completed Matrix. Figure 6.8 is an example of a student's matrix for identifying resources.

After completing her matrix, the student used the rating guide to assess her work. Instructors reviewed her self-assessment and added their own comments. In this particular case, the student decided that her resource matrix exceeded the standards. The teacher and library media specialist concurred with this assessment.

Sample Work B: Completed Checklist. This particular checklist was a handy tool for ongoing assessment of students' bookmaking skills. By using the checklist at critical intervals in the authoring process, the instructors were able to help students revise and improve their work. Periodically, completed copies of the checklist were attached to drafts and submitted for review and feedback, thus providing a system for monitoring individual progress and planning meaningful instruction.

Figure 6.9 is an example of one student's final checklist for his book. The "X" indicates the student's self-assessment. After reviewing the student's rating and comments (S), the teacher (T) and library media specialist (L) added their own comments.

Figure 6.8
Example of student-completed matrix for identifying resources.

Link to the standards: In this lesson I will show that I can find information about my topic in different kinds of print and electronic resources.

Resource Matrix

The title of my book is _Dragonflies in the Wetlands._

My research questions are:

What do dragonflies look like?

What is their life cycle?

How have they adapted to life in the wetlands?

The keywords I will use to search are: <u>dragonflies, insects, wetlands, ponds, and lakes</u>

Source of information (title)	Type of information (format)	One important thing I learned from the source
Dragonflies (Wild Guide) by Cynthia Berger	Book	_I learned that dragonflies are "aerial hunters." (I wonder what that means.)_
Geokids—Tadpoles, Dragonflies, and Caterpillars	Video	_I learned that baby tadpoles, dragonflies, and caterpillars don't look like their parents._
Saving the Wetlands	_A web page_	_I learned that dragonflies are related to damselflies, stick bugs, water striders, and lots of other insects._
Dragonflies of the World by Jill Silsby	Book	_I learned that dragonflies are one of the oldest creatures on earth._

The best source that I found was _Dragonflies (Wild Guide)_

My reason for selecting this is: _It tells what dragonflies look like, how they hunt their food, and what their life cycle is like. It answers most of my questions and it has lots of pictures._

Figure 6.9
Example of student-completed checklist for assessing wetlands books.

Link to the standards: In this lesson I will learn how to improve my work by using a checklist to assess my writing, my art, and my book as a whole.			
Title of the book: *Call of the Canada Goose* Author/Illustrator: Richard Smith			
Assessing My Wetlands Book			
Criteria—what's important?	**Yes**	**No**	**Comments**
Writing			
Do I provide important information about the wetlands?	X		*S: I include lots of important details about description, life cycle, and adaptation.* **L:** You answered all your questions.
Do I have a beginning, middle, and end to my book?	X		**T:** Your introduction grabs attention and hints at what's to come.
Do I use my own words?	X		*S: I use keywords and didn't copy.* **T:** You did a good job.
Do I carefully choose my words to describe the sights and sounds of the wetlands?	X		*S: I try to use words that give good descriptions about things to see and hear.* **L:** I liked phrases you used such as "a round ball of down" and "hang out in meadowy places."
Do I carefully check my spelling, grammar, and punctuation?		X	*S: I used the dictionary and asked my partner to double check but I still made lots of mistakes.* **T:** Hang in there. It's good that you are using dictionaries and partner checks.
Artwork			
Do I accurately show the wetlands in my pictures?	X		**L:** Most of the plants, animals, and landforms look like they belong in the wetlands.
Do my pictures and text go together?	X		*S: I read the text and then drew the pictures. I still need to improve on some of my art.*
Do I use color, design, and composition creatively?		X	*S: I don't know how to do this.* **T:** We need more work on composition.

Figure 6.9 *(Continued)*

Overall presentation			
Do my words and pictures present the wetlands in an interesting way?	X		**L:** I could really see the sights and hear the sounds of the wetlands in your book.
Does my book have an attractive cover?	X		*S: I worked hard on it.* **L:** It is eye-catching and makes me want to read your book.
Does my title page have the title, names of author and publisher, and place of publication?	X		**L:** I like your title!
Do I have four or more pages with text and pictures?	X		*S: I have eight pages.*
Do I list the resources I used to find information?	X		**L:** You have a good variety of resources.
Do I include a section about myself as the author?	X		*S: I wrote about seeing Canadian geese on a fishing trip with my dad.*

S = student, L = librarian, T = teacher

After reviewing his final checklist, the student used the rating guide and indicated that he had met the standards for writing and artwork and that he exceeded the standard for the overall presentation. When asked how the checklist helped him to improve his work, the student responded:

> This is the third time I filled in the checklist. I got better in every-thing but still need more work on writing good sentences and my artwork. The checklist helped by telling me what was important, and the teachers' comments told me what I needed to do to get better. I'm glad I wasn't graded on my first try.

Step 5: Include Samples of Student Reflections

While a consistent rating system might be applied to a range of ru-brics, checklists, matrices, and other graphic organizers, such a system would not be useful for examining reflection logs. The logs contrib-ute a wealth of information about how students think, learn, and feel. They help us understand a student's internal thought processes. Rather than attempt to rate or score them for assessment purposes, however, it would be more meaningful to have students select the log entries that reflect new insights and discoveries for inclusion in the process folios. Figure 6.10 is a student's journal response from the wetlands unit. In this particular response, she explains how she came up with her research questions.

When she selected this particular log for her portfolio, the student explained the reasons for her choice as follows:

> I picked this log because it shows how I came up with my questions. I started out asking why beavers build dams and why they don't get along with people. But when I did the web, I got a lot more ideas for questions to help me write my book. The most important questions were still about building dams and getting along with people.

Figure 6.10
Example of student log for the wetlands unit.

My topic is the beaver. I found out on the Internet that beavers change the land almost as much as men do. I was curious so I clicked on the beaver picture and found out that when they build dams, they make ponds and lakes. It also said that sometimes people and beavers don't get along. Now I had a lot of questions about beavers. The teacher said to make a web so I made one like we did in second grade. My main questions are in ovals. The rectangles show what I want to find out.

My Questions about Beavers

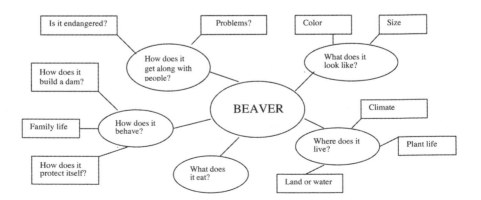

Step 6: Prepare a Summary Sheet for the Process Folio

The summary sheet helps make sense of the data contained in the process folio. As the first page of the document, the sheet provides a big picture view of what the student accomplished, how his learning was measured, and the student's assessment of his accomplishments. The actual work samples, assessment tools, student reflections, and

Figure 6.11
Example of student's summary sheet for the wetlands unit.

Standards/performance indicators	What I did (work samples)	How it was measured (assessment tools)	How well I did (rating)
21st-century learning standards			
Standard 1: Inquire, think critically, and gain knowledge (AASL 2007)			
• Skill 1.1.2: Use prior and background knowledge as context for new learning	*I wrote about what I already knew about the Wetlands.*	*I kept a learning journal.*	*My teacher said I did a good job of writing details about what I knew. I **exceeded** in this.*
• Skill 1.1.4: Find, evaluate, and select appropriate sources to answer questions	*I used books, encyclopedias, and the Internet.*	*I completed a matrix in which I identified the resources I found.*	*My matrix shows I **exceeded** in this skill.*
• Skill 1.1.5: Evaluate information found in selected sources on the basis of accuracy, validity, appropriateness for needs, importance, and social and cultural context	*I evaluated different resources I found.*	*I used a checklist to evaluate the different resources.*	*My checklist shows I **met** this skill. I could have done even better if I had checked to see if the authors were experts on the topic.*
• Disposition 1.2.3: Demonstrate creativity by using multiple resources and formats	*I used over a dozen resources including books, maps, and web sites.*	*I used a tracking sheet to organize my resources by different formats.*	*My tracking sheet shows I **exceeded** in this skill.*
• Responsibility 1.3.4: Contribute to the exchange of ideas within the learning community	*I was a little shy about making suggestions and in sharing with my group.*	*I kept a learning journal.*	*I am in the **approaching** category for this because I need to speak up more.*

(continued)

Figure 6.11 *(Continued)*

• Self-assessment 1.4.1: Monitor own information-seeking processes for effectiveness and progress, and adapt as necessary	*I did pretty well in writing up my information but I had problems with the artwork.*	*I assessed my work using the book-making checklist.*	*I **met** this skill but I could definitely improve in the art stuff.*
Science			
Develop understanding of • Characteristics of organisms • Life cycles of organisms • Organisms and environments (National Research Council 1996)	*I described the alligator in my book, and I talked about its life cycle.*	*I made sure that my information was accurate and important and that I answered the questions.*	*I **met** this standard because I wrote about the alligator.*
Language arts			
Conduct research on issues and interests by generating ideas and questions and by posing problems (Kendall and Marzano 2010)	*I picked the alligator as a topic. I asked what it looks like, how it grows, and why it's in trouble.*	*I used the chart that says what makes a good question.*	*I think I **met** this standard because I asked good questions.*
Instructors' comments: We agree that your work either exceeds or meets the targeted standards in most areas. However, more information is needed to answer all your questions. In particular, you need to explain the relationship between the alligator and the wetlands environment. We will discuss whether your work meets the standard for science.			

Overall ratings:

21st-century learning standards: Inquire, think critically, and gain knowledge	Meets/exceeds standard
Language arts: Conducts research on interests and issues	Meets standard
Science: Understands organisms and their environments	Approaches standard

instructors' comments follow the summary sheet as artifacts to document the learning achievements of a particular student.

Figure 6.11 is an example of a student's summary sheet for the wetlands project. You will note that the teacher and library media specialist reviewed the student's comments and added their own. An agreement was reached with the student before assigning an overall rating representing the child's performance in relation to the specific standards addressed. The summary sheet displays the content standards addressed by the teacher as well as the information literacy standards addressed by the library media specialist.

GETTING STARTED

Participating in portfolio assessment can be a daunting task. What must you consider? Where might you begin? First, teachers at your school must already be experimenting with portfolios. Second, you must be engaged in some level of collaborative instructional planning with your teachers. Third, you might consider the following strategy in experimenting with a portfolio system:

- Start with one teacher with whom you have successfully collaborated.
- Together identify just one unit of work for the portfolio system.
- Select no more than one or two AASL learning standards as the targets for assessment in this unit. (The teacher should also limit the content standards being addressed.)

By limiting the number of teachers and students you are working with and by restricting the units and standards that you wish to assess, you make your initial work with portfolios more manageable. You also have an opportunity to test effective and efficient methods of data collection and organization.

CONCLUSION

With the current emphasis on performance assessment, an increasing number of schools have adopted a portfolio system to measure students' progress in relation to the standards. Donald Graves (1992) states, "portfolios are simply too good an idea to be limited to an evaluation instrument" (1). He views portfolios as a way of helping students assume ownership of their own learning. By identifying work samples, assessing the quality of their performances, and re-flecting on their successes and failures, students become the keepers of their portfolios. Students who use portfolios as a means of com-munication and self-discovery as well as assessment and evaluation develop the confidence needed to become self-directed learners.

While portfolio assessment may be considered on the leading edge for many library media programs, working with the wider school community to develop this type of assessment system would make the benefits of learning through the library tangible and compelling.

CHAPTER 7

Assessing for Critical Understanding

This chapter addresses the following:

- Defining critical understanding
- Acquiring skills needed for critical understanding
- Developing critical understanding through inquiry
- Assessing for critical understanding

A staff development seminar we recently attended opened with a straightforward question: *What is important for students to learn?* Not surprisingly, the question was more difficult than it first appeared. Some participants thought that it was most important for students to learn skills like reading, writing, and computing. Others argued that learning is synonymous with the acquisition of knowledge related to the core disciplines—history, geography, science, and literature.

One teacher in the group commented that when she was in school, she memorized a lot of facts and acquired enough skill to do well on standardized tests, but she still had trouble making decisions and solving problems. Another participant added that many of the things he learned in school have been long since forgotten. He has had to learn new facts and acquire new skills to survive in a technology-driven world. He questioned whether today's schools were preparing students for the unknowns they will surely encounter in a 21st-century world. We were left wondering whether knowledge and skills alone would help students to navigate the complexities of our rapidly evolving society.

DEFINING CRITICAL UNDERSTANDING

Critical thought has many dimensions—affective as well as cognitive. It involves critical thinking, problem solving, and knowledge creation. It may be understood as a set of skills, abilities, dispositions, or habits of mind. All of this leaves educators asking: How do we know that students understand what has been presented?

David Perkins (1993) and his colleagues at Harvard see understanding from the perspective of performance. In their view, students demonstrate understanding through their performances. Perkins (1993) writes: "Knowledge and skill in themselves do not guarantee understanding. People can acquire knowledge and routine skills without understanding their basis or when to use them" (2). Arthur Costa and Bena Kallick (2001) also focus on performance and the need for students to produce knowledge rather than just acquire it. They outline 16 habits of mind that represent a combination of skills, abilities, and dispositions that are characteristic of critical thinkers and problem solvers. The list includes attributes like persistence, attentive listening, flexibility, metacognition, and questioning—all qualities essential to the effective use of information.

Robert Ennis (2000) has contributed a considerable body of work supporting the performance perspective on critical thinking and teaching for understanding. He describes critical thinking in terms of dispositions and abilities that help one decide what to believe and do. His online site devoted to critical thinking offers a comprehensive outline of dispositions and abilities that form the basis for a thinking curriculum.

It is clear from the work of these and other researchers that understanding goes beyond the acquisition of skills and knowledge. There is general agreement that learners demonstrate understanding through actions that are purposeful and thoughtful. Teaching and assessing understanding involves recognition of four interconnected components:

- A strong base of knowledge
- The skills needed to acquire knowledge
- The ability to analyze and think critically about whatever is learned
- The disposition to use knowledge and skills to solve problems, make decisions, and create products and performances

We observe this sense of purpose in the library environment when students demonstrate understanding by:

- Asking meaningful questions related to a topic, problem, or issue
- Planning and executing a search strategy
- Gathering information from a variety of sources
- Evaluating sources and information for accuracy and relevancy
- Challenging assumptions and validating predictions
- Considering multiple points of view before reaching a conclusion

- Creating products that meet or exceed predetermined criteria
- Communicating effectively to share ideas and solicit feedback

ACQUIRING CRITICAL UNDERSTANDING

In recent years, the federal No Child Left Behind legislation has emphasized the importance of content standards and standardized testing. In the view of many, this singular focus on the acquisition of knowledge and skills has led to a neglect of higher-order thinking. Adding to the problem, many educators express confusion about the nature of critical thought and question whether thinking skills can be taught at all.

Perkins (1993), Ennis (2000), Costa (1988), and others argue in favor of a thinking curriculum in which understanding is the ultimate goal. They each offer strategies that instructors might use to develop more thoughtful learners. Drawing from the work of well-known experts like these, we have compiled a list of strategies that library media specialists might use to promote deeper levels of understanding:

- Set both short- and long-term goals for learning.
- Plan activities that encourage interaction and collaboration.
- Ask open-ended questions that invite divergent responses.
- Allow time for students to think before they respond to a question.
- Solicit multiple points of view before shutting down a discussion.
- Involve students in conversations about the quality of work.
- Determine assessment criteria at the beginning of a project.
- Incorporate reflection and self-assessment at critical points in the process.
- Consider developmental factors and scaffold instruction to support learning.
- Teach for transfer.

We recognize that critical understanding is not the outcome of a single lesson or learning experience. It develops over time through involvement in many experiences that are challenging and meaningful to the learner. Because librarians may have, at best, intermittent contact with students, it is imperative that we establish collaborative relationships with teachers and other instructors who share our goals.

Collaboration is a major theme of the *Standards for the 21st-Century Learner* (American Association of School Librarians [AASL] 2007). The introduction to this document clearly states: "School librarians collaborate with others to provide instruction, learning strategies, and practice in using the essential learning skills needed in the 21st century" (4). These are lofty goals that are best achieved when librarians and teachers work together to provide thought-provoking learning experiences.

In the past, library media specialists tended to view their instructional role from the vantage point of the resource provider. They made resources available to students, expecting that the students would absorb the needed information and use it appropriately. The most recent standards document advises school librarians that "skills are best taught through an approach in which the teacher guides learners to construct their own understandings and their application to any learning experience" (AASL 2009b, 18).

In the library setting, students demonstrate understanding in myriad ways—by identifying problems, posing meaningful questions, conducting investigations, and evaluating sources and information. As students learn to reflect, self-assess, and use feedback to improve their work, we see incremental growth in understanding and self-awareness. Consider how knowledge, skills, and thinking are demonstrated in the following performances:

- A high school student demonstrates his understanding of history by preparing a visual timeline explaining the sequence of events leading up to the Civil War. He writes brief annotations explaining each visual and establishing a cause and effect relationship among events. In his log, he expresses his personal views on the war.

- A middle school science class notices a foul smell coming from the pond adjacent to their school. They learn from a local environmental agency that decomposing plant life might be the cause of the odor. Their decision to adopt the pond leads to a semester-long investigation of pond life. They pull weeds, monitor water quality, and introduce snails and other mollusks with a high tolerance for pollution. Throughout the year they keep a video log chronicling the restoration of the pond. The final performance is a webcast that incorporates parts of the video log and concludes with individual students reflecting on how the project contributed to their appreciation for the natural environment.

- A fifth-grade class is looking for a service project. When they learn that the local food bank needs donations of fresh vegetables,

they decide to plant a community garden. With the help of teachers, parents, and interested neighbors, they search for a site on the
school playground that receives plenty of sunshine and has access
to water and electricity. They research what kinds of vegetables
will grow well in their area and decide how much bed space to
allot for each. With teachers' help, they develop and implement
a year-long gardening plan that includes preparing the soil, dig-
ging and planting, feeding and watering, and sharing the fruits of
the harvest.

In each example, students use knowledge and skill to solve problems
and investigate issues of interest to them. In the process, they deepen
their understanding of underlying concepts and increase the likeli-
hood of transferring this knowledge to new and different situations.
Through these types of learning experiences, students acquire knowledge and skill; more importantly, they begin to understand how
their actions can affect the local community and the world in which
they live.

DEVELOPING CRITICAL UNDERSTANDING
THROUGH INQUIRY

Many librarians have been using an inquiry model as an instructional
framework that supports critical understanding. Although several
approaches to inquiry have been developed, they share three strands
related to the targets of learning: content knowledge, skills, and thinking processes (Harada and Yoshina 2004). To plan effectively for inquiry,
each of these goals must be addressed. Figure 7.1 proposes questions
teachers and librarians might use to plan inquiry-based learning experiences that incorporate all three goals.

Inquiry provides a structure for implementing the new American
Association of School Librarians learning standards. The very first
standard sets the expectation that students will be able to inquire, think
critically, and gain knowledge. That overarching goal continues as a
dominant theme throughout the document and signifies a departure
from previous practices. In the past, library instruction has focused on
teaching students skills such as using the online public access catalog
(OPAC) or the Dewey Decimal System to navigate library collections.
In contrast, the current standards encourage librarians to collaborate
with teachers to create learning experiences that foster critical thinking and deeper levels of understanding. Taken as a whole, the new

Figure 7.1
Questions used to plan inquiry lessons.

Learning targets	Questions to guide the planning
Content knowledge	What do we want students to understand?
	What information is needed for understanding to occur?
	Is the content relevant and accessible to students of this age?
	Will this knowledge help students to understand other situations?
Skills	What will students do to demonstrate their understanding of the content?
	What reading, writing, and listening skills are needed at each phase of the inquiry?
	What technology skills are needed?
	How can students be supported as they build on existing skills?
Thinking processes	What thinking skills, abilities, and dispositions are essential to the learning?
	How can we scaffold instruction to help students acquire skills and understand concepts?

standards indicate a greater role for librarians in supporting learning that is authentic, meaningful, and lasting.

In our work with schools we have encountered many approaches to inquiry. After experimenting with several different models, we have adopted Barbara Stripling's (2007) phases of inquiry that identify how inquiry-based research engages students in thinking behaviors:

- Connect: Learners connect to the overarching theme and the essential questions. They explore aspects of the topic that they are familiar with or curious about. They use prior knowledge as a context for constructing new understanding.
- Question: Learners ask questions targeting important aspects of the topic. They wonder what more can be learned. They question the validity of newly acquired information.
- Investigate: Learners plan investigations, identify potential sources, develop search strategies, and evaluate information. They take notes, download relevant information, and cite sources.

- Construct: Learners construct new knowledge by analyzing, organizing, and synthesizing information. They summarize findings, validate hypotheses, and draw conclusions.
- Express: Learners share their knowledge through products and performances. They make appropriate use of media to communicate their understandings with real audiences.
- Reflect: Learners reflect upon what has been learned, how it was learned, and problems encountered. They use criteria to self-assess and make adjustments.

ASSESSING FOR CRITICAL UNDERSTANDING

In this section we describe questions and problems our students have wrestled with through inquiry, and we examine some of the tools and strategies used to assess the scope and depth of understanding. In each scenario we focus on the involvement of the school librarian in teaching and assessing skills outlined in the *Standards for the 21st-Century Learner* (American Association of School Librarians [AASL] 2007).

Scenario A: Assessing Ability to Connect New Learning to Prior Knowledge

Second graders are learning to be salmon stewards. They know that every year fewer salmon return to the local stream to spawn. They have discovered that the Pacific salmon are dying at an alarming rate, and they wonder what can be done to save them.

The children suggest that they could bring attention to the plight of the salmon by preparing a "Save the Salmon" exhibit for the school's Earth Day celebration. This becomes the basis for an inquiry-based unit focused on environmental factors affecting Pacific coast salmon. Two overarching questions provide a framework for learning:

- Why are the salmon not returning to the river where they were born?
- How can we help to bring back the salmon?

The second-grade teachers plan several experiences to build understanding of the issue through active learning. These planned activities include:

- Visiting a salmon hatchery
- Building an incubator for salmon eggs
- Making a diagram to show the life cycle of the salmon

- Creating a "Save the Salmon" project that explains the plight of the salmon and addresses the essential questions for the unit

Teachers decide to use the visit to the salmon hatchery as a kickoff activity, and they ask the library media specialist to help prepare students for the excursion. For his part, the librarian sees this as an opportunity to assess students' ability to use prior knowledge as a foundation for new understanding (AASL 2007, Standard 1.1.2). He decides to use a K-W-L (know, wonder, learn) approach to structure the learning and provide evidence for assessment.

Students are provided with a handout divided into three columns labeled "Know," "Wonder," and "Learn." The librarian asks them to think about something they already know about the Pacific salmon and to exchange ideas with a partner. Using a wall chart, the librarian models the process of writing what students believe to be true in the "Know" column. Following the same procedure, students use their own handouts to write additional ideas.

Next, students share with their partners things they wonder about the salmon. These thoughts are written in the "Wonder" column as questions to be answered. The librarian explains that new questions will be added to the list during the investigation. He also tells the class that the "Learn" column will be filled in later.

During the visit to the hatchery, students are encouraged to pose their questions to guides and to examine informational displays for anything that might help answer their questions. Upon their return to school, they use the "Learn" column to write what they learned about the salmon during the field trip. To bring closure to the lesson, students are asked to compare the "Know" column with the one labeled "Learned" and to reflect on the new knowledge they acquired.

The K-W-L process allows students to recognize gaps in their knowledge and to formulate questions that address those gaps. It permits instructors to see at a glance whether students are building upon a base of knowledge. For busy educators and their students, the K-W-L process is one of the simplest ways to assess learning. Figure 7.2 represents the K-W-L chart described in this lesson along with the guide used for scoring it.

Figure 7.2
K-W-L chart for visit to salmon hatchery.

My learning goals:
I can write things that I **know** about the salmon.
I can write things that I **wonder** about the salmon.
I can write things I **learned** about the salmon that I didn't know in the beginning.

Things I know about the salmon	Things I wonder about the salmon	Things I learned about the salmon

Assessment Guide

Exceeds	I wrote three things that I knew about the salmon in the beginning.
	I wrote three questions I had in the beginning. I added to the list as I found new information.
	I wrote three things I learned about the salmon on the field trip.
Meets	I wrote two things that I knew about the salmon in the beginning.
	I wrote two questions I had about the salmon in the beginning, but I didn't add questions later.
	I wrote two things that I learned about the salmon that I didn't know at the beginning.
Beginning	I wrote one thing that I knew about the salmon in the beginning.
	I wrote one question that I had about the salmon.
	I wrote one thing I learned about the salmon that I didn't know at the beginning.

Scenario B: Assessing Ability to Ask a Range of Questions to Focus the Search for Understanding

The fifth grade has chosen "Mover and Shakers" as the theme for the year. Their essential question is: *How do "movers and shakers" change the world?* In every curriculum area students are introduced to the men and women who have influenced that aspect of human endeavor. In math class they learn about Pythagoras and Archimedes. Through science they become familiar with figures as diverse as Galileo, Marie Curie, and Thomas Edison. The study of American history introduces them to everyone from the early explorers to modern presidents and Civil Rights leaders.

As a culminating activity a closed-circuit TV broadcast is planned featuring interviews with movers and shakers from many spheres of human activity, including: the arts, sports, and entertainment, as well as traditional academic fields. Students work in pairs to identify a person, living or dead, who qualifies as a mover and shaker. They develop a list of questions to ask that person during a live interview. They write a script and practice asking questions and giving responses. Prior to the broadcast, they decide who will be the interviewer and who will play the part of the interviewee. For the real-time production, one student comes dressed like the person being interviewed. The other student plays the role of a TV reporter, equipped with a microphone and a notepad.

Early on, teachers observe that few students are asking questions that might lead to a deeper appreciation of what it means to be a mover and shaker. To the contrary, most questions focus on facts that can be answered in a word or a phrase. For example, a student who selected Jackie Robinson as his topic asks questions like these: "What team did he play for?" and "How many homeruns did he get?"

The library media specialist, an important instructional partner at the school, offers to plan a lesson on questioning. This lesson provides an opportunity to assess students' ability to "Develop and refine a range of questions to frame the search for new understanding" (AASL 2007, Standard 1.1.3). She begins instruction by having students use a T-chart to separate their fact-based questions from those that focus on big ideas. After posting their charts and discussing the differences among the questions, students make the following generalizations:

- Fact-based questions can be answered in a word, a phrase, or a short sentence. You can usually find the answer to these questions by looking in a book or by googling the key words. Most fact-based questions begin with the words *who, what, where, or when.*
- Big idea questions are harder to answer. You may look in many different resources and still not find the answer. Sometimes you have to read between lines and form your own conclusions to come up with an answer. "Big idea" questions often ask *how, why, or what if.*

The library media specialist designs an assessment strategy to determine whether students can transfer what they learned through this exercise to formulating their own interview questions. Students help to determine assessment criteria before writing the questions they will ask during the interview. The criteria they agree on are incorporated into the assessment checklist included in Figure 7.3. The librarian uses students' responses on the checklist along with their interview questions to assess learning and adjust instruction.

Figure 7.3
Checklist for assessing interview questions.

Name of the person to be interviewed: _____

Questions I will ask:

_____

_____

_____

_____

Checklist for Assessing Interview Questions

Learning goal: I will write meaningful questions to ask the person I interview.		
Criteria	Yes. Here is an example.	No. This is what I need to change.
I have questions that ask for simple facts.		
I have questions that focus on big ideas.		
I have questions that will lead to interesting information about the person's life.		
I ask a question that suggests a follow-up question.		
My questions will help me answer the essential question.		

After using the checklist to assess my list of questions, I made the following revisions:

_____

_____

_____

Scenario C: Assessing Ability to Consider Different Points of View toward a Controversial Issue Before Coming to a Conclusion

An 11th-grade social studies class is closely following the national debate on health care reform. Students have been scouring the media to locate articles for and against the movement to reform health insurance in America. They clip newspaper headlines highlighting key points of controversy and share information gathered from blogs and webcasts. As the intensity of the debate increases, they decide to hold a panel discussion to examine all sides of the issue. The panel focuses on answering the question: *Is health care a fundamental right that government is obligated to provide for all of its citizens?*

The class decides to approach the issue from different perspectives—a health care provider (a doctor, a nurse, or a pharmacist), an insurance executive, a hospital CEO, a Congressperson, and an uninsured patient. Groups are formed to gather information and to develop arguments favorable to the interests of these constituencies. Although one person is selected to represent each view on the panel, every member of the team is expected to contribute to the presentation.

The library media specialist is involved with the project in several ways. In addition to providing access to resources, he structures learning to help students develop a deeper understanding of this complex issue. He works with the teacher to plan experiences requiring students to:

- Identify and evaluate sources to help make the case
- Summarize arguments for and against a particular point of view
- Formulate a personal position and support it with facts

The library media specialist uses the forum to assess students' ability to consider multiple points of view before taking sides and making decisions. He creates an assessment tool (Figure 7.4) that focuses on the ability to "employ a critical stance in drawing conclusions by demonstrating that the pattern of evidence leads to a decision or conclusion" (AASL 2007, Standard 2.2.3). The response sheet designed for the forum guides students to think critically about the arguments presented before forming a judgment. It contains the following elements:

- A statement of the learning goals
- A T-chart to sort out arguments for and against reform
- Space for writing a personal opinion on the issue
- Self-assessment criteria to guide students through the process

Figure 7.4
Response form for panel discussion on health care.

___

Learning goals:
I will summarize arguments for and against government involvement in health care reform.

I will consider both sides of the issue before reaching my own conclusion.

Question: Is health care a fundamental right that government is obligated to provide for all of its citizens?

Points made by those who say YES	Points made by those who say NO
• _____	• _____
• _____	• _____
• _____	• _____
• _____	• _____
• _____	• _____

After considering arguments on both sides, I have come to this conclusion:

_____

_____

_____

Criteria for Self-Assessment

I listened carefully to each speaker and wrote down the key points made.

I used the T-chart to separate arguments of those in favor from those opposed to reform.

I have at least one point for and one against health care as a fundamental right.

I have at least one point for and one against government's involvement in health care.

I express my personal point of view and give reasons for my position.

Scenario D: Assessing Ability to Identify Bias

The curriculum for a seventh-grade geography class focuses on National Geographic Standard 18: "How to apply geography to interpret the present and plan for the future" (National Geographic Society Committee on Research and Exploration 1994). Instructors build a curriculum around topics in the daily news that are related to geography. In place of textbooks, students use a variety of media—print, visual, and digital—as information sources. Learning experiences are planned to build understanding through critical reading, listening, and viewing followed by vigorous discussion of the issues.

Global warming is chosen as the first topic of study. Each day three students are assigned to report on a current event that is in some way connected to global warming or climate change. They have the option of selecting news stories from television, Internet sources (including blogs), video presentations, or traditional print media. Prior to making the presentation, the student posts on the bulletin board a headline, article, or advertisement promoting the story, and classmates are asked to predict what the article will be about. Following the presentation, students work in groups to verify their predictions and to express their personal views.

Early on, it becomes apparent that the media's coverage of global warming, like so many other issues, is rife with bias and outright propaganda. The instructional team looks for a way to help students identify bias and misconceptions in the stories they report on. The library media specialist designs a graphic organizer to assist students in evaluating news stories and preparing for their presentations. She wants to assess students' ability to "make sense of information gathered from diverse sources by identifying misconceptions, main and supporting ideas, conflicting information, and point of view or bias" (AASL 2007, Standard 1.1.7).

The matrix she designs serves several purposes:

- It provides a framework for identifying bias in the news.
- It helps students to select news stories on which to report.
- It provides a focus for reporting.
- It encourages students to listen critically to the ideas presented by others.
- It provides students and instructors with a tool to assess learning goals.

As a final assessment, each student chooses three news stories to assess for bias using the tool presented in Figure 7.5.

Figure 7.5
Assessing news stories for bias.

My learning goal: I will use critical reading skills to detect bias in a news story.			
Questions	Article 1	Article 2	Article 3
Who is responsible for the ideas in the article?			
What people or groups are likely to support the views expressed?			
What is the purpose of the article (e.g., to entertain, inform, persuade, express an opinion)?			
What is the main idea expressed in the article?			
What evidence is given to support claims that are made?			
How do other media sources report on the same issue?			

Reflection Questions

Which of these articles expresses the most biased point of view? Why do you think this?

Which article expresses the most balanced point of view? Why do you think this?

Scenario E: Assessing the Ability to Draw Conclusions

"A Sense of Place" is the overarching theme addressed throughout the fourth-grade curriculum. In geography, students grapple with the question: *Why do people around the world look, speak, and live in different ways?* Through their study of literature, they explore the relationship between place and character development. In math class, reference books like *The World Almanac* are used to collect and analyze statistics related to population, wildlife, vegetation, geographic features, and other categories related to the concept of place.

A science unit brings the focus on place closer to home. The big question to be answered is: *What lives in my neighborhood?* Learning begins with a walking tour around school grounds. The objective is for students to connect with their own sense of place by:

- Observing sights, sounds, and smells that indicate life
- Reflecting on the meaning of what was observed
- Formulating questions related to the observations
- Using an inquiry process to validate assumptions

The library media specialist wants to test students' ability to "to draw conclusions from information and apply knowledge to curricular areas, real-world situations, and further investigations" (AASL 2007, Standard 2.1.3). She collaborates with teachers to develop an independent learning activity modeled after the schoolyard project. Students paste a handout with the following directions inside their observation journals:

- Take a walking tour of your backyard.
- Observe sights, sounds, smells, and other signs of life.

Figure 7.6
Map for assessing ability to draw conclusions.

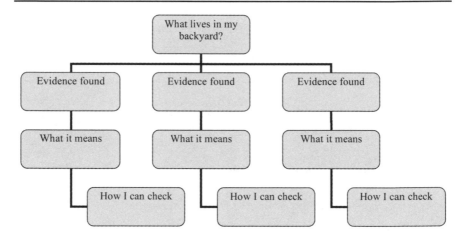

My Self-Assessment Guide

Assessment Criteria	Comments
I use my senses to observe sights, sounds, and smells of living things in my backyard.	
I find evidence of at least three things that live in my backyard, and I take notes on my organizer.	
I consider what the evidence means and write what I think lives in my backyard.	
I write about how I can check my conclusions and find more information.	

- Write notes about your observations.
- Use your observations to form conclusions about what lives in your backyard.
- Reflect on your experience by answering the questions on the graphic organizer (Figure 7.6).

Scenario F: Assessing Ability to Effectively Communicate Understanding

An eighth-grade environmental class hears about hundreds of fish lying dead on the banks of a nearby stream. Puzzled by the mysterious event, students hypothesize that the fish died from pollution caused by human activity. A field trip is planned to test the hypothesis. Students take photographs and collect water samples from different parts of the watershed. Back in the school lab they test the samples for dissolved oxygen, phosphates, nitrates, and PH levels, and they scrutinize pictures and videos taken at the scene for evidence of human activity. They formulate a list a questions for a guest speaker from the U.S. Fish and Wildlife Service, and they explore the full range of library resources to gather information related to understanding the cause of the problem and exploring possible solutions.

As a final project, the class decides to launch a public relations campaign aimed at improving water quality in local streams for the benefit of people as well as fish and other wildlife. Teams of students prepare and present their case to various school and community groups, including: the school's environmental club, the site-based management team, the school board, and the city council committee on environmental issues. The big question put before each group is: *How can we save the watershed for ourselves and future generations to use and enjoy?* In their presentations, student teams address the following questions:

- What caused the fish to die?
- What do the levels of oxygen, phosphates, nitrates, and PH in the water mean?
- How do we know that human activity is responsible for the fish-kill?
- If we agree that the problem was caused by people, how can people also be part of the solution?

Under the guidance of the school's media team, consisting of the librarian and the technology coordinator, students develop slide presentations

Figure 7.7
Rubric for assessing slide presentation.

Learning goal: I will create a slide presentation that explains the cause of the problem and suggests a solution.			
Criteria	Beginning	Proficient	Exemplary
Content	Only one or two facts are given. Some facts are not accurate or relevant.	The information is accurate, but some points need clarification. Most facts are relevant.	All of the information is accurate and relevant. There is enough information to make a strong case.
Originality	No new ideas are offered. Everything is copied from another source.	Some new ideas are offered. Most ideas are borrowed from other sources.	New ideas and insights are offered. Original thoughts are supported with information from credible sources.
Organization	There is no clear organization, just a list of facts about the topic.	Headings and bullets are used to organize the text. However, some ideas may be out of place.	The content is organized to make a strong case. Headings, bullets, fonts, and spacing are used to organize ideas logically.
Sources	Only one or two sources are listed. Citations are incomplete.	Sources are given for data and other facts. Some citations are incomplete.	Full citations are provided for data, charts, and other facts. All sources are reliable.
Message effectiveness	The purpose of the presentation is not clear.	The purpose of the presentation is stated in opening and closing frames. Some of the content does not support the message.	The purpose of the presentation is stated in the opening frame and restated at the end. The content supports the message.

My Self-Assessment

These are the strong points of my slide presentation:

These are some improvements that I can make:

to make their case before these various audiences. They create slides that:

- Describe the problem
- Identify possible causes of the problem
- Predict consequences of neglecting the problem
- Suggest actions that ordinary citizens might take to forestall the effects of the problem

The librarian uses the slide presentation to assess students' ability to "conclude the inquiry-based research process by sharing new understandings and reflecting on learning" (AASL 2007, Standard 3.1.1). After involving students in a discussion of criteria for assessment, she develops a rubric focusing on aspects of the presentation that relate to the development of understanding. Students use the rubric presented in Figure 7.7 as a guide for ongoing self-assessment, and instructors use it to measure the attainment of learning goals.

CONCLUSION

In this chapter, we have examined the importance of critical thinking in achieving deeper levels of understanding. We have identified the kinds of learning experiences that support the renewed emphasis on critical thinking, problem solving, and communication. We have looked at the expanded role of the library media specialist that is implicit in the *Standards for the 21st-Century Learner* (AASL 2007). Most importantly, we have explored ways in which librarians might collaborate with colleagues to craft meaningful experiences that enhance understanding and provide students with the knowledge and skills needed for lifelong learning.

CHAPTER 8

Assessing for Dispositions

This chapter addresses the following:

- Defining dispositions
- Acquiring dispositions
- Assessing for dispositions
- Using portfolios

The ability to thoughtfully manage oneself is essential in today's ever-changing workplace. Self-directed individuals are able to independently manage, monitor, and modify their behaviors when they are confronted with complex and demanding tasks (Costa and Kallick 2004). Such individuals exhibit the following types of behaviors (Conley 2008; Costa and Kallick 2004):

- Being aware of one's current level of mastery and understanding (and misunderstandings) of a problem or subject
- Approaching tasks by clarifying outcomes
- Identifying and systematically employing a range of strategies to achieve desired results
- Persisting when presented with a novel, difficult, or ambiguous task
- Thinking flexibly and developing alternative strategies
- Transferring learning and strategies from familiar settings and situations to new ones
- Reflecting on what worked and what needed improvement regarding a particular challenge

The *Standards for the 21st-Century Learner* (American Association of School Librarians [AASL] 2007) clearly indicates that successful learning behaviors include self-awareness, self-monitoring, and self-control. These tend to transcend content areas. As we mentioned in Chapter 7, *dispositions* and *responsibilities* are interwoven with the students' ability to assess their own learning journeys in the new AASL standards.

DEFINING DISPOSITIONS

While library media specialists are comfortable with *skills* as building blocks for learning, the notion of *dispositions* is less familiar. Dispositions have been described as "habits of mind, attitudes and learning behaviors" (AASL 2009b, 40). They reflect a tendency to exhibit frequently, consciously, and voluntarily a pattern of behavior that is directed to a broad goal (Katz 2000). They are a "set of problem-solving skills that a student calls on when he is faced with an unfamiliar situation or challenge" (Moreillon and Fontichiaro 2008, 65).

It's important to note that a disposition is more than simply knowing how to do something; it is actually doing it. Dispositions involve more than the cognitive ability to perform tasks; they also involve the affect, and embrace the whole learner. The AASL *Standards for the 21st-Century Learner* provides a rich spectrum of dispositions that today's students must display. They include the following:

- Initiative, curiosity, and engagement—learners pose questions and venture beyond fact gathering
- Creativity and flexibility—they use multiple resources and formats
- Adaptability—they change their focus and questions based on newly discovered information
- Resilience—they adjust strategies when results are not satisfactory and continue experimenting with different options to achieve desired outcomes
- Productivity—they plan strategically, clarify goals, establish reasonable deadlines, and work efficiently
- Openness—they seek and respect divergent perspectives and points of view
- Social responsibility and collaboration—they contribute to exchanges of questions and ideas in teams

ACQUIRING DISPOSITIONS

Much as skills cannot be taught in isolation from content, dispositions cannot be practiced in a vacuum. *Instructors foster these important attitudes by embedding them in content-based instruction.* Collaborating with teachers, library media specialists can help to foster these behaviors. Here are two quick examples:

- Elementary grade students are debating the literary and artistic merits of a traditional fairy tale against a Disney-produced film version of it. This is the opportune time to have them practice and reflect on an open-minded approach to examining the strengths and unique features of both works. They might also form teams to investigate these works and demonstrate their ability to collaborate on opinions based on supporting evidence from the works. The library media specialist can nurture an open discussion by introducing brainstorming strategies and graphic organizers that challenge teams to consider a range of ideas and suggestions.

- High school physics students are constructing a solar-powered car for a national competition. Their target, of course, is a winning final product. At the same time, however, the teacher and library media specialist want students to think deeply about how they solve problems and make decisions. To do this, they have students create wiki logs of their daily progress. They provide the following types of prompts that focus on students' productivity and resilience: What was your target today? How successful were you in achieving it? What problem did you encounter? How might you tackle this differently?

Several important points to consider about cultivating dispositions are:

- They develop over time and through numerous opportunities to practice responsibility and positive behaviors.
- It's not possible or desirable to flag the development of dispositions or responsibilities by grade-level benchmarks. For example, a very young student might display amazing persistence at a task when he or she is motivated, while an unmotivated high school student might be satisfied with cutting and pasting information from an online encyclopedia.
- Adult mentors—teachers, library media specialists, other support specialists, community experts, and family members—must model the desired behaviors and create situations and experiences that allow students to also demonstrate their abilities.
- Self-awareness and self-assessment are critical in this process of building lifelong inclinations to pursue learning. Simply doing is not enough; there must be times when learners step back to thoughtfully reflect on what's happening, why it's happening, and how they feel about the experience.

ASSESSING FOR DISPOSITIONS

All the tools and strategies described in Chapters 3, 4, 5, and 6 might be used to assess for dispositions. In the following six brief scenarios that range from primary grades to high school examples, we indicate how library media specialists and teachers might engage students in the assessment process as they work on inquiry-focused studies. The scenarios are merely suggestive of the range of possible approaches to assessing for dispositions.

Scenario A: Assessing for Initiative

Grade 1 students study the endangered green sea turtle. The big question for them is: How can we save the turtle? As their final product, the students create a school mural that portrays what must be done to protect this endangered species. To help the students go beyond questions that can be answered with *yes* or *no* responses, the library media specialist models how to generate questions that also ask *how, why,* and *what if,* among others. She also teaches them how to develop a question web using Kidspiration, a Web-based tool that allows students to combine text, numbers, and pictures. Students have guided practice time to create their individual question webs.

The library media specialist and teacher want to assess if students are able to "display initiative and engagement by posing questions and investigating the answers beyond the collection of superficial facts" (AASL 2007, Standard 1.2.1). They stage a gallery walk in which students post their question webs. Students participate in the gallery walk, examining each web carefully and placing stars beside all questions that go beyond yes/no responses. They do this for the webs created by their peers as well as their own webs. After the gallery walk, students reflect on what they have done (Figure 8.1).

Figure 8.1
Postgallery walk: Questions to assess for initiative.

- Which of my questions required more than yes or no answers?

- What help did I need to come up with these questions? Who helped me?

- After the gallery walk, could I think of additional questions that required more than yes or no answers?

- If so, what were the questions?

Scenario B: Assessing for Flexibility

Grade 5 students investigate how to be hygiene smart. Working with the teacher and library media specialist, the students identify important hygiene issues for kids and gather information on healthy practices by interviewing health professionals as well as reading and viewing various resources. The computer resource specialist helps the students create storyboards with their information and teaches them how to produce animated videos. They ultimately produce two-minute videos of their findings that are aired on the community television network during National Hygiene Week.

The instructors want to assess if students "demonstrate flexibility in the use of resources by adapting information strategies...and by seeking additional resources when clear conclusions cannot be drawn" (AASL 2007, Standard 2.2.1). Students maintain an electronic log of their information searches during the project. By responding to the types of prompts in Figure 8.2, they maintain a trail of the sources they used and the reasons for adapting and modifying their searches.

Figure 8.2
Log prompts to assess for flexibility.

- What information source did I use today?

- What was I looking for?

- How did it work out?

- What should I try next, and why?

- How do I feel about my progress so far?

Scenario C: Assessing for Persistence

Grade 7 students develop an online history of their community that combines text-based and multimedia materials (adapted from a unit described by Weigel and Gardner 2009). With guidance from their social studies and language arts teachers as well as the library media specialist and technology resource teacher, the students interview older residents in the community, upload the interviews to the project's online wiki, and convert the audio recordings of the interviews into downloadable podcasts. In the process, students hone their writing and information and communication technology skills and gain a broader appreciation of their community.

The instructional team wants to assess students' ability to "display persistence by continuing to pursue information to gain a broad perspective" (AASL 2007, Standard 1.2.7). To do this, they devise a rating scale that also requires students to provide evidence supporting their ratings (see Figure 8.3).

Figure 8.3
Rating scale to assess for persistence.

1. I have a clear idea about what I need to find out.   Just starting —1—2—3—4—5—6—7—8—9—10 Doing a good job **Support for my rating:
2. I am curious and not afraid to ask questions.   Just starting —1—2—3—4—5—6—7—8—9—10 Doing a good job **Support for my rating:
3. I seek new ways to find information when one approach doesn't work.   Just starting —1—2—3—4—5—6—7—8—9—10 Doing a good job **Support for my rating:
4. I search for alternative solutions when I encounter a problem on this project.   Just starting —1—2—3—4—5—6—7—8—9—10 Doing a good job **Support for my rating:
5. I learn from my mistakes and use them to improve my work on this project   Just starting —1—2—3—4—5—6—7—8—9—10 Doing a good job **Support for my rating:

Scenario D: Assessing for Literary Appreciation

Grade 8 students participate in independent reading projects in their English class. To launch this project, the teacher and library media specialist administer a reading interest inventory to find out what students want to read. Based on the results of the inventory, the library media specialist plans a series of book talks in a range

Figure 8.4
Reading tracker to assess for literary appreciation.

Rating scale: Use this to rate your reads	
****	You have to read this!
***	Pretty good
**	Not that great
*	Forget this one!

Date	Title/Author	Genre	Rating
Reasons for the rating:			
Date	**Title/Author**	**Genre**	**Rating**
Reasons for rating:			
Date	**Title/Author**	**Genre**	**Rating**
Reasons for the rating:			
Date	**Title/Author**	**Genre**	**Rating**
Reasons for the rating:			
Date	**Title/Author**	**Genre**	**Rating**
Reasons for the rating:			

of genres, invites the local public librarian to also join in book talks, creates a Web page with recommended reads and links to interesting resources, and encourages students to participate in a librarian's blog on reads too good to miss.

The teacher and library media specialist want to see if students "show an appreciation for literature by electing to read for pleasure and expressing an interest in various literary genres" (AASL 2007, Standard 4.2.4). Students maintain electronic reading trackers that allow them to document what they are reading and how they are responding to the various works (Figure 8.4).

Scenario E: Assessing for Openness

Grade 10 students gain a deeper understanding of intellectual freedom by studying books that have been challenged in the United States (adapted from a unit described by Stephens 2008). Students select specific works from the American Library Association's *100 Most Frequently Challenged Books: 1990–2000* (2008). The social studies and English teachers enlist the help of the library media specialist for this project. Besides reading the selected book, the student locates national reviews and news items dealing with challenges to the book as well as reports of actions taken by the community and courts. Students produce response journals of the issues for and against the challenged work. They also develop their own conclusions defending or opposing the challenge. While they work independently for the first half of this project, they ultimately collaborate on a class-produced video documentary titled *Burn That Book!* that they enter in a K–12 technology competition in their school district.

The instructional team wants students to demonstrate an "openness to new ideas by considering divergent opinions, changing opinions or conclusions when evidence supports the change, and seeking information about new ideas encountered through academic or personal experiences" (AASL 2007, Standard 4.2.3). They devise a graphic organizer that allows students to document their findings and present their conclusions (Figure 8.5).

Scenario F: Assessing for Social Responsibility

Grade 12 students in a global studies class read foreign affairs columnist Thomas Friedman's bestseller, *The World Is Flat* (2005). They participate in the award-winning Flat Classroom Project designed

Figure 8.5
Graphic organizer to assess diverse points of view and conclusions.

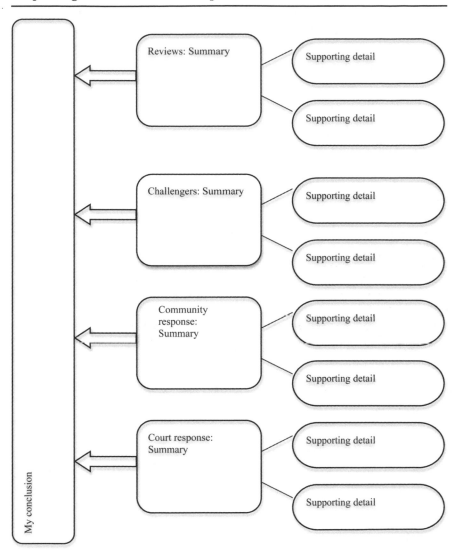

by Julie Lindsay and Vicki Davis (2009), that enables students from around the world to study major events and innovations that have flattened the world. They extend their understanding by engaging in wide-ranging discussions about the impact of these events on business, government, politics, education, art, and science. During each cycle of the project, student teams in different countries partner to create a thematic wiki page on a topic related to the book. They share their completed projects with their fellow participants on-line (Weigel and Gardner 2009). The teacher, library media specialist, and computer resource specialist assist the students in deeper research on the topics selected and serve as guides on the side as their students collaborate with students from campuses around the globe.

The instructors are particularly interested in the students' abilities to "show social responsibility by participating actively with others in learning situations and by contributing questions and ideas during group discussions" (AASL 2007, Standard 3.2.2). They also want

Figure 8.6
Rubric to assess for social responsibility.

Respect for others

○	3.	I always listen to others without interruption. I always consider the opinions and ideas of others. I learn from others by consistently encouraging feedback.
○	2.	I usually listen to others without interruption. I sometimes consider their opinions and ideas. I sometimes ask for feedback.
○	1.	I have difficulty listening to others without interruption. I rarely consider their opinions and ideas. I almost never ask for feedback.

Cooperative work style

○	3.	I encourage contributions toward the group's work. I help others to focus on the task. I frequently share materials and ideas.
○	2.	I don't lead but I contribute my fair amount to the group's work. I sometimes share materials and ideas.
○	1.	I contribute to the group's work when I am prompted. I rarely share materials and ideas unless required to do so.

Collaborative problem solving

○	3.	I take leadership in identifying problems with which the group must deal. I frequently suggest alternative ways to resolve the problem. I take the lead in helping my group reach consensus.
○	2.	I provide appropriate input as a team member in identifying a problem. I contribute my share to resolving the problem.
○	1.	I have trouble identifying a problem. I play a small role in resolving the problem.

Figure 8.6 *(Continued)*

Idea generation

○	3.	I continuously look for new ways of looking at things. I use different information and communication technology tools independently to generate new and innovative ideas that help my group's work.
○	2.	I don't usually come up with original ideas, but I often provide useful information to support these ideas. I use different information and communication technology tools but need guidance.
○	1.	I don't come up with original ideas, and I rarely provide information to support these ideas. I use different information and communication technology tools but need lots of help.

Ethical behavior

○	3.	I always honor the rules and processes established for online group work. I always practice acceptable computer etiquette. I always practice legal and ethical uses of technology and information.
○	2.	I usually follow the rules established for online group work. I usually practice acceptable computer etiquette as well as ethical uses of technology and information.
○	1.	I rarely follow the rules established for online group work. I have to be constantly reminded to practice acceptable computer etiquette and ethical uses of technology and information.

to have students "demonstrate teamwork by working productively with others" (AASL 2007, Standard 3.2.3). The instructors and students collaboratively design a rubric that can be used for assessment by individuals and peers as well as instructors (Figure 8.6).

USING PORTFOLIOS

In Chapter 6, we elaborated on the benefits of portfolios and how they might be used in assessing student learning. In this chapter, we suggest that portfolios are especially valuable in enhancing student reflection and metacognition. They help students seriously consider the big question, "who is in charge of your learning"? (Costa and Kallick 2004, 44).

Through entries in their portfolios, students tell their own stories about how they learned and how they felt about their learning. They might capture their reflections through journal-type entries or they might create letters to their instructors, parents, community mentors, or peers. In the process of doing this, they define their own progress and how their behaviors and attitudes have changed over time. In short, "portfolios can tell us who we are and who we want to be. This is an ideal opportunity for students to provide evidence and reflect on what makes them feel efficacious, what engages them, and how they view themselves as learners" (Costa and Kallick 2004, 65). Figure 8.7 provides examples of portfolio prompts that might be used to assess dispositions.

Figure 8.7
Portfolio prompts to assess dispositions.

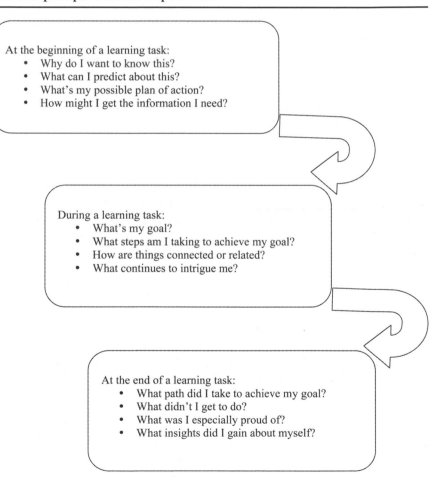

At the beginning of a learning task:
- Why do I want to know this?
- What can I predict about this?
- What's my possible plan of action?
- How might I get the information I need?

During a learning task:
- What's my goal?
- What steps am I taking to achieve my goal?
- How are things connected or related?
- What continues to intrigue me?

At the end of a learning task:
- What path did I take to achieve my goal?
- What didn't I get to do?
- What was I especially proud of?
- What insights did I gain about myself?

CONCLUSION

Developing enduring habits of learning is a guided adventure in continual growth and improvement. Judi Moreillon and Kristin Fontichiaro (2008) liken this to tending a garden where seeds are carefully planted and gently nurtured. They indicate that dispositions "integrate naturally into thoughtful instructional design" (Moreillon and Fontichiaro 2008, 66). To effectively foster self-directed practices, educators must build the language of dispositions along with the actions of dispositions. The goal is to have students develop a thirst for learning "and not depend solely on the judgment of others to determine the value of what they are learning" (Costa and Kallick 2004, 68).

Ultimately, we want students to predict consequences of their decisions and expand their repertoire of techniques and strategies. Self-assessment energizes these types of dispositions that lead to lifelong learning. Helping students to own their learning is true self-empowerment. By highlighting dispositions in collaborative teaching, "we can watch our student seedlings grow...[it] can be a time for all of us to blossom together!" (Moreillon and Fontichiaro 2008, 67).

CHAPTER 9

Assessing for Tech-Integrated Learning

This chapter addresses the following:

- Defining the digital landscape
- Acquiring the essential skills in a digital world
- Identifying implications for library media specialists
- Assessing for tech-integrated learning

DEFINING THE DIGITAL LANDSCAPE

The revolution in digital expression has transformed how we read, write, listen, and speak by allowing us to manipulate a number of new media forms involving sound, graphics, and moving images. As a result, the way we communicate, solve problems, and learn from others continues to change dramatically (Hamilton 2009). New communication tools invite both individual and collaborative construction and publication through blogs and such services as MySpace, Google Docs, and YouTube (Ohler 2009, 10). Tech users also have the capacity to integrate new media forms into a single narrative—for example, a Web page, blog, or digital story (Ohler 2009, 10). In short, literacy in the 21st century is "not just learning to read a book" (Scherer 2009, 7). It's about harnessing collective intelligence in a global landscape (Strickland 2008).

ACQUIRING SKILLS FOR SUCCESS
IN A DIGITAL WORLD

Educators are well aware that online communication tools are a natural part of most students' daily lives outside of school. Not-so-startling statistics from a report by the Pew Internet and American Life project (Pew Research Center 2007) indicate that 59 percent of youngsters ages 12 to 17 share artistic creations online via videos, Web pages, and blogs, and that 55 percent of them have profiles on social networking sites like Facebook. Doug Johnson (2009) says that the Internet generation is "postliteracy's poster child" (20). These young people can read but choose to meet their primary information and recreational needs through audio, video, graphics, and gaming (Johnson 2009, 20). The Net generation demands spaces that allow freedom, customization, and collaboration (Darrow 2009, 80). As these Web 2.0 technologies find their way into classrooms and library media centers, a new world of experiences is opening up for students (New Media Consortium 2009).

What are the implications for schools? First, the use of these technologies allows students to take the reins: they move from being consumers of the Internet to creators on the Web (Knobel and Wilber 2009; Lamb and Johnson 2009). The optimum learning environment allows the use of personal communication devices (MP3 players, handhelds, laptops) and provides wireless network access for these devices.

Does this mean that students are making wise use of the technologies? Not necessarily. Bill Ferriter (2009) says "there's not a lot of thoughtful discourse going on among teenagers blasting their way through Halo on their PlayStations" (85). He observes that students "have no trouble connecting, but no one has taught them about the power of these connections" (86). To put it simply, access alone is not sufficient for students to effectively and responsibly use these various applications and tools. They need to acquire the skills, cultivate the dispositions, and assume the responsibilities necessary to constructively use these technologies. The 2009 Horizon Report prepared by the New Media Consortium emphasizes the value of collaboration in the workplace, as people must work across geographic and cultural boundaries. Many educators are finding that online tools provide rich opportunities to develop teamwork skills and tap into the perspectives of people around the world (New Media Consortium 2009). To effectively use these tools, students must value and practice ethical and responsible social behavior. They must be able to personally assess the appropriateness of their online communication. Doug Fodeman and Marje Monroe (2009) drive this particular point home in the following quote:

> We know that the greatest motivating factor for children to use technology in grades 7 and up is to connect to others, to socialize. Their irresistible need to connect with their peers, coupled with the development of 24/7 accessible technologies, can make the use of

sites like Facebook all-consuming. It gives the false sense of privacy along with the feeling of anonymity and lack of social responsibility that develops from using text-centered telecommunications. Students can post embarrassing and hurtful content in text, photos, and videos. We need to teach them that nothing is private online. (36–37)

IMPLICATIONS FOR LIBRARY MEDIA SPECIALISTS

Pam Berger (2007) states:

> Just as basic literacy means more than decoding alphabetic symbols, digital literacy involves more than the mere ability to use software or operate a digital device; it includes a variety of technical, cognitive, social, and emotional skills that users need in order to function effectively in a digital environment. (116)

The *Standards for the 21st-Century Learner* (American Association of School Librarians [AASL] 2007) mirrors Berger's sentiments that the emphasis is no longer on information literacy alone but on immersion in multiple ways to access, understand, and use information. If this is indeed the case, today's library media specialist must be knowledgeable about how learning takes place in a hypertext environment. While there is much freedom in accessing large amounts of information, the sheer volume and nonlinearity of the information can result in hopelessly losing oneself in cyberspace. In addition, Web-based hypermedia environments encourage broad explorations of information rather than in-depth investigations. Checking e-mail, googling, blogging, and instant messaging tend to distract rather than focus digital natives on the "deep reading and reflection" that are so critical for "associative thinking, synthesis, and understanding" (Berger 2007, 117).

Library media specialists are in a potentially vital position to team with teachers and other learning specialists on staff to integrate and use new technologies. By partnering with teachers, they can help all students "assimilate technology into their lives in a way that will enhance—not eclipse—skills like sustained thinking and connecting to fellow humans" (Sprenger 2009, 34). Daniel Pink (2005) refers to these critical skills as high concept and high touch. High concept refers to people's ability to discern patterns, connect ideas, and construct new knowledge. High touch is being able to empathize and respect others and to encourage and even inspire collaborative discoveries. As key members of teaching teams, library media specialists can nurture both high concept and high touch. They can help students strike a healthy balance between being "connected through technology and connecting with real people" (Sprenger 2009, 37).

ASSESSING FOR TECH-INTEGRATED LEARNING

The 2009 Horizon Report (New Media Consortium 2009) states that assessment is a theme repeatedly introduced in discussions of current and emerging technologies. Educators at all levels are challenged when it comes to assessing student work in the new media. They are also struggling to evaluate how much an individual student contributes to or learns from a collaborative project. In the following six brief scenarios that range from elementary grades to high school examples, we indicate how library media specialists and teachers might engage students in the assessment process as they incorporate the use of technology to organize data, create and communicate new understandings, and interact socially to construct new knowledge. The reader is reminded that these scenarios are merely suggestive of the range of possible approaches to assessment. As demonstrated in the examples that follow, many of the tools and strategies described in Chapters 3, 4, 5, and 6 might be used to assess for tech-integrated learning.

Scenario A: Assessing Online Discussions

Grade 4 students join scientists and students from other elementary schools across the nation to track the migration of the humpback whale as part of their year-long study of endangered species. The library media specialist helps the class establish an online forum where students can share what they are learning, raise questions, and provide links to interesting facts and images relating to this marine mammal.

As a critical part of this project, the library media specialist and teacher engage the students in assessing their use of "social networks and information tools to gather and share information" (AASL 2007, Standard 4.1.7). They also focus on students' ability to "participate in the social exchange of ideas, both electronically and in person" (AASL 2007, Standard 4.3.1). The instructors design a rating scale that requires students to provide reasons for their ratings (Figure 9.1).

Figure 9.1
Rating scale to assess online collaborative teamwork.

Rating:
3 = I do this all the time.
2 = I do this some of the time.
1 = I almost never do this.

Criteria	3	2	1	My reason(s) for the rating
I complete all tasks I am assigned by the group.				
I post my work on time so that the group can move forward.				
I raise questions and make comments that help the group understand the work.				
I come up with ideas for different ways to work on a problem.				
I always communicate respectfully.				

Scenario B: Assessing Blogs

Grade 5 students engage in researching their favorite fiction writers. Working with the library media specialist and teacher, each student selects a living author to study. The students read several books by the authors selected and generate questions they would like to ask the author about his or her works and future plans for stories. They interview the authors using Skype and share their summaries via blogs. This Web-based journal entry platform also allows fellow readers to comment.

The teacher and library media specialist have the students focus on using "technology and other information tools to organize and display knowledge and understanding in ways that others can view, use and assess" (AASL 2007, Standard 3.1.4). Students work with the instructors in creating a rubric (Figure 9.2) to assess their blog entries. The students as well as the instructors use the rubric to continually reflect on whether the entries are clear, organized, and effective in communicating points the students wish to convey.

Figure 9.2
Rubric to assess blog entries.

Criteria	Proficient	Developing	Beginning
Content	My post covers the following areas: (1) the author's reasons for writing, (2) his/her feelings about the stories, and (3) his/her future ideas for stories.	My post focuses on two of the three areas mentioned for "proficient."	My post focuses on only one of the three areas mentioned for "proficient."
Organization	My entire post is well organized and clear.	Most of my post is organized and clear.	Most of my post is confusing and rambling.
Response	In my response to someone else's post, (1) I made connections between my classmate's post and my own, (2) I asked questions if something was unclear, and (3) I shared new ideas and opinions.	My post focuses on two of the three areas mentioned for "proficient."	My post focuses on only one of the three areas mentioned for "proficient."

Scenario C: Assessing Podcasts and Vodcasts

Grade 7 students are studying the impact of technology on their lives. One of the hot issues is cyber bullying. The students discuss how teenagers can use cell phones, instant messaging, Twitter, and a number of other interactive technologies to post hateful messages that hurt and torment their peers. The discussions evolve into a project where the students work in teams to create podcasts and vodcasts describing what cyber bullying is, why people do it, how to prevent it, and how to take action against it. They decide to use the products as public service announcements to inform and educate the school and general community.

Students learn that podcasts are online audio content that is delivered via an RSS feed (Web feed format that publishes frequently updated works), while vodcasts are online video clip content delivered via the feeds. The library media specialist and computer resource teacher collaborate with the classroom teacher in having the students draft storyboards and create podcasts and vodcasts.

The instructional team and students focus on the importance of using "information and technology ethically and responsibly" (AASL 2007, Standard 3.1.6). They use a rating scale (Figure 9.3) to assess their products. Along with this assessment tool, the students maintain electronic logs, or e-logs, describing their progress. In their e-logs, they respond to prompts such as:

- What is the message we wish to communicate? Why?
- What is the most effective way to present our message?

Figure 9.3
Rating scale to assess podcasts and vodcasts.

Rating:
3 = We did a terrific job.
2 = We did a satisfactory job.
1 = We need to be a much better job.

Criteria	3	2	1
Our purpose is clearly stated.			
The major points of our podcast/vodcast are accurate and clearly communicated.			
Our graphics and videos are relevant to the content.			
Our podcast/vodcast is well organized and flows smoothly.			
Our conclusion clearly summarizes our major points.			
The sound is clear.			
The slides effectively display the points we want to make.			
The podcast/vodcast is linked to other useful resources.			
We accurately cite our sources.			

- Where can we find information to help us support our message?
- What are we learning as we conduct our research?
- What additional questions are we asking as we work on this project?
- How do I personally feel about our progress?
- How do I personally feel about our final product?
- How will we know if our product effectively delivered our message?

Scenario D: Assessing Wikis

Grade 8 students in a health education course are concerned about current health issues in their community. They decide to establish a wiki page to compile and present information on health concerns focusing on teens. They learn that wikis provide easy-to-use tools for

Figure 9.4
Checklist to assess a wiki page.

Criteria	Yes	No	Specific Evidence and Examples
Content: • We clearly stated the purpose of our contribution. • We supported our opinions with accurate facts.			
Structure: • We made effective use of hyperlinks to connect information and ideas. • Our wiki was logically organized: alphabetical, chronological, hierarchical, geographical, thematic, etc.			
Teamwork: • Everyone in the team had a chance to contribute. • We shared the tasks equally. • We all met deadlines.			

creating, editing, and sharing digital documents, images, and media files. Multiple participants can enter, submit, manage, and update a single Web workspace, thereby creating a community of authors and editors (Lamb and Johnson 2009, 48). Importantly, they are excited about using wiki tools to engage in collaborative learning experiences that promote reading, writing, and high-level thinking across content areas and grade levels (Knobel and Wilbur 2009, 24).

In producing their wiki page, the students search for information in multiple formats, interview health professionals, and conduct focus group sessions with their peers on topics ranging from anorexia and obesity to depression and self-mutilation. They embed photos and videos in the wiki, create hyperlinked pages, and edit each other's writing.

The teacher and library media specialist involve the students in assessing the quality of the class-created wiki page. They focus on the use of "technology and other information tools to analyze and organize information" (AASL 2007, Standard 2.1.4). The teacher and library media specialist study different checklists that might be used for assessment purposes (e.g., Lamb and Johnson 2009) and devise a checklist that requires students to also include supporting evidence (Figure 9.4).

In addition to the checklist, the class uses the history tool on a wiki page to trace the additions and changes made by individual students. The students reflect on the nature of contributions they make—that is, whether their contributions are helping the team clarify or elaborate on content or discover new alternatives or ideas.

Scenario E: Assessing Digital Narratives

Pacific Ocean High School has a large English as a Second Language (ESL) student population. As a social studies/sociology project, grade 11 students focus on immigrants in their community. They delve into some of the following issues: how cultural differences affect individuals and groups in the community, how immigrants contribute to community life, and problems that develop from immigrant assimilation. The students are excited about creating personalized stories of the immigrant experience. They see digital storytelling as a way to shape and share information in a way that engages the interest and emotions of their viewers. They collaborate with their teacher, the library media specialist, and the technology resource teacher in developing story outlines, doing the background research, and designing and producing

Figure 9.5
Rubric to assess a digital narrative.

Criteria	Exemplary	Proficient	Approaching
Subject	All key ideas are supported with details and examples based on research conducted.	Most key ideas are supported with details based on cited research.	Key ideas are supported with personal opinions rather than cited research.
Story line	The message is clear and the entire narrative holds the attention of the audience. The entire story flows logically from one sequence to the next.	The message is clear and most of the narrative holds the attention of the audience. Most of the story flows logically from one sequence to the next.	The message is unclear and the narrative does not hold the attention of the audience. The story jumps around and is hard to follow.
Originality	Product successfully incorporates creative approaches to presenting the story.	Product reflects some creativity but not everything works.	Product does not reflect creativity.
Storyboard	Storyboard is fully developed. It includes the following: dialogue, camera angles, time, scene, and sketch. Storyboard was used extensively during project development.	Storyboard is missing one of the following: dialogue, camera angles, time, scene, or sketch. Storyboard was used periodically during project development.	Storyboard is missing two or more of the following: dialogue, camera angles, time, scene, or sketch. Storyboard was not used during the project development.
Multimedia content	All multimedia components explain and reinforce the main points of the story.	Most multimedia components explain and reinforce the main points of the story.	Most multimedia components tend to stray from the main points of the story.
Narration/ sound	Voice quality is clear and consistently audible throughout the narrative.	Voice quality is clear and audible through most of the narrative.	Voice quality is frequently muffled and inaudible throughout the narrative.

Figure 9.5 *(Continued)*

Criteria	Exemplary	Proficient	Approaching
Pace	The pace fits the story line and helps the audience really get into the story.	The pace is occasionally too fast or too slow for the story line.	The pace is often too fast or too slow for the story line.
Cited sources	All citations are documented in the desired format.	Most citations are documented in the desired format.	Citations are not documented in the desired format.

digital narratives to share at a school-sponsored cultural symposium that is open to the public.

Students discover that they have access to almost unlimited combinations of text, audio, and video for this project. They use Web 2.0 tools such as VoiceThread (http://voicethread.com) to enable audio and video interactions where they can comment on an image or document through speech, text, audio files, or video. They employ Flickr (http://www.flickr.com), an online photo-sharing site, to add annotations and links directly to pictures, creating connected stories and conversations. They not only bookmark sites, but they share these favorites using social bookmarking sites like Delicious.com where others can find them (Richardson 2009, 30).

The instructional team and students focus on "using the writing process, media and visual literacy, and technology skills to create products that express new understandings" (AASL 2007, Standard 2.1.6). They also "connect understanding to the real world" (AASL, 2007, Standard 2.3.1). To assess progress, students compose log entries in a wiki (wiki-logs) that allow them to post entries and also to comment on each other's logs. They reflect on the following types of questions:

- What do I already know about this topic?
- What do I really want to find out?
- What sources can I use to get the information I need?
- How can I organize my story?
- How can I best tell my story?

Along with the wiki-logs, students use a rubric (Figure 9.5) to assess their progress and evaluate their final products.

Scenario F: Assessing Wiki Pathfinders

High school students in an industrial arts academy work in teams to select a community issue such as vandalism or homelessness and work on research-based industrial designs to help deal with the selected issue. For example, students might design a type of stone bench that would discourage skateboarders from using them for unsafe skating practices, or they might design a temporary shelter for the homeless. Part of the predesign work involves doing the investigative research that might be collected in an annotated wiki pathfinder—for example, online resources, interviews, community contacts, podcasts, and video clips with annotations. As part of the project, each team also develops a wiki pathfinder that they can jointly edit throughout their

Figure 9.6
Reflection rubric to assess a wiki pathfinder.

Criteria	Exceeding	Meets	Needs work
Introduction	Opening paragraph clearly defines the topic and organization of the pathfinder.	Opening paragraph clearly defines the topic but does not explain the organization of the pathfinder.	Opening paragraph simply states the topic and does not explain the organization of the pathfinder.
Reflection			
Resources	Includes a range of resources in four or more formats including print, graphic, online, and community experts. All resources are of consistently high quality.	Includes resources in at least three different formats. Most resources are of high quality.	Includes resources only in one or two formats. Many resources are questionable.
Reflection			
Annotations	All annotations are evaluative and effectively convey the value of the sources.	Several annotations are descriptive rather than evaluative.	Some entries have no annotations. Existing annotations are largely descriptive rather than evaluative.

Figure 9.6 *(Continued)*

Criteria	Exceeding	Meets	Needs work
Reflection			
Keywords	At least three appropriate keywords are included.	At least two appropriate keywords are included.	Only one appropriate keyword is included.
Reflection			
Sequence	All information is organized in a clear, logical way.	Most information is organized in a logical way.	There is no evidence of a clear plan for the organization.
Reflection			
Text—font and format	Font formats (e.g., color, bold, italic) have been carefully selected to enhance readability and content.	Font formats have been carefully selected to enhance readability but not content.	Font formats detract from reader's ability to understand the content and view the material.
Reflection			
Citation	All citations are complete and correctly entered in required format.	Two or three citations are incomplete.	Most of the citations are incomplete.
Reflection			

work. They use Google Docs (http://docs.google.com) to upload annotations, create links, and edit their work with team members. The library media specialist also incorporates the pathfinders on the library's Web page, and students have access to the pathfinders from the library's Web-based catalog.

By successfully creating these pathfinders, students "demonstrate mastery of technology tools for accessing information and pursuing inquiry" (AASL 2007, Standard 1.1.8). They also "demonstrate confidence and self-direction by making independent choices in the selection of resources and information" (AASL 2007, Standard 1.2.2). To assess students' performance, students and instructor use a reflection rubric (Figure 9.6) that combines a rubric with spaces for reflective comments.

CONCLUSION

Access to the learning tools afforded by technology give students an opportunity to "experience learning in multiple ways, to develop a public voice, to make connections with others around the world, and to compare their own ideas with those of their peers" (New Media Consortium 2009, 7). Web 2.0 technologies coupled with emerging learning standards demand that learners be personally productive, socially responsible, and collaborative with diverse team members both face-to-face and online. Students not only gain new knowledge from their individual reading, but they are also expected to confidently generate and share knowledge with other members of a globally networked community (Coiro 2009, 60–61).

As information professionals, library media specialists need to teach safe protocols and etiquette on the Internet to our students so they do not inadvertently make the errors that place them in jeopardy socially, financially, emotionally, and even physically (Farr 2009, 32). Being able to assess how the current media results in the construction and communication of new knowledge allows everyone in the learning community to reflect on how the technologies empower us to learn in ways we never imagined before.

CHAPTER 10

Outcome-Based Approach: Elementary Grade Example

This chapter:

- Introduces an outcome-based strategy to lesson planning
- Presents a sample project in an elementary school setting
- Describes outcome-based planning for sample library lessons related to the project

OUTCOME-BASED APPROACH

In assessment-focused instruction, library media specialists start with an idea of what the students must be able to do *at the end of the learning experience.* Grant Wiggins and Jay McTighe (1998) have popularized the term "backward design" (146) to describe this important concept in curriculum planning. Other educators (Perkins 1992; Wiske 1994; Mitchell, Willis, and The Chicago Teachers Union Quest Center 1995; Luongo-Orlando 2003) have advocated similar approaches to instructional design. This type of planning challenges instructors to identify the outcomes first and the means by which outcomes will be measured before creating the activities themselves. This is counter to common practice in which instructors begin by creating lesson procedures and then tacking on objectives. In this latter type of planning, assessment is frequently ignored. Figure 10.1 displays the differences between the two approaches.

Starting with a clear notion of the end goal applies not just to planning a unit of study; it should also be reflected in creating individual lessons. There are two critical questions involved in this process (Harada and Yoshina 2004):

- What must students be able to demonstrate or perform by the end of this experience?
- How can we measure how well students have achieved this goal?

Figure 10.1
Conventional versus outcome-based planning.

Conventional planning	Outcome-based planning
Start with ideas for activities	Start with a standard and a performance indicator selected from the skills strand
	Identify dispositions and/or responsibilities to be addressed
Select activity for lesson	Define learning task based on performance indicator
Develop lesson procedure	Determine criteria to assess student performance
	Design tool or method to do the assessment
Determine lesson objectives based on lesson activity	Develop instructional procedure that is directly connected to learning task and assessment. Include the following:
Decide on assessment technique (often viewed as ancillary and optional)	• Direct instruction with modeling • Guided practice with informative feedback • Independent practice with self-monitoring based on criteria • Reflection and self-assessment

The following steps are crucial in this type of planning:

- Begin by identifying the broad standard being addressed.
- Articulate a more specific performance indicator related to the standard.
- Describe a learning task based on the performance indicator. This may be referred to as a performance task.
- Determine the criteria that will be used to assess how well students perform the learning task.
- Design the tool or method to measure proficiency.

The Figure 10.2 captures these steps in a visual form.

Although skills remain a critical focus for instruction and assessment, the *Standards for the 21st-Century Learner* (American Association of School Librarians [AASL] 2007) reminds us that dispositions and responsibilities represent long-term goals and important instructional outcomes that complement the skills strand.

In Chapters 10, 11, and 12, we focus on how lessons implemented in the library media center might demonstrate an outcome-based

Figure 10.2
Relationship between standards and assessment.

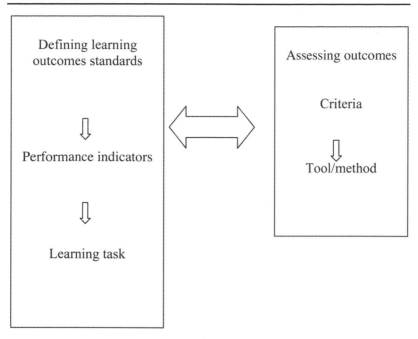

approach to student learning. In this chapter, we share library lessons that might be part of a classroom project in an elementary school. In Chapters 11 and 12, we apply the same outcome-based approach to lessons in middle and high school settings. The organization of all three chapters is identical. First, the project itself is summarized. This is followed by two sample lessons, each organized under the following major headings.

OUTCOMES: WHAT MUST STUDENTS BE ABLE TO DEMONSTRATE AT THE END?

Standards and performance indicators addressed

Dispositions and/or responsibilities developed through the learning experience

Products and performances that demonstrate learning

(continued)

**ASSESSMENT: HOW WILL STUDENT
PERFORMANCE BE MEASURED?**

Learning goal that states how students will show what they
know
    Criteria for assessing performance
    Self-assessment strategies
    Tools for collecting, recording, and quantifying data

**LEARNING PLAN: HOW WILL THIS
LESSON BE DELIVERED?**

What will instructors do?
What will students do?

It's critical to note that school library media specialists can start
with assessment tools they are already using (e.g., rubrics, checklists, rating scales) and, with minimal effort, refocus them for the
student by substituting "I," "me," and "my" in the tools (Marjorie
Pappas, personal communication). The instructional process or
learning plan has four overlapping components: (1) direct instruction with modeling, (2) guided practice with informative feedback,
(3) independent practice with self-monitoring based on criteria, and
(4) reflection and self-assessment. Our examples are based on the
assumption that there is some degree of cooperation or collaboration between library media specialists and teachers. The outcome-
focused approach to lesson planning is most effective when teaching
in the library media center is directly aligned with the learning targets of the classroom.

SUMMARY OF PROJECT

A third-grade class is learning about the wetlands. Early on, students
decide they want to produce their own books with the information
gathered. Their essential questions are project-focused: What is important to share about wetlands? Where might we find this information?

To stimulate their curiosity, instructors take students on virtual
tours of the Everglades, Okefenokee Swamp, and the Louisiana coastal
marshes. The students deepen their knowledge by participating in a
field trip to a nearby wetlands area where they photograph and take

notes on what they see and hear. In the library media center, they comb through trade books, encyclopedias, and the Internet to find additional information about the plants and animals they encountered on their field experience. A simple authoring program guides students through the process of planning, drafting, editing, and revising the writing.

With the help of the teacher and library media specialist, students learn how to enhance their projects by uploading pictures taken with digital cameras. They eventually share their completed works at an authors' showcase in the library media center where they celebrate their accomplishments with families and other third-grade classes.

SAMPLE LESSONS

How might the library media specialist contribute to this project? We suggest two possibilities in this chapter and invite readers to think of other lessons that might be integrated into this unit:

- Lesson 1: Finding information in a variety of sources
- Lesson 2: Developing criteria to assess student-produced books

Lesson 1: Finding Information in a Variety of Sources

In the classroom, children create webs and generate questions to guide the search for information. At this point, the library media specialist helps students with the task of identifying potential information sources. The objective of this lesson is to locate a variety of print and electronic sources to use in the project and to determine which of those sources would be most useful.

Outcomes Desired

Standards and Performance Indicators: Because this lesson represents the collaborative efforts of the classroom teacher and the library media specialist, content area standards for language arts and science are addressed along with appropriate performance goals from the *Standards for the 21st-Century Learner* (Figure 10.3).

Disposition/Responsibility: Not every lesson can realistically address both dispositions and responsibilities as identified in the *Standards for the 21st-Century Learner* (American Association of School Librarians [AASL] 2007). However, one or the other should be possible

Figure 10.3
Standards and performance indicators addressed in lesson 1.

Content areas	Standards	Performance indicators
Language arts	Gather and use information for research purposes Use reading skills and strategies to understand and interpret a variety of informational texts (Kendall and Marzano 2010)	Use electronic media to gather information (Kendall and Marzano 2010)
Science	Acquire skills necessary to do scientific inquiry (National Research Council 1996)	Develop the abilities necessary to do scientific inquiry Demonstrate understanding of scientific inquiry (National Research Council 1996)
Library (21st-century learner)	Inquire, think critically, and gain knowledge (American Association of School Librarians 2007)	Follow an inquiry process in seeking knowledge: Find, evaluate, and select appropriate sources to answer questions (American Association of School Librarians 2007)

in most lessons. In this particular example, the following disposition is addressed: Students will demonstrate confidence and self-direction by making independent choices in the selection of resources and information (AASL 2007, Standard 1.2.2).

Product/Performance: Students use a matrix (Figure 10.4) to identify at least four relevant information sources for their projects. They describe the format of each source and state one thing that might have influenced their selection. They compare their sources to decide which is most helpful for their projects, and they explain their choices.

Figure 10.4
Organizer for identifying resources.

Link to the standards: In this lesson I will...

- Use the online public access catalog to locate at least one book that helps answer my questions
- Use an electronic database to locate an online article
- Find the Web site of a wildlife organization that will help answer my questions
- Find information related to my questions in a print or electronic encyclopedia
- Give the title, author, and format for each source
- Evaluate each resource based on how accurate the information is and whether it will help me with my project

Resource Matrix

The topic of my wetlands book is _____

My research questions are

_____

_____

_____

The keywords I will use to search are

_____

The resources I think will be most useful for my project are:

Source of information (title, author, date)	Type of information (format)	One answer I found in this source

The best source that I found was _____

_____

This is the best source because _____

_____

Assessment

Learning Goal: Students explore various information centers to find, evaluate, and select resources that are relevant and appropriate.

Assessment Criteria: Figure 10.5 outlines the criteria for measuring how well students perform in relation to the performance indicators.

Self-Assessment Strategies: Students work with their instructors to construct the "I will" statements presented earlier in Figure 10.4. Instructors refer to these statements to provide informative feedback throughout the activity, and students use them to monitor their performance and improve their work. In addition, students use their learning logs to reflect on the experience and identify the resources they might examine for additional information.

Tools for Collecting, Recording, and Quantifying Data: The resource matrix presented in Figure 10.4 serves as a tool for both instruction and assessment. The library media specialist also designs a rating system (Figure 10.6) to analyze students' responses on the matrix and to assess their performance in relation to the learning goals.

Learning Plan

The learning plan outlined in Figure 10.7 is designed to scaffold the learning experience so that students will develop the skills and dispositions required for inquiry learning. The lesson plan outlines four interrelated steps:

- Direct instruction with modeling: Instructors explain the task and model what a solid performance or product might look like. Students help determine criteria for an acceptable performance.

Figure 10.5
Criteria for locating and evaluating a variety of sources.

I will...

- Use the online public access catalog to locate books related to the inquiry
- Use an electronic database to locate online articles
- Use the Internet to access Web sites of organizations that provide information related to the inquiry (e.g., Sierra Club or Environmental Protection Agency)
- Evaluate resources and information based on accuracy, relevancy, and accessibility
- Cite sources selected and evaluated

Figure 10.6
Rating system for identifying resources.

Number of resources used	
Not met	I found one resource for my topic.
Approaches	I found two resources for my topic.
Meets	I found three resources for my topic.
Exceeds	I found at least four resources for my topic.
Range of resources used	
Not met	I found only a print or an electronic source.
Approaches	I found one print and one electronic source.
Meets	I found more than one print and electronic source.
Exceeds	I found print, electronic, and people sources.
Information found	
Not met	I didn't find anything to report.
Approaches	I reported something I learned from at least one resource.
Meets	I reported something I learned from each resource.
Exceeds	I reported something I learned from each resource. I also selected the best resource and told why I chose it.

The librarian works with students to develop a resource map (Figure 10.8) to provide a framework for independent learning.

- Guided practice with feedback: Students practice the task. Instructors provide informative feedback by asking questions that focus on established criteria.
- Independent practice with self-monitoring: Students work independently on their projects. They use criteria to make ongoing adjustments. Instructors provide help as needed.
- Reflection and self-assessment: Students use learning logs to reflect on what they are doing, how they are learning, and problems they are having. They use criteria to self-assess each stage of the learning and to make improvements.

Figure 10.7
Learning plan for identifying information resources.

Instructional design	What will instructors do?	What will students do?
Direct instruction with modeling	Explain the task and present the matrix. Ask students how we can find the answers to our questions? Where can we look? Model the process of filling in the matrix. Guide the discussion by creating a map showing the information sources that might be accessed through the library (Figure 10.8). Help students to compose "I will" statements to be used during guided and independent practice.	Write personal topic and research questions on the matrix. Brainstorm a list of possible resources. Contribute ideas to resource map. Work in small groups to craft "I will" statements similar to those found in Figure 10.5.
Guided practice with informative feedback	Provide technical assistance and informative feedback as students access and evaluate both print and electronic resources. Assist students who need help filling in the matrix.	Visit each of the information centers identified on the resource map (Figure 10.8). Use feedback to make adjustments.
Independent practice with self-monitoring based on criteria	Encourage independence by referring students to the "I will" statements. Continue to provide informative feedback as students work on their matrices. Focus on students who need additional help locating sources.	Use search words to access potential sources. Fill in information required by the matrix. Refer to the "I will" statements to self-monitor and make adjustments.

Figure 10.7 *(Continued)*

Reflection and self-assessment	Encourage reflection and self-assessment by having students keep logs. Provide appropriate prompts such as: —*How did you know which resources would be most helpful?* —*What problems did you have filling out your matrix?* —*What kind of help do you need finding more resources for your project?*	Use "I will" statements to self-assess and make improvements. Accept feedback from instructors and peers. Reflect on the experience and write personal thoughts in learning logs.

Figure 10.8
Map of information sources.

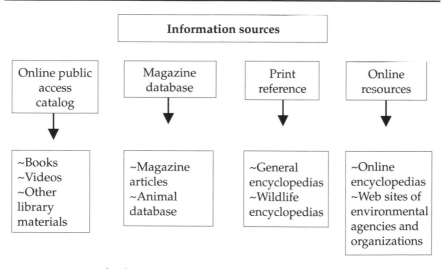

Lesson 2: Developing Criteria to Assess Student Books

The library media specialist undertakes the development of assessment criteria with the students as part of a bookmaking workshop. While the classroom teacher focuses on the writing process and the artwork, the library media specialist helps students understand how books are put together.

Outcomes Desired

Standards and Performance Indicators: Figure 10.9 presents the standards targeted in the bookmaking portion of the project.

Figure 10.9
Standards and performance indicators addressed in lesson 2.

Content areas	Standards	Performance indicators
Language arts	Use general skills and strategies of the writing process (Kendall and Marzano 2010)	Draft and revise: Use strategies to revise written work Edit and publish: Use strategies to publish written work Evaluate own and others' writing (Kendall and Marzano 2010)
Library (21st-century learner)	Share knowledge and participate ethically and productively as members of democratic society (American Association of School Librarians 2007)	Use writing and speaking skills to communicate new understandings effectively Use technology and other information tools to organize and display knowledge and understanding (American Association of School Librarians 2007)

Disposition/Responsibility: While lesson 1 included a disposition, this particular lesson more appropriately addressed the following responsibility identified in the *Standards for the 21st-Century Learner:* Students follow ethical and legal guidelines in gathering and using information (AASL 2007, Standard 1.3.4).

Product/Performance: With instructors' assistance, students develop a list of criteria to guide and assess the bookmaking project. The criteria provide quality indicators for writing, the use of technology, and the overall presentation.

Assessment

Learning Goal: Students use the established criteria to guide them through the process of creating an original book about the wetlands.

Assessment Criteria: Students work with their instructors to determine the criteria that will be used to assess the final product.

These criteria relate to the process of developing a book as well as the final product. Figure 10.10 is an example of the criteria.

Self-Assessment Strategies: Students use the criteria outlined in Figure 10.10 to make ongoing improvements as they work on each phase of the bookmaking project. They also work with a partner to practice asking questions that will improve their work. Some of their questions include:

- Does the beginning of my book introduce the topic? Does it capture the reader's attention?

Figure 10.10
Criteria for evaluating student-created books.

Writing

- Content—It provides important information about the topic.
- Organization—There is a beginning, middle, and end.
- Voice—It is written in the author's own words.
- Sentence fluency—It is written in complete sentences that flow naturally.
- Word choice—Words are carefully chosen to represent wetlands accurately.
- Conventions—There are no mistakes in spelling, grammar, or punctuation.

Use of Technology

- Writing and technology skills are used to create books.
- Production tools (authoring software and digital cameras) are used to organize information and create projects.

Overall Presentation

The book is attractive to look at and easy to read.

- The pictures show the wetlands accurately.
- The pictures complement the text.
- Color, design, and composition are used creatively.

The book has the following parts:

- An attractive cover.
- A title page that has the title of the book, the author's name, the publisher's name, and the place of publication.
- At least four pages containing text and illustrations.
- A list of resources.
- A "Something about the Author" section that includes personal reflections about the inquiry and the process of authoring a book.

- Do I have enough details to make my book interesting and informative?
- What other important information should I include? Where can I find it?
- Have I chosen pictures that help tell my story? Do my pictures show the wetlands accurately?
- Does my list of resources include books and other printed materials, online sites, places I visited, and people I talked to?

Tools for Collecting, Recording, and Quantifying Data: The library media specialist works with teachers to devise a checklist (Figure 10.11) that incorporates the agreed-upon criteria as well as some of the questions suggested by students as they worked on their projects. While instructors use the checklist to assess performance, students also use it to self-monitor and make improvements as they work on their books. The same checklist is used as a final evaluation.

Figure 10.11
Checklist for assessing wetlands books.

Link to the standards: In this lesson I will learn how to improve my work by using a checklist to assess my writing, my ability to use technology, and my book as a whole.

Title of the book: _____

Author/illustrator: _____

Assessing Your Wetlands Book

Criteria—what's important?	Yes	No	Comments/ explanation
Writing			
Do I provide accurate information about the wetlands?			
Does my story have a beginning, middle, and end?			
Do I support my main ideas with details?			
Do I use my own words?			

(continued)

Figure 10.11 *(Continued)*

Do I write in complete sentences that make sense?			
Do I choose my words carefully to describe the sights and sounds of the wetlands?			
Do I have any mistakes in spelling, grammar, or punctuation?			
Use of technology			
Did I use authoring software to create my book?			What is the name of the program?
Did I effectively use a digital camera to take photos?			
Overall presentation			
Do my words and pictures present the wetlands in an interesting way?			
Does my book have an attractive cover?			
Does my title page have the book's title, the names of the author and publisher, and the place of publication?			
Do I have four or more pages with text and pictures about the wetlands?			
Do I have a list of the resources used?			
Do I have a "Something about the Author" section that includes my reflections on the process and the final product?			

Suggested scoring guide for instructors

3—*Exceeds standards by achieving*
- At least six of seven criteria for writing
- Both criteria for use of technology
- At least four out of six criteria for overall presentation

2—*Meets standards by achieving*
- Four or five of seven criteria for writing
- One of two criteria for use of technology
- Three of six criteria for overall presentation

1—*Approaches standards by achieving*
- Two or three of seven criteria for writing
- Neither criterion for use of technology
- One or two criteria for overall presentation

Learning Plan

The goal of this particular lesson is for students to identify possible criteria for assessing their books. The library media specialist uses *A Wetland Walk,* by Sheri Amsel, to introduce this lesson. Figure 10.12 summarizes what instructors and students do to achieve the desired outcome.

Figure 10.12
Learning plan for developing assessment criteria with students.

Instructional design	*What will instructors do?*	*What will students do?*
Direct instruction with modeling	Introduce *A Wetland Walk*. Call attention to: – The book cover – The title page – Illustrations – List of references – Information about the author Pose questions to encourage predictions such as: – *Is it fiction or nonfiction? What makes you think so?* – *What do you expect to learn about the wetlands from the book?* Write responses on white board.	Students draw from experience and prior knowledge to make predictions about the story. Their comments might include: – *It will tell what plants and animals live in the wetlands.* – *It may explain why the wetlands are important.* – *It will describe the wetlands and tell how they are formed.* – *It should tell what you would see and hear on a walk through the wetlands.*
Guided practice with informative feedback	Read the story aloud, stopping to encourage comments that relate to predictions: – *What words help you to see, hear, feel, and smell?* – *What do you think the author's message is? How does she get it across?* – *Does the author explain why the wetlands are important?* Organize students into groups to brainstorm answers to the question: What qualities make	Demonstrate critical listening skills by responding to the reading and participating in the discussion. Meet in small groups to discuss the qualities of a good book. Record ideas on a handout modeled after the chart. Responses might include:

(continued)

Figure 10.12 *(Continued)*

Instructional design	What will instructors do?	What will students do?
	A Wetland Walk a good nonfiction book? **What qualities make a good nonfiction book?** Writing Overall presentation Ask for feedback from each group and record responses under the headings *writing* and *overall presentation*.	<u>Writing</u> – *It sticks to the topic.* – *Everything is about the wetlands.* – *The words help you to see, hear, and feel what the wetlands are like.* <u>Overall presentation</u> – *All the parts are there—title page, illustrations, list of sources, etc.* – *The cover is attractive. It makes you want to read it.*
Independent practice with self-monitoring based on criteria	Incorporate criteria into a checklist (Figure 10.11) to be used by students as they work independently on their books. (A category for the use of technology is added to the criteria suggested by students.) Scaffold the learning and provide support to meet the needs of individual students.	Work independently using authoring software to create text and import pictures. Use the criteria expressed on the checklist to self-monitor and to make needed adjustments.
Reflection and self-assessment	Refer to the criteria on the checklist to provide informative feedback. Use assessment data provided by the checklist and student reflections to make timely adjustments in instruction.	Engage in ongoing reflection and self-assessment. Use the criteria on the checklist to self-monitor and to make needed changes. Reflect on learning by responding to prompts such as: – *How did technology help you with your project?* – *What tools did you use? Were they helpful?* – *What problems did you have?* – *How did you solve them?*

Figure 10.13
Lessons for grade 3 wetlands project: Focus, outcome, task, and assessment.

Lesson focus	Desired outcomes	Learning task	Assessment tool
Lesson 1 Finding information in various sources	Find, evaluate, and select appropriate resources to locate information	Explore information sources and indicate titles, authors, and types of information found	**Matrix** that guides the instructional process and serves as a tool for assessment (Figure 10.4)
		Compare and evaluate sources based on usefulness to the project	**Reflection log** prompts focusing on goals (embedded in Figure 10.7)
Lesson 2 Developing criteria to evaluate the final product	Use criteria to revise, improve, and update self-generated knowledge	Develop a list of criteria to assess the student-made books on topics relating to the wetlands	**Checklist** that includes criteria for assessing the writing, use of technology, and overall presentation (Figure 10.11)
	Use technology tools to create products and share knowledge		

CONCLUSION

The key to effective learning starts with students having a clear idea of what they must demonstrate. To measure how well students achieve the expected goal requires a careful delineation of criteria and the selection of an appropriate tool or strategy for the assessment. The learning plan is ultimately shaped by the targeted outcome. Figure 10.13 summarizes the key elements of the lessons in this chapter.

In the next chapter, we present a middle school example of how lessons taught in the library media center might reflect an outcome-based approach to instructional design.

CHAPTER 11

Outcome-Based Approach: Middle School Example

This chapter:

- Reviews an outcome-based strategy to lesson planning
- Presents a sample project in a middle school setting
- Describes outcome-based planning for sample library lessons related to the project

OUTCOME-BASED APPROACH

In Chapter 10, we began with a description of outcome-based instruction and presented examples of lessons in an elementary grade project that were planned in that manner. We present more examples in this chapter, this time at the middle school level. We start with a summary of a classroom-library project and follow this with two related lessons that might be taught in the library media center. Each lesson is formatted as follows.

OUTCOMES: WHAT MUST STUDENTS BE ABLE TO DEMONSTRATE AT THE END?

Standards and performance indicators addressed

Dispositions and/or responsibilities developed through the learning experience

Products and performances that demonstrate learning

(continued)

ASSESSMENT: HOW WILL STUDENT PERFORMANCE BE MEASURED?

Learning goal that states how students will show what they know
    Criteria for assessment
    Self-assessment strategies
    Tools for collecting, recording, and quantifying data

LEARNING PLAN: HOW WILL THIS LESSON BE DELIVERED?

What will instructors do?
What will students do?

SUMMARY OF PROJECT

When eighth graders read the stories of Anne Frank and other Holocaust victims, they react with dismay and disbelief. Their need to make sense of this tragic event leads to thoughtful questions that demand honest, if difficult, explanations. Recognizing the need for background information, teachers solicit the help of the library media specialist, who contributes to the project by suggesting additional resources and instructional assistance as students seek answers to their questions. In the classroom, students work in literature circles to read and discuss critical aspects of selected literary pieces. Three questions provide a framework for the study:

- What can we learn about the Holocaust from this piece of literature?
- How does this work compare with other accounts of the Holocaust?
- What questions will help me to learn more about the Holocaust?

Concurrently with the literature study, students engage in inquiry projects related to the Holocaust. During this phase of the project, the library media specialist works closely with teachers to help students choose a focus for inquiry, pose meaningful questions, identify potential resources, and collect and evaluate information. When the class expresses an interest in creating a virtual museum as a culminating project, the library media specialist offers both technical and instructional support.

SAMPLE LESSONS

We present two library-based lessons that are critical for this project:

- Lesson 1: Asking the right questions
- Lesson 2: Selecting and evaluating resources

Lesson 1: Asking the Right Questions

Quality research begins with questions that serve as a guide for reading and note taking. They tell students what to look for as they survey resources. They help to define the topic by targeting the most important and relevant information in terms of both the topic and the product. Meaningful questions help students decide which resources to use, which notes to take, and how to organize the information for an effective presentation. This library lesson seeks to determine: What is a good research question? How do we write one?

Outcomes Desired

Standards and Performance Indicators: This information is presented in Figure 11.1.

Figure 11.1
Standards and performance indicators addressed in lesson 1.

Content areas	Standards	Performance indicators
Language arts	Gathers and uses information for research purposes (Kendall and Marzano 2010)	Gathers data for research topics (e.g., prepares and asks relevant questions) (Kendall and Marzano 2010)
History	The student conducts historical research (National Center for History in the Schools 1996)	Formulates historical questions from encounters with historical documents, eyewitness accounts, letters, diaries, and other records from the past (National Center for History in the Schools 1996)
Library (21st-century learner)	Inquire, think critically, and gain knowledge (American Association of School Librarians 2007)	Develop and refine a range of questions to frame the search for new understanding (American Association of School Librarians 2007)

Disposition/Responsibility: This lesson addresses the following disposition: Display initiative and engagement by posing questions and investigating the answers beyond the collection of superficial facts (American Association of School Librarians [AASL] 2007, Standard 1.2.1).

Product/Performance: Students develop a list of three to five questions to focus their inquiry on a topic related to the Holocaust.

Assessment

Learning Goal: Students use a rubric to develop and refine questions related to their research topics.

Assessment Criteria: Students help to determine criteria for good research questions by examining work samples representing different levels of performance. Working in small groups, they discuss the characteristics of meaningful questions and list criteria for assessing them. Figure 11.2 presents the types of criteria upon which instructors and students might agree.

Self-Assessment Strategies: The assessment rubric for generating questions (Figure 11.3) is an example of what instructors and students might use as a guide for self-assessment and improvement. During the guided and independent practice phases of learning, students compare their questions with the criteria presented in the rubric. At the end of each session, students use exit passes to reflect on what they have learned and to explain why they think their questions meet, exceed, or approach the standards.

Tools for Collecting, Recording, and Quantifying Data: The same rubric that serves as a guide for self-assessment provides a means to determine each student's level of proficiency in generating thoughtful questions. Before students embark upon the task of collecting information, they review their questions with an instructor using the rubric displayed in Figure 11.3. Questions are revised based upon this assessment. Instructors measure growth by comparing the initial and final assessments.

Figure 11.2
Possible criteria for questions.

Good research questions:

- Relate to the essential questions
- Lead to important information about the topic
- Ask "how" and "why" as well as "who," "what," "when," and "where"
- Encourage comparisons and connections
- Target information needed to complete the project

Figure 11.3
Assessment rubric for generating questions.

	Link to the standards: My goal for this lesson is to write questions that will focus the research on important information that will help with the project.

Exceeds standards	• Research questions help answer the essential question. • Questions target important facts and basic information about the topic. • Some questions ask "how" and "why." • All questions are clear and to the point. • Questions call for comparisons or connections with other events in history or with other pieces of literature.
Meets standards	• The questions target important facts and basic information about the topic, but it is not always clear how they answer the essential question. • There is at least one question that asks "how" or "why." • The questions are clear but may be too general. • At least one question calls for comparisons or connections to be made.
Approaches standards	• The questions ask "who," "what," "when" and "where." • None of the questions ask "how" or "why." • The point of some questions is not clear. • The questions lead to a list of facts rather than a deeper understanding of the topic.

Learning Plan

The groundwork for this lesson was laid in the classroom where students have been reading fiction and nonfiction selections about the Holocaust including:

- Anne Frank's *The Diary of a Young Girl*—a memoir or personal narrative
- David Adler's *We Remember the Holocaust*—a history based on personal narratives
- Milton Meltzer's *Rescue: The Story of How Gentiles Saved Jews in the Holocaust*—historical accounts
- Ida Vos's *Hide and Seek*—a novel
- Hana Volavkova's *I Never Saw Another Butterfly: Children's Drawings and Poems*—a collection of artwork and poetry by children of the Holocaust

In the library media center, students extend their background knowledge of the Holocaust by taking a virtual tour of the U.S. Holocaust Memorial Museum (http:www.ushmm.org/).They draw upon insights developed through the literature and the museum experience to select their research topics. Following the procedures outlined in Figure 11.4, students develop questions to focus their own search for information.

Lesson 2: Selecting and Evaluating Resources

Lesson 2 combines the teaching role of the library media specialist with that of resource provider. In this dual capacity, he or she assists with identifying the resources for learning, presents them in a way that is appealing and meaningful, and helps students to analyze and compare what they read, see, and hear.

Outcomes Desired

Standards and Performance Indicators: This information is presented in Figure 11.5 (see p. 174).

Disposition/Responsibility: In this lesson, the following responsibility is addressed: Recognize that resources are created for a variety of purposes (AASL 2007, Standard 4.3.2).

Product/Performance: Students complete a matrix for each of the pieces they choose to evaluate. They use a blog created for that purpose to recommend one of their selections to other students and to provide a convincing argument stating why it should be read or viewed. They make at least one additional blog posting in response to comments or suggestions by other students.

Assessment

Learning Goal: Students select three resources, representing different formats and genres, and complete a response form for each. They use a blog to discuss their choices and to interact with other students.

Assessment Criteria: The criteria that are used to assess achievement of the learning goals are presented in Figure 11.6 (see p. 174).

Self-Assessment Strategies: Students respond to the following prompts in their reflection logs:

Figure 11.4
Learning plan for lesson on generating questions.

Instructional design	What will instructors do?	What will students do?
Direct instruction with modeling	Strategies for introducing the lesson—tap prior knowledge by asking questions: – *What do you know about the Holocaust?* – *What other questions do you have?* – *Why is it important to learn about the Holocaust?* – *How do you think we can learn more about it?* Strategies for developing questions to focus the research – *Revisit the Holocaust Museum Web site to focus on "frequently asked questions."* – *Ask students to differentiate between questions that focus on facts and those that target big ideas.* – *Explain how to use the K-W-L (know, wonder, learn) chart to generate both fact-based and big idea questions.*	Students meet in existing literature circles to work on the first column of a K-W-L chart, where they brainstorm what they already know about the Holocaust. Groups post and compare charts. The class discusses why it is important to learn about the Holocaust and where information might be found. Students work in teams to construct a T-chart for the "frequently asked questions" on the museum site. Fact-based Big idea questions questions The class compares charts and discusses the characteristics of each type of question. Literature circles work on column two of the K-W-L chart—What do we want to find out about the Holocaust? Questions might include: – *Why do we remember the Holocaust?* – *How is Hitler connected to the Holocaust?* – *What was life like for the Jewish people before the war? During the war?* – *Who besides Jews were victims of the Holocaust?*

(continued)

Figure 11.4 *(Continued)*

Instructional design	What will instructors do?	What will students do?
	Present and explain a model showing a hierarchy of questions: **Essential questions for the unit:** • Why is it important to remember the Holocaust? • How do the lessons of the Holocaust affect us today? **Focus question:** What was the Holocaust? **Questions to guide the information search:** Where did it happen? When did it happen? Who was involved? What happened to victims? How did this event change the world? Why is it important to remember the victims? What other events in history can it be compared with?	Using the questions modeled by the instructors and those on their K-W-L charts, students consider the criteria for good research questions. Each group selects five criteria to share with the class. The class comes to a consensus on the criteria for good research questions.
Guided practice with informative feedback	Instructors use the criteria contributed by students to create a rubric for research questions. As students work on their questions, instructors refer to the rubric to make informative feedback.	Working in pairs, students develop a list of questions specific to their own topics. They provide feedback to each other based on the rubric.
Independent practice with self-monitoring based on criteria	Instructors present a list of possible questions to model the use of the rubric.	Students analyze, revise, and refine their research questions. Each student writes a list of three to five questions to focus his/her inquiry. The rubric serves as a guide for self-assessment.

Figure 11.4 *(Continued)*

Instructional design	What will instructors do?	What will students do?
Reflection and self-assessment	Instructors provide prompts for exit passes. They allow five minutes for students to write a response at the conclusion of each session.	Self-assessment is built into the learning process as students continually compare their work with the criteria described in the rubric.
	Sample prompts: *What are the three most important questions you have about the Holocaust?* *Why do we need both fact-based and big idea questions? Give an example of each.* *Why do we need to write research questions before we start to look for information?* *Based on the rubric, how well do your research questions meet the criteria? Explain your answer.*	Students use exit passes to reflect on what was learned each day. Acceptable pieces should: – *Respond clearly to the question that is asked in the prompt* – *Provide details and examples to elaborate and clarify* – *Indicate an understanding of critical ideas embodied in the lesson*

- What have I learned about the Holocaust from the three resources I evaluated?
- Which resource will I recommend to others through the blog? Why did I choose this resource?
- What contributions have I made to the blog? What have I learned from others by using the blog?
- Why is it important to explore information in a variety of formats and genres?

Tools for Collecting, Recording, and Quantifying Data: Students complete a response sheet (Figure 11.7) for each of their selections. The scoring guide accompanying the response sheet provides a tool for assessing and quantifying the student's ability to analyze and personalize the literature. An average score from the three selections is recorded as evidence of learning. To assess their contributions to the blog, students complete the self-assessment tool presented in Figure 11.8.

Figure 11.5
Standards and performance indicators addressed in lesson 2.

Content areas	Standards	Performance indicators
Language arts	Read a wide range of literature from many periods and in many genres to develop an understanding of the dimensions of human experience (Kendall and Marzano 2010)	Use reading skills and strategies to understand and interpret a variety of literary passages and texts Understand point-of-view in a literary text (Kendall and Marzano 2010)
Library (21st-century learner)	Draw conclusions, make informed decisions, apply knowledge to new situations, and create new knowledge Pursue personal and aesthetic growth (American Association of School Librarians 2007)	Consider diverse and global perspectives in drawing conclusions Participate in the social exchange of ideas, both electronically and in person (American Association of School Librarians 2007)

Figure 11.6
Criteria for assessing resources in different formats.

I am able to:

- Select resources that represent different formats and genres.
- Evaluate three different resources that will be useful for the project. I complete a separate response sheet for each resource.
- Write a blog entry that recommends one resource to other students and explains how that selection has contributed to my personal understanding of the Holocaust.
- Use the blog to interact with other students, to share thoughts, and to make comparisons.

Figure 11.7
Response sheet for assessing resources.

Author or person responsible: _____

Title: _____

Format or genre: _____

Questions	My thoughts	Evidence from the work
From which point-of-view is the story told?		
How did the piece contribute to my understanding of the Holocaust?		
What did I like best about this piece?		
What did I like least about this piece?		
How does it compare to other things I have read or viewed about the Holocaust?		

Suggested scoring guide
 	
3—*Exceeds standards*
  ° Answers each question with an appropriate and relevant personal response.
  ° Provides strong evidence from the piece to support each personal response.
  ° Selects pieces from more than three different formats or genres.
2—*Meets standards*
  ° Gives an appropriate response to each question.
  ° Provides some evidence to support personal responses.
  ° Selects pieces from three different formats or genres.
1—*Approaches standards*
  ° Provides responses that do not indicate an understanding of the selection.
  ° Does not support personal statements with evidence from the work.
  ° Selects pieces that represent a single format or genre.		

Learning Plan

This lesson begins in the classroom where the assignment is made to select, read, or view at least three pieces of literature related to the Holocaust experience and to recommend at least one selection to other students. In anticipation of class visits, the library media specialist

Figure 11.8
Self-assessment tool for contributions to blog.

	Yes, I did it independently. Here is an example to support my assessment.	Yes, but I needed some help. These are some things that I needed help with.	No, I wasn't able to do this. These are some things I can change or improve.
Did I use the blog to recommend a resource that added to my understanding of the Holocaust?			
Did I explain why this resource should be read or viewed by my peers?			
Did I use the blog to respond or react to postings made by teachers and other students?			

Figure 11.9
Learning plan for selecting and evaluating resources.

Instructional design	What will instructors do?	What will students do?
Part 1: Introductory activity		
Direct instruction with modeling	Compare a segment from the DVD *Anne Frank Remembered* with book being read in class. – *Refer to* Diary of a Young Girl. – *Ask how the DVD might compare with the book.* – *Show a 10-minute segment.*	Engage in active viewing and listening. Use a T-chart to jot down similarities and differences while viewing. Similarities | Differences

Figure 11.9 *(Continued)*

Instructional design	What will instructors do?	What will students do?
Guided practice with informative feedback	Synthesize the discussion around points made by students. These may include: – *Both the book and video provide information about the same person.* – *The same situation is presented in both.* – *The author of the book tells the story in her own words.* – *The video gives an outsider's point-of-view.* – *The book tells the story with words. The video tells the same story with pictures and sound.* Read a poetry selection related to the Holocaust (e.g., "Daniel" by Laura Crist, available at www.mtsu.edu/~baustin/daniel.html)	Form groups to discuss the DVD and compare charts. Create a group chart that summarizes the discussion. Post charts and share key ideas. Discuss as a group: *How does the poem contribute to our understanding of the Holocaust experience?*
Part 2: Selecting and evaluating resources		
Direct instruction with modeling	Present list of Holocaust resources and explain the assignment. Model the process of completing a response form (Figure 11.7).	Review the list of resources. Select three pieces to read or view.
Guided practice with informative feedback	Provide informative feedback as students work on one of the forms. Invite students to ask questions for clarification.	Complete a response form for one of the selections. Self-assess and make revisions.

(continued)

Figure 11.9 *(Continued)*

Instructional design	What will instructors do?	What will students do?
Independent practice with self-monitoring based on criteria	Explain how to use the scoring guide to self-assess work on the evaluation matrix. Continue to provide feedback as students evaluate three resources and complete the response sheets.	Evaluate three Holocaust resources using the matrix provided on the response form (Figure 11.7). Complete a separate response form for each selection. Improve work by referring to the criteria represented in the scoring guide.
	Part 3: Writing a blog entry	
Direct instruction with modeling	Explain the second part of the assignment: *Write a blog entry that recommends one of your resources to others. Respond to blog entries of other students.* Provide models of blog entries. Synthesize discussion of criteria for blog entries. Post criteria that everyone agrees on.	Form groups to analyze and discuss sample blog entries. Brainstorm criteria for an effective blog entry—for example: − *Tells how the resource contributes to understanding of the Holocaust.* − *Writes clearly with few errors.* − *Explains why this resource should be read or viewed.*
Guided practice with informative feedback	Allow time for students to draft their blog entries. Provide assistance with both the content and the technical aspects of the assignment.	Compose blog entries that recommend one of their selections to the class. Use criteria to self-assess. Revise writing.
Independent practice with self-monitoring based on criteria	Provide computer access so that students can post their blog entries. Remind students to self-assess by referring to criteria.	Post entries recommending one resource on the Holocaust. Read other students' blogs and respond to at least one.

Figure 11.9 *(Continued)*

Reflection and self-assessment	Provide prompts that encourage students to reflect on what they are learning and how they are learning. Use scoring guide to assess literature response sheets. Read and respond to students' blog entries.	Consistently use criteria to improve work. Assess original postings and responses using the matrix provided in Figure 11.8. Write journal responses that demonstrate deeper levels of understanding.

compiles a list of videos, dramatic scripts, poetry collections, historical works, biographies, and novels available in the media center. He or she also works with teachers to establish a blog that students use for communication, interaction, and discussion. Figure 11.9 outlines the plan used to support learning in the library media center.

CONCLUSION

In both Chapters 10 and 11 we have provided examples of lessons that might be integrated into existing classroom projects. In each case, the library media specialist begins the lesson construction process with careful attention to what students need to demonstrate by the end of the learning experience. The assessment tools are designed with these targets in mind. As mentioned in Chapter 10, library media specialists can start with assessment tools they are already using (e.g., rubrics, checklists, rating scales) and, with minimal effort, refocus them for the student by substituting "I," "me," and "my" in the tools (Marjorie Pappas, personal communication). Figure 11.10 summarizes the key elements of the lessons in this chapter.

In the next chapter, we present a high school example of how lessons taught in the library media center might reflect an outcome-based approach to instructional design.

Figure 11.10
Lessons for grade 8 Holocaust unit: Focus, outcome, task, and assessment.

Lesson focus	Desired outcome	Learning task	Assessment tool
Lesson 1 Generating questions	Formulate questions based on information needs	Generate three to five questions related to students' research areas	**Rubric** that identifies the quality of questions based on requirements of accuracy, relevance, and scope
Lesson 2 Selecting and evaluating resources	Derive meaning from information presented in a range of formats and genres	Read and respond to three literary pieces presented in three different formats Write a blog entry recommending one resource	**Response sheet** that requires student to evaluate resources in different formats **Blog entry** that recommends one of the resources

CHAPTER 12

Outcome-Based Approach: High School Example

This chapter:

- Reviews an outcome-based strategy to lesson planning
- Presents a sample project in a high school setting
- Describes outcome-based planning for sample library lessons related to the project

OUTCOME-BASED APPROACH

In Chapters 10 and 11 we presented examples of lessons that library media specialists incorporated into elementary and middle school projects. In each instance, we demonstrated how effective lesson planning starts with the careful identification of learning standards and related performance indicators that target specific outcomes. With these outcomes as the focus, library media specialists then determined how to assess student performance and how to shape the learning experience to help students achieve the desired outcomes.

The sample lessons in this chapter are part of a high school senior project assignment. As we did in the earlier chapters, we begin with a summary of the overall project and follow this with two related lessons that might be taught in the library media center. Each lesson is formatted as follows.

OUTCOMES: WHAT MUST STUDENTS BE ABLE TO DEMONSTRATE AT THE END?

Standards and performance indicators addressed

Dispositions and/or responsibilities developed through the learning experience

Products and performances that demonstrate learning

(continued)

ASSESSMENT: HOW WILL STUDENT PERFORMANCE BE MEASURED?

Learning goal that states how students will show what they know

    Criteria for assessment

    Self-assessment strategies

    Tools for collecting, recording, and quantifying data

LEARNING PLAN: HOW WILL THIS LESSON BE DELIVERED?

What will instructors do?

What will students do?

SUMMARY OF PROJECT

The senior project is becoming as much a part of the high school landscape as SATs, GPAs, and commencement exercises. Many schools have adopted it as a way for students to demonstrate their competencies through an in-depth study of a topic of their choice.

Proponents of the senior project describe it as a culminating activity that allows students to apply what they have learned to a project that is personally meaningful. By providing opportunities to develop and polish a range of skills and competencies, it prepares high school graduates for college and the workplace. Properly implemented, the senior project has the potential for creating rich opportunities for rigorous challenges and engagements.

Senior projects promote the goals of information literacy by engaging students in a process that involves producing, applying, and communicating knowledge. Typically, students work with mentors who help them to set goals, generate questions, locate sources, and design a method of investigation. The students use a wide range of online tools to interact with teachers and mentors, to access information, and to organize and present their findings. They share their conclusions through research papers, science experiments, multimedia presentations, and a host of other products and performances. As they work on their projects, students engage in a continuous stream of reflection, revision, and self-discovery (O'Grady 1999).

Although districts have set different guidelines for fulfilling the senior project requirement, most schools see the project as a vehicle for students to demonstrate learning by:

- Showing what they know and are able to do
- Engaging in a focused investigation related to an area of interest or a career choice
- Using an inquiry process to build knowledge and understanding
- Utilizing feedback to revise and improve their work
- Preparing and presenting findings to a panel of judges

SAMPLE LESSONS

In our example, the faculty supports a team approach to guide students through the project. The library media specialist serves as an important resource to instructional teams consisting of content area specialists, the technology coordinator, and a representative of the counseling staff. At the beginning of the year, an informational meeting is held to explain requirements and to address the questions and concerns of students and their parents. During the meeting, three components of the project are identified and described. These include:

- A research paper dealing with a student-selected topic
- A project that has a logical connection to the research
- An online presentation to be reviewed by a panel of judges representing the faculty, the student body, and the larger community

The technology coordinator works with a group of interested students to create a senior project Web page that is linked to the school's Web site. The Web page allows for the dissemination of general information pertaining to the goals of the project and serves as a mechanism for posting requirements, deadlines, and assessment tools. It also includes a wiki where students can post their project proposals and seek community mentors. Parents can also learn more about the senior projects by visiting the Web page.

As a part of the instructional team, the library media specialist agrees to provide instruction on critical aspects of the research process. Two of the lessons that prove to be most valuable are:

- Lesson 1: Evaluating Web sites
- Lesson 2: Preparing an annotated bibliography

Lesson 1: Evaluating Web Sites

Teachers work with the library media specialist to develop guidelines for the research component of the project. Considerable emphasis is placed on the selection, evaluation, and use of both print and electronic resources. However, early in the process, it becomes evident that many students are relying on the Internet to the exclusion of other information sources. Teachers also observe that students are selecting sites indiscriminately without regard to issues of accuracy, reliability, or relevance. In response to these concerns, the library media specialist designs a lesson focusing on Web site evaluation.

Outcomes Desired

Standards and Performance Indicators: This information is presented in Figure 12.1.

Disposition/Responsibility: This lesson addresses the following disposition: Maintain a critical stance by questioning the validity and accuracy of all information (American Association of School Librarians [AASL] 2007, Standard 1.2.4).

Figure 12.1
Standards and performance indicators addressed in lesson 1.

Content Areas	Standards	Performance Indicators
Language arts	Gathers and uses information for research purposes (Kendall and Marzano 2010)	Use a variety of criteria to evaluate the validity and reliability of primary and secondary sources (Kendall and Marzano 2010)
Library (21st-century learner)	Inquire, think critically, and gain knowledge (American Association of School Librarians 2007)	Evaluate information found in selected sources on the basis of accuracy, validity, appropriateness of needs, importance, and social and cultural context (American Association of School Librarians 2007)

Product/Performance: Students select, evaluate, and compare three Web sites to use with their projects.

Assessment

Learning Goal: Students will use criteria to select and evaluate information found on selected Web sites. The overarching goal is for students to become discriminating users of online resources.

Assessment Criteria: Students work with instructors to develop criteria for evaluating Web sites. These criteria reflect the focus on content, authority, and presentation. It is important that they are written in the language of students. Figure 12.2 lists examples of criteria suggested by students.

**Figure 12.2
Criteria for evaluating Web sites.**

Content
- Information is accurate and complete.
- Information is related to the topic and helps answer the research questions.
- Both sides of the issue are presented.
- The reading level is neither too hard nor too easy.
- The information is current. Dates of publication and the last update are given.
- The information will be helpful for this project.

Authority/credibility
- The person or organization responsible for the information is stated.
- The URL indicates that the sponsor is a government agency, an academic institution, or an organization with a reputation in the field.
- There is no obvious bias for or against a particular point of view.
- The purpose of the page is to inform or explain—not to entertain, sell a product, or influence public opinion.

Presentation and ease of use
- The page loads easily.
- The links are easy to use.
- Topics, headings, and bullets are used to break up text.
- Graphics, artwork, and other features enhance the presentation and contribute to understanding.
- There are no obvious errors in spelling, grammar, or other conventions.

Self-Assessment Strategies: Students respond in their learning logs to the following prompts: *Why is it important to evaluate Web sites? What are some ways of finding out more about the author, the content, or the purpose of the Web site? How can we improve the Web site evaluation tool to make it more helpful and less confusing?* Responses to these questions are attached to the tool for assessing Web sites and used as a basis for assessment and further instruction.

Tools for Collecting, Recording, and Quantifying Data: The library media specialist uses the criteria developed with students to design a rating scale for Web site evaluation (Figure 12.3). Students use this tool to evaluate Web sites dealing with their topics.

Figure 12.3
Tool for assessing Web sites.

Web Site Evaluation Tool

Name of Web site: _____ URL: _____

Content	Poor	Adequate	Excellent	Explain your rating
Does the information appear to be accurate?				
Is the coverage of the topic comprehensive?				
Does the information relate to my topic and questions?				
Are different points of view represented?				
Is the reading level appropriate for me?				
Is the information current? (Check the last update, usually found at the bottom of the page.)				
Will the information help with my project?				

Figure 12.3 *(Continued)*

	Poor	*Adequate*	*Excellent*	*Explain your rating*
Authority/credibility				
Is the name of the author or sponsoring organization stated?				
Is the author qualified to speak on the topic?				
Is the writing free of bias?				
Is the purpose to explain or provide information, rather than to sell or influence public opinion?				
Presentation and ease of use				
Does the page load easily?				
Are links provided to appropriate Web sites? Are they active?				
Are topics, headings, and bullets used to break up text?				

Suggested scoring guide

3—Exceeds standards by using the rating scale to satisfactorily evaluate more than three Web sites.
2—Meets standards by using the rating scale to satisfactorily evaluate three Web sites.
1—Approaches standards by using the rating scale to satisfactorily evaluate one or two Web sites.

Learning Plan

The purpose of the lesson is twofold: (1) to establish guidelines for evaluating Web sites and (2) to have students use the rating scale presented in Figure 12.3 to evaluate and select Web sites for their projects. Figure 12.4 describes the procedure used to develop competency in Web site evaluation.

Figure 12.4
Learning plan for evaluating Web sites.

Instructional design	What will instructors do?	What will students do?
Direct instruction with modeling	Strategies for introducing the lesson: Tap prior knowledge by asking: What makes a Web site useful for research? How do you choose one site over another on the same topic? Present a scenario like the following: *Students are asked to write in their journals about their areas of interest, their hobbies, and career goals. One student writes that he has two compelling interests: baseball and architecture. He thinks he might focus his research on baseball stadiums. For his project, he wants to use his personal Web page to create a photo gallery with pictures, maps, architectural drawings, and other interesting information about historic ballparks. He begins his inquiry by doing an Internet search using the keywords "baseball stadiums."* The library media specialist presents a list of Web sites along with brief descriptions of items retrieved for "baseball stadiums."	Students offer their ideas about what makes a good Web site. Responses might include: – *It's easy to use.* – *It has good information.* – *It answers your questions.* – *It uses bullets and headings.* – *It includes pictures and graphics.* – *It has a "search" button.* Group work: Students meet in small groups to examine the list and predict what the theme and scope of each Web site will be. They decide which sites are most likely to help with the essential question and report their findings to the class. Students offer ideas on how accuracy can be determined. Suggestions might include: – *Check it out in a print source or another Internet site.* – *See if the author is an expert.* – *Check the date to see if it's current.* – *Look at the domain name to see what kind of site it is.*

Figure 12.4 *(Continued)*

Instructional design	What will instructors do?	What will students do?
	The following question is posed: Which of these sites are likely to answer the student's essential question: "What do historic stadiums say about the history of baseball?" Follow-up question: How can you tell if the information is accurate when just about anyone can put up a Web site? Call attention to URLs and domain names. Ask: What do these indicators mean? How might the domain name help you predict the usefulness of the page? Synthesize discussion by sharing examples of Web sites with different domain indicators. Emphasize the relationship between the domain name and the purpose of the site.	Students identify the following domain indicators: com, edu, gov and org. They discuss the connection between the domain name and the purpose and content of the site.
Guided practice with informative feedback	Provide each group with printouts downloaded from Web sites retrieved through a search for "baseball stadiums." Printouts are from sites like the following: – *Baseball Hall of Fame: http://www.baseball halloffame.org*	Group activity – Distribute articles—one per student. – Identify URL and the domain indicator. – Predict the purpose and content of the page. – Read for information. – Report to the group on purpose and content.

(continued)

Figure 12.4 *(Continued)*

Instructional design	What will instructors do?	What will students do?
	— *Bleacher Report: http://bleacherreport.com/articles/38103-what-are-the-most-historic-baseball-stadiums* — *Fairness of Major League Baseball Stadiums: http://students.imsa.edu/* — *Major League Baseball Stadium and Ballpark Photo Gallery: http://www.digitalballparks.com/MLBIndex.html* Provide directions for group activity. Synthesize discussion with questions like the following: — *Which are most useful for the project? Why?* — *Which sites do the best job of comparing the stadiums?* — *How can we use domain names to determine the potential for a site?* — *What other factors should we consider in evaluating Web sites?* Encourage students to generate a list of questions to help with Web site evaluation. Suggest that questions be organized around the categories of content, authority, credibility, and presentation and technical quality. Use questions to create a tool for evaluating Web sites.	— Compare differences in treatment. — Discuss clues about purpose and content provided by URL. — Suggest other factors to consider in selecting a Web site for research. Group work Students brainstorm a list of questions to use in evaluating Web sites. Questions might include: — *Who created the page?* — *Does the author have expertise on the subject?* — *What information can we get from the domain indicator?* — *When was the article published?* — *When was it last updated?* — *Is it easy to load?* — *Are there links to other pages? Do they work?* — *Is it easy to read and understand?* — *Are all sides of the issue presented?* — *How does it compare with other sites on this topic?* Practice assessing one site using the rating scale.

Figure 12.4 *(Continued)*

Instructional design	What will instructors do?	What will students do?
	Demonstrate the process of filling in a rating scale (Figure 12.3) for one of the sites provided.	
Independent practice with self-monitoring based on criteria	Provide instructions for independent practice: – *Locate three Web pages for your research topic.* – *Evaluate each site using the rating scale (Figure 12.3).*	Students will: – Search the Web for sites related to their topics. – Select and print out information from three different sites to use with their projects. – Use the rating scale (Figure 12.3) to evaluate selected Web sites.
Reflection and self-assessment	Explain the learning log and its purpose. Use rating scales and students' reflections to measure progress toward the learning goals and to make appropriate instructional adjustments.	Students respond to prompts like the following: *Why is it important to evaluate Web sites? What are some ways of finding out more about the author, the content, or the purpose of the site?* Use assessment feedback to become more efficient users of the Internet.

Lesson 2: Preparing an Annotated Bibliography

An important requirement for the senior project is an annotated bibliography. This allows the library media specialist to assess several aspects of information literacy, including the ability to locate, evaluate, and use information for a specific purpose. Although students have previous experience preparing bibliographies for their research papers, the library media specialist sees the senior project as an opportunity to assess aspects of information literacy related to the appropriate and ethical use of sources.

Outcomes Desired

Standards and Performance Indicators: The information is presented in Figure 12.5.

Figure 12.5
Standards and performance indicators addressed in lesson 2.

Content areas	Standards	Performance indicators
Language arts	Gathers and uses information for research purposes (Kendall and Marzano 2010)	Uses standard format and methodology for documenting reference sources (Kendall and Marzano 2010)
21st-century learning	Inquire, think critically, and gain knowledge Share knowledge and participate ethically and productively as members of our democratic society (American Association of School Librarians 2007)	Respect copyright/intellectual property rights of creators and producers Use information and technology ethically and responsibly (American Association of School Librarians 2007)

Disposition/Responsibility: This lesson addresses the following responsibility: Follow ethical and legal guidelines in gathering and assessing information (AASL 2007, Standard 1.3.3).

Product/Performance: Students help determine criteria for citing sources and preparing annotated bibliographies. They use these criteria to write annotations for at least three sources selected for their projects.

Assessment

Learning Goal: Students use a style sheet to fully and consistently cite sources they use in their projects. Each citation is accompanied by an annotation that evaluates the source on the basis of accuracy, relevancy, authority, and comparison with other sources.

Assessment Criteria: Students develop criteria to use in evaluating their bibliographies. Figure 12.6 presents some of the ideas they generate.

Self-Assessment Strategies: Students evaluate their citations by referring to the style sheet. They use the rubric provided in Figure 12.7 to monitor their work and to make necessary improvements.

Figure 12.6
Criteria for assessing annotated bibliographies.

I am able to:

- Include citations for print, electronic, and personal resources
- Make evaluative statements that address relevance, authority, accuracy, and usefulness for the project in question
- Use a consistent style to properly cite each source
- Follow conventions outlined in the style sheet provided

Figure 12.7
Rubric for assessing annotated bibliographies.

Criteria	Exceeds	Meets	Approaches
Range	I cite *more than three* different kinds of sources (e.g., a book, an article, a personal interview, an Internet source).	I cite *three* different kinds of sources.	I cite *fewer than three* sources.
Citation style	I provide a complete citation for each source. I observe conventions and use a consistent style for citations.	I provide complete citations. I observe most conventions, but the style is not always consistent.	Some of my citations are incomplete. I don't always follow a consistent style.
Summary of contents	I briefly describe the scope or the central theme of the source.	I give specific information from the source rather than a summary of main ideas.	I list some facts found but I don't attempt to summarize ideas.

(continued)

Figure 12.7 *(Continued)*

Criteria	Exceeds	Meets	Approaches
Evaluation of source	I consider the authority and expertise of the authors. I point out strengths and weaknesses of sources. I explain in detail how each source helped with the project. I compare each item with other sources. I give reasons for my opinion.	I identify authors but don't explain why they are credible. I point out strengths and weaknesses for one or two sources. I explain how some sources helped with the project. I make some statements comparing sources.	I don't consider the expertise of the authors. I make no attempt to point out strengths and weakness. I attempt to explain how at least one source was helpful. I make simple comparisons (e.g., good, better, best) without providing details.

Tools for Collecting, Recording, and Quantifying Data: The library media specialist uses the criteria that the students have contributed to develop the aforementioned rubric for developing and assessing annotated bibliographies.

Learning Plan

As students work on the research phase of their projects, they keep bibliographic records of the sources they use. This information provides a starting point for the work on annotated bibliographies. The lesson has three desired outcomes—students:

- Follow conventions and use a consistent style to cite information sources
- Write an annotation for three of the sources
- Demonstrate ethical use of information

Figure 12.8 describes the instructional procedure used in the library media center to assist students with their bibliographic work.

Figure 12.8
Learning plan for developing bibliographies.

Instructional design	What will instructors do?	What will students do?
Introduction to the lesson		
Direct instruction with modeling	Tap prior knowledge through focused discussion. Ask: *Why is a bibliography required for the project?* Synthesize the discussion by making the following points about the reasons for a bibliography: – *To demonstrate respect for intellectual property rights by crediting those responsible for the information* – *To validate the information presented.* Pass out an example of a bibliography. Ask students to compare the bibliography with the lists of resources they have compiled for their projects. Ask: *What is the difference between a list of resources and a bibliography?*	Group discussion Students offer their ideas on the need for a bibliography. Ideas might include statements like the following: – *Show where I got the information* – *Give credit to the author* – *Prove that I didn't make it up* – *Support my arguments* – *Show that I did my research* Students work in groups to discuss the differences between a resource list and a bibliography. A T-chart is used to record responses. Resource List Bibliography
Part 1—writing the citation		
Direct instruction with modeling	Provide copies of a style sheet to be used for senior projects. Explain the organization of the style sheet and how to use it to write citations.	Select one resource to practice citing. Use the style sheet to locate the correct citation style for the source.

(continued)

Figure 12.8 *(Continued)*

Instructional design	What will instructors do?	What will students do?
Guided practice with informative feedback	Provide guidance and feedback as students work on a citation for one of their sources. Call upon students to share citations for different resource formats. Provide additional instruction as necessary.	Write a citation for the source selected. Work with a peer to assess the citation using the style sheet as a reference. Make necessary adjustments based on feedback.
Independent practice with self-monitoring based on criteria	Direct students to write citations for each resource used in their projects. Note: This may be completed as a homework assignment.	Write citations for sources used in their projects. Correctly cite sources representing at least three different formats.
Reflection and self-assessment	Invite questions and provide additional instruction as needed.	Self-assess by referring to the style sheet. Make necessary adjustments.
Part 2—writing the annotation		

Direct instruction with modeling	Provide examples of annotated bibliographies.
	
	Ask: *What is the purpose of the annotation in relation to the senior project? What should the annotation include?*
	
	Synthesize discussion by developing steps for writing an annotation:
	Step 1: Write one or two sentences to summarize the scope or theme of the item.
	Step 2: Write two or three evaluative sentences. These might:
	  – *Address the author-ity or credibility of the author(s)*
		Students offer their ideas on the purpose of the annotation. Comments might include:
		  – *Gives a general idea of what the item is about.*
		  – *Tells why the source was selected.*
		  – *Explains how the source helped with the project.*
		  – *Compares the item with other sources.*
		
		Work with a partner to write an annotation for one of the examples provided by instructors.
		
		Use the rubric to assess and modify the annotation.

Figure 12.8 *(Continued)*

Instructional design	What will instructors do?	What will students do?
	– Point out the strengths and weaknesses of the item *– Explain how the source helped with the project* Step 3: Compare the source with other items on the same topic. Explain the rubric for assessing annotated bibliographies (Figure 12.7).	
Guided practice with informative feedback	Provide guidance and informative feedback by referring students to the rubric.	Practice writing an annotation for one of their own sources. Use the rubric to self-assess and make adjustments.
Independent practice with self-monitoring based on criteria	Establish a timeline for completing annotated bibliographies. Conference with students on an informal basis. Note: Students complete this portion of the lesson on their own time.	Continue to write annotations for each of their project sources. Finalize annotated bibliographies to include with their projects.
Reflection and self-assessment	Use the rubric (Figure 12.7) to monitor progress, to adjust instruction, and to provide a focus for evaluation.	Use the rubric to engage in a continuous process of self-assessment and improvement.

CONCLUSION

Outcome-based learning and teaching challenges all instructors to consider dramatic shifts in both pedagogy and curriculum development practices (Luongo Orlando 2003; Wiggins and McTighe 1998). It begins with establishing learning that focuses on standards. It requires

Figure 12.9
Lessons for senior project: Focus, outcome, task, and assessment.

Lesson focus	Desired outcome	Learning task	Assessment tool
Lesson 1 Evaluating Web sites	Evaluate information critically and competently	Evaluate three Web sites as appropriate information sources for their projects	**Rating scale** that includes analysis of the accuracy, relevance, and comprehensiveness of a Web source
Lesson 2 Preparing annotated bibliographies	Practice ethical behavior in regard to information use	Create citations and annotations for at least three information sources in different formats	**Rubric** that covers consistency and completeness in citations and evaluative annotations that focus on relevance, authority, and accuracy

developing targeted goals, assessment tools, and performance tasks based on the standards. Figure 12.9 summarizes the key elements of the lessons in this chapter.

Student engagement in self-assessment and reflection is essential in the learning process. In all the lessons presented, students question, contemplate, and determine the quality of their own work. By being partners in assessment, they critically examine the process and products of their efforts. They become increasingly aware of the strengths and needed improvements in their work and determine the quality of their performances. Assessment in this context is not assessing learning but truly becomes assessing *for* learning.

CHAPTER 13

Communicating Evidence of Learning

This chapter:

- Focuses on how assessment data collected in the library can be used to support school goals
- Makes a case for the importance of communicating assessment results to various stakeholders
- Provides scenarios and samples of how results can be synthesized and communicated to different audiences

The most critical uses of assessment data are to allow students an opportunity to reflect on their own progress and to provide instructors with crucial information on what students are learning and how teaching might be shaped to help students do even better. With the current emphasis on accountability, however, still another important use of assessment information has emerged: the need for synthesizing and presenting summaries of students' learning achievements to various stakeholder groups. In short, communicating evidence of what is being learned through library instruction is a valuable advocacy tool.

In this chapter, we share examples of how assessment data collected in the library can be shared with different school audiences. In the past, the evaluation of library media programs has been based on factors like circulation statistics, the size of the collection, the frequency of instructional sessions, and a physical count of students in the library. Evidence-based practice has shifted the focus for evaluation from statistics about resources to the contributions made by the library media program to academic achievement. The critical question for 21st-century library media specialists is not "How many books are we circulating?" but "Are our programs and practices making a difference in terms of student learning?"

Ross Todd (2001a) advises that key people, including teachers, administrators, and members of the larger community need to see "explicit local evidence of how collaborative learning communities can enable and foster significant learning outcomes of students" (1). As librarians work with teachers to plan a curriculum based on standards and grade-level benchmarks, they need to systematically document the influence of information literacy instruction on the achievement of the school's learning goals.

HOW CAN ASSESSMENT DATA BE USED TO SUPPORT SCHOOL-WIDE GOALS?

In earlier chapters we described different assessment methods and the context in which they might be used to improve teaching and learning. In this chapter, we explore ways of using the same data to show how the library media program supports school-wide achievement goals. This involves taking assessment beyond its instructional applications and using it to validate the essential role of information literacy instruction in areas like critical thinking, problem solving, decision making, and literacy.

Collecting evidence is not an end in itself. Todd (2001a) stresses the importance of analyzing and synthesizing selected evidence to create an accurate picture of achievement. Figure 13.1 outlines a process that starts with data collection and ends with the communication of results.

Embedded in this process is the notion that evidence-based practice should bring together research-based evidence with professional knowing and experience to inform critical decisions and result in actions of best practice (Todd 2008).

WHY IS IT IMPORTANT TO COMMUNICATE RESULTS?

All educators are being called upon to present evidence that their programs are contributing in a substantive way to student achievement.

Figure 13.1
Steps involved in evidence-based assessment.

Steps	Guiding questions
1. **Collect** evidence of achievement.	What data do we collect to document learning?
2. **Analyze** evidence.	What does this data show?
3. **Synthesize** findings.	What conclusions can be drawn based on evidence?
4. **Communicate** results.	How do we report our findings?

The question for library media specialists is: How can our assessment practices be used to show the link between standards-based instruction and student learning? We need to go beyond educated guesses and anecdotal reports by providing verifiable evidence that what we are doing does make a difference. From the plethora of data collected during the instructional process, evidence must be carefully selected for specific purposes, such as:

- Showing how libraries are helping students to meet the standards
- Confirming that students are learning to work as a group
- Validating the benefits of collaborative teaching partnerships
- Demonstrating that students are able to inquire, think critically, gain knowledge, and use it to create and share new knowledge

In the remainder of this chapter, we present examples of how the assessment data might be summarized and communicated to different target audiences.

In the following scenario, the teachers have identified an information need. They want to see evidence that clearly shows how well their

COMMUNICATING WITH TEACHERS

The media center in an urban elementary school has always operated on a fixed schedule with half-hour sessions meeting every other week. In the past, the primary role of the library media specialist was to instruct students in the use of the library and to provide teachers with release time for planning. A new library media specialist has been hired. She wants to encourage more integrated and cooperative instruction. Three third-grade teachers accept her invitation to partner on a project. Together they develop and implement the wetlands unit described in Chapter 10.

One of the instructional goals of the unit is for students to access and evaluate information found in both print and electronic resources. During planning meetings, teachers express some skepticism about how learning outcomes might be measured. They ask: "How do we know that this integrated approach to instruction will help our students meet grade-level benchmarks?"

students are doing in terms of reading and understanding information found in various sources. With this as a starter, the library media specialist follows the steps laid out in Figure 13.1 to address the teachers' concerns.

Step 1: Collect Evidence of Achievement

The library media specialist decides that her first task is to show the correlation between the American Association of School Librarians (AASL) learning standard for inquiring and gaining knowledge and a related standard for reading—uses reading skills and strategies to understand and interpret a variety of informational texts (Kendall and Marzano 2010). Although science standards are also addressed in the unit, teachers elect to assess science content using more traditional testing methods. Her next step is to identify work samples, assessment tools, and reflections that document both language arts and AASL learning standards. She collects the following pieces of evidence from each student:

- Responses to the journal prompt: "Which resources did you find most helpful? Explain why you think this."
- Resource matrix
- Rubric used to assess performance on the resource matrix

A resource matrix was used in Chapter 10 to guide students through the process of locating information about the wetlands in a variety of sources. It is reproduced in Figure 13.2. Completed matrices provided evidence of the student's ability to locate, evaluate, and compare information found in both print and electronic resources.

The instructors use a rubric (Figure 13.3) to rate each student's resource matrix.

Step 2: Analyze Evidence

The real work of analysis is an ongoing and integral part of the instructional process. Students use the rubric as a guide as they work on their resource matrices. The same rubric provides a system for analyzing how well each student has achieved the desired outcome: to access and evaluate information in a variety of print and electronic sources. The resource matrix and the rubric, along with responses to the journal prompt, are analyzed to see what they say about each student's performance.

Figure 13.2
Matrix for identifying resources (work sample).

Link to the standards: In this lesson I will show that I can find information
about my topic in different kinds of print and electronic resources.

Resource Matrix

The topic of my book is _____.
My research questions are

_____

_____

_____

The keywords I will use to search are _____.

Source of information (title)	Type of information (format)	One important thing I learned from the source

The most helpful resource I found was _____

The reason I think this is _____

Step 3: Synthesize Findings

The library media specialist develops a profile that summarizes the data for a class. Figure 13.4 is a profile created for one of the three classes.

Note that comments are included to explain why some students exceeded or failed to meet standards. Some teachers feel that a class profile is incomplete without an explanation about why a student received a particular rating. Teachers who feel this way may write comments for each student, or they may choose to comment only on performances at the extremes, those that do not meet or that exceed the standards. Other teachers may write no comments at all. They believe that the ranking is all that is needed to synthesize the data. Since the comments do not factor into the final computation, they are an optional part of the class profile.

Figure 13.3
Rubric for assessing the resource matrix (assessment tool).

Rating	Criteria
Does not meet standards	Does not include both print and electronic sources Takes notes from a single source Identifies only the resource that was used without explaining what was learned or how it was helpful
Approaches standards	Identifies both print and electronic sources Finds only one print and one electronic source Identifies what was learned from some resources Tells which resource was most helpful but doesn't explain why
Meets standards	Identifies both print and electronic sources Finds at least three different information sources Explains what was learned in each resource Tells which resource was most helpful and explains why
Exceeds standards	Identifies several print and electronic sources Uses four or more different information sources Explains what was learned in each resource Evaluates resources by explaining their strengths and weaknesses

By creating profiles for all three classes, the instructors are able to compare and make the following types of generalizations:

- 5 percent of the students do not meet the standards.
- 20 percent of the students are approaching the standards.
- 55 percent of the students meet the standards.
- 20 percent of the students exceed the standards.

The library media specialist uses these conclusions to make the case that 75 percent of third-grade students involved in the project are either meeting or exceeding the criteria for accessing and evaluating information found in a variety of sources.

Step 4: Communicate Results

Communication can take many forms. In this case, the library media specialist shares the class profiles with the teachers in an informal setting that invites interaction and further analysis. The purpose of the

Figure 13.4
Sample of grade 3 class profile.

Class list	Standards-based assessment	Comments
Abigail	Exceeds	Identifies eight different sources and explains why some are better than others.
Benjamin	Meets	
Carrie	Meets	
Daniel	Approaches	
Emi	Exceeds	Finds five sources, both print and electronic. Tells something important learned from each. Identifies the best source.
Frank	Meets	
Isaac	Does not meet	Uses only one source—an encyclopedia. Does not evaluate or compare sources.
Jill	Approaches	
Kathryn	Meets	
Lily	Meets	
Mark	Meets	
Matthew	Exceeds	Identifies five sources of different kinds. Evaluates each source.
Nina	Meets	
Peter	Meets	
Ricky	Meets	
Sam	Approaches	
Suzie	Meets	
Tim	Exceeds	Identifies six sources, both print and electronic. Explains what was found in each.
Vanessa	Approaches	
Will	Meets	

meeting is to emphasize that the goals of information literacy and other content areas can be accomplished through a collaboratively planned, integrated unit of instruction. The results can now be used to plan future projects.

COMMUNICATING WITH PRINCIPALS AND SCHOOL COUNCILS

Faced with budget cutbacks and limited resources, the principal of a rural middle school has asked the entire staff to submit evidence that their programs are contributing to the school's achievement goals. The school advisory council will use this information to make decisions regarding the allocation of personnel and fiscal resources for the coming school year.

Recognizing the high stakes involved, the library media specialist seeks ways to correlate information literacy with the school-wide goal to improve reading proficiency. Together with the eighth-grade teachers, she develops the literature-based unit described in Chapter 11. Students read a variety of literary genres and research different aspects of the Holocaust to answer the guiding questions: "Why is it important to remember the Holocaust?" and "How can we apply the lessons of the Holocaust to our lives today?" The library media specialist contributes to the unit by identifying appropriate literary selections and guiding students through the process of gathering information related to the Holocaust experience.

In Chapter 11 we described two of the lessons conducted by the library media specialist:

Lesson 1: Asking the right questions
Lesson 2: Selecting and evaluating resources

Because the school's focus is on reading improvement, the library media specialist decides to use assessment data from the second lesson to show the relationship between information literacy instruction and the school-wide reading goal.

In the preceding scenario, the library media specialist seeks to answer the following questions:

- How does the library program contribute to the goal of improving reading comprehension?
- How can the contributions of information literacy instruction be validated?

Step 1: Collect Evidence of Achievement

The standards and performance indicators for reading and information literacy that have been identified for this unit (Figure 13.5) provide a starting point for the selection and evaluation process.

Using the standards as a guide, the library media specialist collects evidence to show how information literacy instruction helps to bring about improvement in the critical analysis of resources. She has the students use the response form for each resource selected. It comes with a scoring guide.

The Holocaust unit calls for students to select at least three titles from a list of Holocaust resources to read or view independently. The

Figure 13.5
Alignment of standards and performance indicators for reading and information literacy.

Content areas	Standards	Performance indicators
Language arts	Uses reading skills and strategies to understand and interpret a variety of literary texts (Kendall and Marzano 2010)	Use reading skills and strategies to understand a variety of literary passages and texts Understand point-of-view in a literary text (Kendall and Marzano 2010)
Library (21st-century learner)	Draw conclusions, make informed decisions, apply knowledge to new situations, and create new knowledge Pursue personal and aesthetic growth (American Association of School Librarians 2007)	Consider diverse and global perspectives in drawing conclusions Participate in the social exchange of ideas, both electronically and in person (American Association of School Librarians 2007)

items they choose must represent different genres and formats. For example, a student might choose to read a memoir and a play and to watch a video. The literature response forms (Figure 13.6) that the student completes for each item are used to assess his proficiency in terms of the targeted standards.

Figure 13.6
Literature response form.

| Author or person responsible: _____ |
| Title: _____ |
| Format or genre: _____ |

Questions	My thoughts	Evidence from the work
From which point-of-view is the story told?		
How did the piece contribute to my understanding of the Holocaust?		
What did I like best about this piece?		
What did I like least about this piece?		
How does it compare to other things I have read or viewed about the Holocaust?		

Suggested scoring guide

3—*Exceeds standards*
- Answers each question with an appropriate and relevant personal response.
- Provides strong evidence from the piece to support each personal response.
- Selects pieces from more than three different formats or genres.

2—*Meets standards*
- Gives an appropriate response to each question.
- Provides some evidence to support personal responses.
- Selects pieces from three different formats or genres.

1—*Approaches standards*
- Provides responses that do not indicate an understanding of the selection.
- Lacks supporting personal statements with evidence from the work.
- Selects pieces that represent a single format or genre.

Step 2: Analyze Evidence

The response form documents the student's ability to interpret a piece of literature in relation to the central theme and driving questions. The accompanying scoring guide is used to analyze how well students are able to read, interpret, and appreciate literature in different formats and genres. In this instance, the library media specialist wants to find out about the variety and range of the student's reading selections. She also examines the responses to determine how well students

- Identify the point of view expressed in the story
- Explain how the piece contributed to their understanding of the Holocaust
- Provide a personal perspective by stating what they liked best or least about the piece
- Compare pieces of literature on the Holocaust theme

Step 3: Synthesize Findings

The instructors use the scoring guide and share the task of analyzing each student's performance. The library media specialist records each student's rating on a class profile. At the request of the teacher, she also includes brief comments to justify each rating. One class's profile is displayed in Figure 13.7.

Data from the class profiles provide the following snapshot of students' achievement:

- 5 percent of students did not meet the standards.
- 15 percent of students are approaching the standards.
- 60 percent of students are meeting the standards.
- 20 percent of students exceed the standards.

Step 4: Communicate Results

The library media specialist decides that a multimedia slide presentation would be the most effective way to share her findings with the school advisory council. Her aim is to convince the council that information literacy instruction has a direct bearing on reading improvement. To make this correlation, she presents her evidence under the following major points:

Figure 13.7
Sample of grade 8 class profile.

Class list	Standards-based assessment	Comments
Anita	Exceeds	Responds to five pieces of literature (a novel, two poems, a video, and a biography). Answers questions thoughtfully with reference to text.
Brian	Meets	Responds to a novel, a poem, and a video. Responses show insight into the tragedy of the event.
Cindy	Approaches	Reads only fiction pieces. Responses are very brief. No reference to text.
David	Exceeds	Completes response forms for four works (a video, a biography, a poem, and a history). Supports opinions with analysis of text/script.
Emily	Meets	Responds to a novel, a poem, and a TV show. Tells what she learned from each. Refers to text in her responses.
Frank	Meets	Responds to a TV documentary, a video, and a novel. Tells what he likes best about each and makes comparisons with books read in class.
Gina	Exceeds	Reads five pieces of literature (two novels, a biography, and two poems). Explains how each contributed to her understanding.

Figure 13.7 *(Continued)*

Class list	Standards-based assessment	Comments
Heather	Approaches	Reading is limited to personal narratives. Says what she likes about each, but doesn't refer to text to answer most questions.
Ian	Meets	Responds to a novel, a video documentary, and a biography. Refers to text in his answers.
Jodi	Does not meet	Completes only one response form for a video. Responses are very general and lacking in detail.
Mike	Meets	Reads a novel and a biography. Also responds to a TV documentary. Makes good comparisons with specific references to text.
Patrick	Approaches	Reads two personal narratives. Tells what he thinks, but makes limited reference to text.

- What she taught
- What students were expected to do (the performance task and the assessment criteria)
- How well students performed

She uses the graph displayed in Figure 13.8 to make the point that 80 percent of the students either met or exceeded the targeted standards for reading and information literacy.

The library media specialist carefully words her presentation so that it is jargon free, and it is warmly received. Lay members on the council are duly impressed and ask thoughtful questions about

Figure 13.8
Profile of achievement.

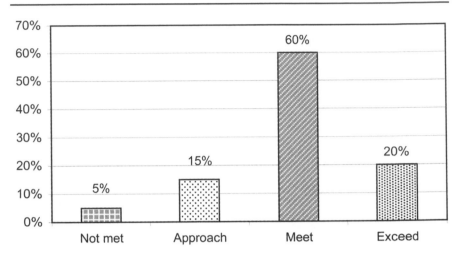

collaborative instruction and the involvement of the library media specialist. The presentation itself and the ensuing discussion provide convincing evidence that the library program has a significant role to play in achieving the school's goals. Accordingly, the council agrees to maintain the current funding for library resources and to seek cuts elsewhere in the school budget.

COMMUNICATING WITH THE LARGER COMMUNITY

There has been an ongoing debate within the community about whether students graduating from high school are adequately prepared to enter the workforce. The high school establishes a blue-ribbon panel, composed of community and business leaders, to study the issue and make recommendations. The community group begins its investigation by identifying the skills and competencies needed in a 21st-century workplace. Among the skills they identify as most critical is the ability to use technology to perform workplace tasks.

During the fact-finding phase of the investigation, the panel asks the school to verify the place of educational technology in

(continued)

the curriculum. The school task force charged with providing this information organizes a presentation around four major themes:

- Technology as a tool for learning
- Technology as a tool for communication
- Technology as a tool for research
- Social and ethical issues related to the use of technology

In this scenario the community group wants to know what is being done to prepare students for a workplace driven by technology. The challenge for school personnel is to describe how technology-based activities help students to learn, to communicate, and to produce knowledge.

As a key member of the technology committee, the library media specialist agrees to address technology as a tool for research. He decides to focus his presentation on two phases of the search process where technology is used extensively: locating information and presenting knowledge.

Step 1: Collect Evidence of Achievement

For his part of the presentation, the library media specialist randomly selects 30 (out of 200) senior projects representing a heterogeneous group of students engaged in a diverse range of studies. He also assembles student-produced process folios for each of the selected projects to document the research and production processes. The library media specialist plans to analyze and summarize information from the following items in the process folios:

- Annotated bibliographies prepared by students
- Plans for the final presentations
- Students' reflections on how they used technology to access information and make their presentations

The annotated bibliographies include citations for all of the resources used by students during the information search process. The library media specialist creates a tally sheet (Figure 13.9) to track the various types of technology sources cited by individual students in their bibliographies.

Early in the process, students begin working on their presentation plans. These plans are reviewed at different phases of the research. The library media specialist refers to the plans illustrated in Figure 13.10 to determine how many students used technology tools for their final presentations as well as the types of tools employed.

Figure 13.9
Sample of tally sheet.

Student	Web sites	Electronic encyclopedia	Periodical database	Video/TV	E-mail
Student 1					
Student 2					
Student 3					

Step 2: Analyze Evidence

The analysis focuses on two questions related to the contributions of technology to the senior projects:

- How do students use technology to *locate* information?
- How do students use technology to *present* their projects?

To find out how technology is used to locate information, he gathers data by examining students' annotated bibliographies and making hash marks on the tally sheet to indicate sources that were accessed through technology.

His next step is to find out how many students use technology in their presentations. He gathers this information by examining students' presentation plans, in which they indicated the technology tools they planned to use and the adjustments they made to their plans. While students are encouraged to incorporate multimedia, video, and Web technology into their presentations, the use of technology is not a requirement, nor is it always appropriate.

Finally, the library media specialist reviews students' reflections to find out how they felt about the contributions of technology to their projects. Students have been asked to reflect on these questions:

- What technologies did you use for your project?
- How did they contribute to the final outcome?
- Could you have done it without the technology? Explain your response.

Here is how one student responds:

My project was about finding ways to protect our beaches from erosion. Most of my information came from the Internet. I found five different web sites on beach erosion that answered my research questions and that I could understand. I listed them in my bibliography.

Figure 13.10
Plan for presentation.

The topic of my project: _____

My audience: _____

Date, time, and place of the presentation: _____

My statement of purpose (what I hope to show,
do, or demonstrate): _____

How I will present my project: _____

Technology tools I plan to use:

_____Video

_____Presentation software (e.g., PowerPoint)

_____Multimedia software (e.g., HyperStudio)

_____Web authoring tool (e.g., Google Docs)

Other resources I will need: _____

Adjustments I made to my plan: _____

I also used e-mail to get information from an expert on beach erosion at the university. My bibliography also has his name and the dates when we corresponded.

I made a display board to show the results of my research, but I needed to use computers to show my data and to write my conclusions. I used a word processing program (Microsoft Word) and a graphics program for my graphs and charts. I could have drawn my figures, but it wouldn't have looked as good.

I don't think I could have done this project without technology. There aren't many books about beach erosion, and the information is outdated. The information on the Web is the most up-to-date. I also got a lot of help from the university professor. He is working on beach erosion in Hawaii and had a lot of data. He had one of his students answer the questions that I sent through e-mail. That was very helpful.

After reading the student's response, the library media specialist indicates with a plus sign that the student expresses a positive attitude toward technology use. He analyzes each student's response in the same way, using a minus sign for those who do not find it beneficial to use technology and an equal sign for those with a neutral attitude.

Step 3: Synthesize Findings

The library media specialist now has three sets of data to create a picture of how technology has been employed in the senior projects. Figure 13.11 shows the composition of these data sets.

Using hash marks to keep a running tally, the library media specialist tabulates the data. Figure 13.12 displays how many students use each type of technology as well as the total number of students using some form of technology to locate information and to present their projects. The library media specialist also keeps a tally on the attitudes expressed by students in their reflection journals.

Figure 13.11
Synthesizing data about the use of technology.

	Purpose	*Data source*	*Data collected*
Set 1	Find out how students use technology to locate information	Annotated bibliographies Tool for analyzing bibliographies	Number of citations for technology-based resources Technology tools used to locate information
Set 2	Find out how students use technology to present knowledge	Plan for final presentation	Number of students who use technology to present Kinds of technology used to present
Set 3	Find out how students feel about technology use	Reflection logs	Attitudes toward technology use

Figure 13.12
Tallying data related to technology use.

Technology Used to Locate Information (N = 30)					
Web sites	E-mail	Periodical database	Electronic encyclopedia	Video/ TV	Total # of students using technology
///// ///// ///// ///// ///// / (26) 87%	//// (4) 13%	///// ///// // (12) 40%	///// // (7) 23%	///// //// (9) 30%	///// ///// ///// ///// ///// ///// (30) 100%

Technology Used to Present Knowledge (N = 30)						
Video production	Multimedia	PowerPoint	Web authoring	Spreadsheet	Graphic software	Total # of students using technology
//// (4) 13%	///// / (6) 20%	///// /// (8) 26%	/// (3) 10%	/ (1) 3%	///// //// (9) 30%	///// ///// ///// ///// / (21) 70%

Attitudes about Technology (N = 30)		
Positive	Negative	Neutral
///// ///// ///// ///// ///// / (26) 87%	/ (1) 3%	/// (3) 10%

Used in conjunction with samples of student work, this type of data synthesis makes a compelling case that the technology enhances learning by increasing access to information and providing tools for productivity.

Step 4: Communicate Results

The presentation to the blue-ribbon panel is a collaborative effort involving the technology coordinator, a science teacher, the library media specialist, and two students who talk about how technology helped them with their projects. The group carefully plans the presentation to show how technology-related activities in the school prepare students for a 21st-century workplace environment.

As mentioned earlier, the library media specialist is responsible for explaining how students used technology as a tool for research. He begins his portion of the group presentation by sharing several senior projects and engaging the audience in a lively discussion about how technology might have contributed to the outcome. Following the discussion, he shares a multimedia presentation emphasizing three important points:

- Point 1: Every student in our sample used at least one technology tool to locate information. The types of technology used are displayed in Figure 13.13.
- Point 2: In the sample of projects analyzed, 21 out of 30 students used some kind of technology in their presentations. Figure 13.14 shows the technologies used and the percentage of students who used each type of technology.
- Point 3: An analysis of students' journal entries shows that 26 out of 30 students believe that technology was a valuable tool for research. These attitudes toward technology are summarized in Figure 13.15.

The library media specialist uses the data to draw the following conclusions:

Figure 13.13
Percentage of students using technology to locate information.

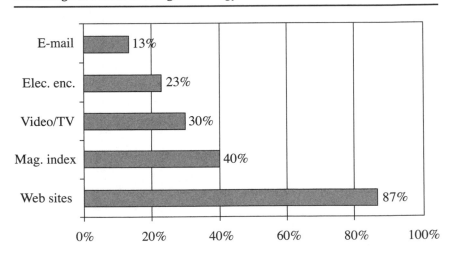

Figure 13.14
Percentage of students using technology to present information.

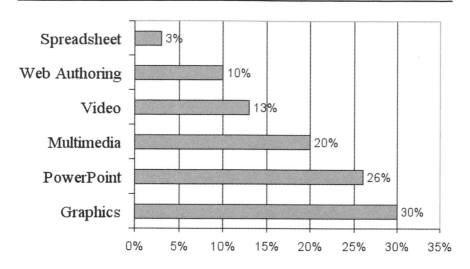

Figure 13.15
Student attitudes toward technology.

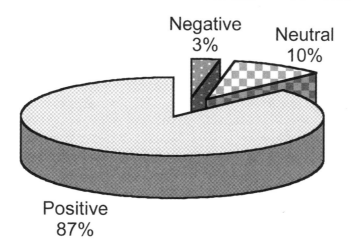

- With appropriate instruction, students become proficient at using technology to locate information.
- Given a choice, students use technology to make their presentations.
- Students who use technology in school develop positive attitudes toward technology as a tool for research and learning.

After the presentation, members of the blue-ribbon panel are encouraged to ask questions of the school representatives. The visual display of data, along with the work samples, assessment tools, and reflections woven into the presentation, help to convince the blue-ribbon panel that technology instruction is critical.

MAKING THE TESTING CONNECTION

Federal initiatives, particularly No Child Left Behind, have exposed schools to an overflow of testing (Chappuis, Chappuis, and Stiggins 2009). This has critical implications for the school library media specialist (Snyder and Roche 2008). Juanita Warren Buddy (2009) states:

> Standardized testing is part of the fabric of American education. For this reason, school librarians should continue to expand the role and importance of the school library in improving student achievement and lifelong learning by having the ability to understand and use standardized test results. This understanding can then serve to help correlate standardized test results to the work done through the school library to meet learning needs of students, raising the awareness of teachers, administrators, parents, and community members. (21)

Doug Johnson (2007) and Michael Eisenberg (2004) recommend that school librarians view testing as an opportunity to work with faculty on long-term efforts to improve student learning. Eisenberg (2004) emphasizes the need for library media specialists to "get detailed and specific in focusing our attention on state standards and tests and the connection to core library media functions" (23). This requires that library media specialists

- Become familiar with various state tests in terms of their focus, format, and content
- Analyze state standards and test items to determine direct connections to learning standards applied in the library media center
- Collaborate with faculty to have students apply the relevant information-related skills and dispositions related to the specific standards
- Evaluate the impact of the instruction on student performance on the test items
- Document the actions taken and the results (Eisenberg 2004).

Consider the following scenario that demonstrates how a library media specialist might become part of a school team to examine and act on test data.

Administration and faculty at a rural high school are deeply concerned about grade 10 students' poor showing in reading on the statewide assessment test. The reading test is composed of both multiple choice and constructed response items and focuses on three broad areas—reading comprehension, conventions and skills, and literary response and analysis. The average 10th-grade reading score is 290, which places the school in the "approaches proficiency" category. Broken down by the three areas of reading being tested, the disturbing results reveal the following:

- Reading comprehension: 79 percent of the students are at the "below proficiency" or "approaches proficiency" levels
- Conventions and skills: 81 percent of the students are at the "below proficiency" or "approaches proficiency" levels
- Literacy response and analysis: 88 percent of the students are at the "below proficiency" or "approaches proficiency" levels

The administration and faculty address the following critical questions in examining the test data:

- What are the specific skills in reading that must be addressed?
- How might we address these skills as a school community?

Faculty and administration in this scenario realize that the first crucial step in connecting test data with student academic improvement is to keep the investigation tightly focused on their critical questions. They acknowledge that they are "data rich, but information poor" (Ronka et al. 2009, 18). They do extensive readings about best practices in analyzing student test data. To organize their efforts, they establish a team to build their data literacy. The library media specialist recognizes that membership on this team will provide an invaluable opportunity to raise awareness that she is a teaching partner and curriculum leader. She volunteers to be a member of the team that is composed of the principal and subject-area teacher representatives.

The team meets regularly for collaborative data-driven conversations and brainstorming discussions on how to connect data analysis to clear action steps.

Step 1: Collect Evidence of Achievement

The team disaggregates the data to identify specific reading gaps. They begin by matching the test items to the state's content standards and benchmarks in language arts. In doing the match, the team identifies the following specific benchmarks:

- Reading comprehension: using annotation to evaluate the use of evidence while reading various texts
- Conventions and skills: using grade-appropriate vocabulary including content area vocabulary; using a variety of strategies to gain information from print and online resources, both primary and secondary, as part of a research plan
- Literary response and analysis: using multiple interpretations of text to support or modify an opinion; explaining how genre conventions and literary devices support an author's message and purpose

Step 2: Analyze Evidence

The data analysis provides vital information about specific benchmarks that must be addressed in the school. As a member of the team, the library media specialist immediately realizes where she might provide targeted instruction to support classroom intervention strategies. She decides to work with students on different techniques to gain relevant information from print and online resources. To accomplish this, she collaborates with the English and Social Studies Departments on their integrated history projects with grade 10 and 11 students. She introduces some of the following teaching and learning strategies:

- Hands-on, guided practice
- Facilitative questioning
- Cross-checking information
- Use of graphic organizers including idea trees and grids
- Peer tutoring and critiquing
- Checklists and rubrics

- Debriefing circles
- Response journals

Step 3: Synthesize Findings

The library media specialist collects her own assessment data for the instruction she provides. Here is an example: one area that she covers is the difference between primary and secondary sources and how to analyze information from primary sources. She administers a simple pretest and a posttest to gauge students' comprehension of key elements including authority and origin of the artifact, stated or inferred purpose, and content clarity. Figure 13.16 is an example of how she synthesizes and displays the student results for the individual teachers.

Step 4: Communicate Results

The library media specialist works with the faculty to ensure that students include a summary of the library assessment data in their learning portfolios. Students share these portfolios at student-led parent conferences. In addition, the library's contribution to strengthening reading skills is noted in the data team's multimedia report on

Figure 13.16
Example of student test results on analyzing primary sources.

Exceeds or meets proficiency = successfully completes 85% to 100% on tests
Approaches proficiency = successfully completes 50% to 84% on tests
Below proficiency = completes 49% or less on tests

Student name	Pretest			Posttest		
	Exceeds or meets	Approaches	Below	Exceeds or meets	Approaches	Below
Student A		x		x		
Student B			x		x	
Student C		x			x	

(1) interventions implemented to improve students' reading skills and (2) results of the effort. The report is presented to the school administration, parents, and district leaders.

Over the years, the faculty analyzes the statewide test results to see whether or not the intervention work influences the students' performance on the tests. The library media specialist remains a crucial partner in this effort. While positive test results may not be directly attributed to any specific intervention, student self-assessment journals and teacher observations support the notion that the library interventions are indeed helpful.

CONCLUSION

At the most fundamental level, assessment provides both students and instructors with information about how well students understand and apply what they are learning. It also allows instructional partners to measure the effectiveness of their teaching and to use the information in shaping improvements. A third function of assessment is communicating the results to various stakeholders in the school community. This last chapter has focused on using assessment data in this way to tell our story.

Evidence-based practice involves collecting critical assessment data, but it does not stop there. It requires analyzing and synthesizing the information and being able to draw conclusions from it. Sharing these results with different stakeholder groups necessitates that the library media specialist

- Knows what the stakeholder values and wants to know
- Identifies the specific data that will answer the stakeholder's questions
- Assembles and presents the evidence in a visually effective and verbally articulate manner

Providing tangible evidence about the power of learning through libraries is an enormous challenge facing our profession. It is a challenge we cannot afford to ignore if we are to remain an integral part of the school's teaching and learning community. To be visible and influential partners in meeting the charge of schools—to prepare our students to be knowledgeable and responsible citizens—we must demonstrate and communicate how our instruction contributes to the school's learning targets. Assessing for learning cannot be an afterthought; it must be a central part of our mission.

References

Adkison, Stephen, and Stephen Tchudi. 2000. "Assessing Growth in English and the Language Arts: The Case for Evaluation as Pedagogy." In *Assessing Student Learning: A Practical Guide* [CD-ROM], ed. Kent Seidel. Cincinnati, OH: Alliance for Curriculum Reform.

American Association of School Librarians. 2007. *Standards for the 21st-Century Learner.* http://www.ala.org/aasl/standards (accessed March 22, 2010).

American Association of School Librarians. 2009a. *Empowering Learners: Guidelines for School Library Media Programs.* Chicago, IL: American Association of School Librarians.

American Association of School Librarians. 2009b. *Standards for the 21-Century Learner in Action.* Chicago, IL: American Association of School Librarians.

American Library Association. 2008. *The 100 Most Frequently Challenged Books: 1990–2000.* Chicago, IL: American Library Association.

Andrade, Heidi G. 2000. "Using Rubrics to Promote Thinking and Learning." *Educational Leadership* 57, no. 5 (February): 13–18.

Asp, Elliott. 1998. "The Relationship between Large-Scale and Classroom Assessment: Compatibility or Conflict?" In *Assessing Student Learning: New Rules, New Realities,* ed. Ron Brandt. Arlington, VA: Educational Research Service, pp. 17–46.

Association for Supervision and Curriculum Development. 2007. *The Whole Child: The Learning Compact Redefined: A Call to Action: A Report of the Commission of the Whole Child.* Alexandria, VA: Association for Supervision and Curriculum Development.

Ausubel, David. 1967. *Learning Theory and Classroom Practice.* Ontario, Canada: The Ontario Institute for Studies in Education.

Badke, William. 2009. "Stepping Beyond Wikipedia." *Educational Leadership* 66, no. 6 (March): 54–58.

Bellanca, James. 1992. *The Cooperative Think Tank: Graphic Organizers to Teach Thinking in the Cooperative Classroom.* Palantine, IL: Skylight Publishing.

Berger, Pam. 2007. "Literacy and Learning in a Digital World." In *School Reform and the School Library Media Specialist,* ed. Sandra Hughes-Hassell and Violet H. Harada. Westport, CT: Libraries Unlimited, pp. 111–27.

Black, Paul, and Dylan William. 1998. "Inside the Black Box: Raising Stan-
    dards through Classroom Assessment." *Phi Delta Kappan* 80, no. 2
    (October): 139–48.

Brookhart, Susan, Connie Moss, and Beverly Long. 2008. "Formative Assess-
    ment That Empowers." *Educational Leadership* 66, no. 3 (November):
    52–57.

Brooks, Jacqueline Grennon, and Martin G. Brooks. 1993. *In Search of Under-
    standing: The Case for Constructivist Classrooms.* Alexandria, VA: Associa-
    tion for Supervision and Curriculum Development.

Buddy, Juanita Warren. 2009. "Standardized Testing Review 101." *School Li-
    brary Monthly* 26, no. 4 (December): 18–21.

Callison, Daniel. 2003. *Key Words, Concepts and Methods for Information Age
    Instruction: A Guide to Teaching Information Inquiry.* Baltimore, MD: LMS
    Associates.

Callison, Daniel. 2009. "Instructional Trends from AASL Journals: 1972–2007.
    Part 1." *School Library Media Activities Monthly* 25, no. 8 (April): 22–26.

Chappuis, Stephen, Jan Chappuis, and Rick Stiggins. 2009. "The Quest for
    Quality." *Educational Leadership* 67, no. 3 (November): 14–19.

Chappuis, Stephen, and Richard J. Stiggins. 2002. "Classroom Assessment for
    Learning." *Educational Leadership* 60, no. 1 (September): 40–43.

Coatney, Sharon. 2003. "Assessment for Learning." In *Curriculum Connections
    through the Library,* ed. Barbara K. Stripling and Sandra Hughes-Hassell.
    Westport, CT: Libraries Unlimited, pp. 157–68.

Cohen, Michael. 2008. "Improving College Preparation: Lessons from the
    American Diploma Project." *New England Journal of Higher Education* 22,
    no. 5 (spring): 21–23.

Coiro, June. 2009. "Rethinking Online Reading Assessment." *Educational Lead-
    ership* 66, no. 6 (March): 59–63.

Col, Jeananda. 2010. "All about Rainforests." Zoom Rainforest. http://www.
    enchantedlearning.com (accessed March 15, 2010).

Conley, David T. 2008. "Rethinking College Readiness." *New England Journal
    of Higher Education* 22, no. 5 (spring): 24–26.

Costa, Arthur L. 1988. "Teaching for Intelligence: Recognizing and Encour-
    aging Skillful Thinking and Behavior." *Transforming Education* (IC#18).
    http://www.context.org/ICLIB/IC18/Costa.htm (accessed April 2, 2010).

Costa, Arthur. 2008. "The Thought-Filled Curriculum." *Educational Leadership*
    65, no. 5 (February): 20–24.

Costa, Arthur L., and Bena Kallick. 2001. "What Are Habits of Mind?" http://
    www.instituteforhabitsofmind.com/what-are-habits-mind (accessed
    April 2, 2010).

Costa, Arthur L., and Bena Kallick. 2004. *Assessment Strategies for Self-Directed
    Learning.* Thousand Oaks, CA: Corwin Press.

Costa, Arthur L., and Bena Kallick. 2010. "It Takes Some Getting Used To: Re-
    thinking Curriculum for the 21st Century." In *Curriculum 21: Essential*

Education for a Changing World, ed. Heidi Hayes Jacobs. Alexandria, VA: Association for Supervision and Curriculum Development, pp. 210–26.

Costa, Arthur, and Rosemarie Liebmann. 1995. "Process Is as Important as Content." *Educational Leadership* 52, no. 6 (March): 23–24.

Damon, William. 2008. *The Path to Purpose: Helping Our Children Find Their Calling in Life.* New York: The Free Press.

Darrow, Rob. 2009. "School Libraries Are Essential." *Knowledge Quest* 37, no. 5 (May/June): 78–82.

Davies, Anne, Caren Cameron, Colleen Politano, and Kathleen Gregory. 1992. *Together Is Better: Collaborative Assessment, Evaluation and Reporting.* Winnipeg, Canada: Peguis Publishers.

Donham, Jean. 1998. *Assessment of Information Processes and Products.* Chicago, IL: Follett Software Co.

Earl, Lorna. 2003. *Assessment as Learning: Using Classroom Assessment to Maximize Student Learning.* Thousand Oaks, CA: Corwin Press.

Education Commission of the States. 2002. *No State Left Behind: The Challenges and Opportunities of ESEA 2001.* Washington, DC: Education Commission of the States.

Eisenberg, Michael B. 2004. "It's All about Learning: Ensuring That Students Are Effective Users of Information on Standardized Tests." *Library Media Connection* 22, no. 6 (March): 22–30.

Ekhaml, Leticia. 1998. "Graphic Organizers: Outlets for Your Thoughts." *School Library Media Activities Monthly* 14, no. 5 (January): 29–33.

Ennis, Robert H. 2000. *An Outline of Goals for a Critical Thinking Curriculum and Its Assessment.* CriticalThinking.net. http://www.criticalthinking.net/goals.html (accessed April 2, 2010).

Falk, Beverly. 2000. *The Heart of the Matter: Using Standards and Assessment to Learn.* Portsmouth, NH: Heinemann.

Farmer, Lesley S. J. 2003. *Student Success and Library Media Programs: A Systems Approach to Research and Best Practice.* Westport, CT: Libraries Unlimited.

Farr, Greg. 2009. "*Mad* Magazine to Facebook: What Have We Learned?" *Teacher Librarian* 36, no. 5 (June): 30–32.

Ferriter, Bill. 2009. "Taking the Digital Plunge." *Educational Leadership* 67, no. 1 (September): 85–86.

Fisher, Douglas, and Nancy Frey. 2007. *Checking for Understanding: Formative Assessment Techniques for Your Classroom.* Alexandria, VA: Association for Supervision and Curriculum Development.

Fodeman, Doug, and Marje Monroe. 2009. "The Impact of Facebook on Our Students." *Teacher Librarian* 36, no. 5 (June): 36–40.

Friedman, Thomas. 2005. *The World Is Flat.* New York: Farrar, Straus, and Giroux.

Gathercoal, Paul, Douglas Love, Beverly Bryde, and Gerry McKean. 2002. "On Implementing Web-Based Electronic Portfolios." *Educause Quarterly* 2: 29–37.

Gordon, Carol A. 2007. "The Real Thing: Authentic Teaching through Action Research." In *School Reform and the School Library Media Specialist*, ed. Sandra Hughes-Hassell and Violet H. Harada. Westport, CT: Libraries Unlimited, pp. 161–78.

Graves, Donald. 1992. "Portfolios: Keep a Good Idea Growing." In *Portfolio Portraits*, ed. Donald Graves and Bonnie Sunstein. Portsmouth, NH: Heinemann, pp. 1–12.

Guskey, Thomas R. 2003. "How Classroom Assessments Improve Learning," *Educational Leadership* 60, no. 5 (February): 6–11.

Hamilton, Buffy J. 2009. "Transforming Information Literacy for Nowgen Students." *Knowledge Quest* 37, no. 5 (May/June): 48–53.

Harada, Violet H. 2002. "Personalizing the Information Search Process: A Case Study of Journal Writing with Elementary-Age Students." *School Library Media Research*. http://www.ala.org/ala/mgrps/divs/aasl/aaslpubsandjournals/slmrb/slmrcontents/volume52002/harada.cfm (accessed April 2, 2010).

Harada, Violet H., and Joan Yoshina. 1997. "Improving Information Search Process Instruction and Assessment through Collaborative Action Research." *School Libraries Worldwide* 3, no. 2 (July): 41–55.

Harada, Violet H., and Joan M. Yoshina. 2004. *Inquiry Learning through Librarian-Teacher Partnerships*. Worthington, OH: Linworth Publishing.

Haycock, Ken. 1999. *Foundations of Effective School Library Media Programs*. Englewood, CO: Libraries Unlimited.

Heath, Marilyn. 2005. "Are You Ready to Go Digital? The Pros and Cons of Electronic Portfolio Development." *Library Media Connection* 23, no. 7 (April/May): 66–70.

Herman, Joan L., Pamela R. Aschbacker, and Lynn Winters. 1992. *A Practical Guide to Alternative Assessment*. Alexandria, VA: Association for Supervision and Curriculum Development.

International Society for Technology in Education. 2007. *National Educational Technology Standards for Students: The Next Generation*. http://www.iste.org/Content/NavigationMenu/NETS/For_Students/NETS_S.htm (accessed April 2, 2010).

Jaquith, Wanda Adams. 2005. "Not for the Faint of Heart." *Knowledge Quest* 34, no. 2 (November/December): 42–44.

Johnson, Doug. 2007. "Can School Media Programs Help Raise Standardized Test Scores?" http://www.doug-johnson.com/dougwri/can-school-media-programs-help-raise-standardized-test-score.html (accessed April 2, 2010).

Johnson, Doug. 2009. "Libraries for a Postliterate Society." *Multimedia & Internet@Schools* 16, no. 4 (July/August): 20–22.

Kansas Association of School Librarians Research Committee. 2001. *The Handy 5: Planning and Assessing Integrated Information Skills Instruction*, ed. Robert Grover, Carol Fox, and Jacqueline M. Lakin. Lanham, MD: Scarecrow Press.

Katz, Lillian G. 2000. "Dispositions as Educational Goals." *ERIC Digest.* http://www.ericdigests.org/1994/goals.htm (accessed April 2, 2010).

Kendall, John S., and Robert J. Marzano. 2010. *Content Knowledge: A Compendium of Standards and Benchmarks for K-12 Education.* 4th ed. Aurora, CO: Mid-Continent Research for Education and Learning.

Knobel, Michele, and Dana Wilber. 2009. "Let's Talk 2.0." *Educational Leadership* 66, no. 6 (March): 20–24.

Kuhlthau, Carol Collier. 2004. *Seeking Meaning: A Process Approach to Library and Information Services.* 2nd ed. Westport, CT: Libraries Unlimited.

Lamb, Annette, and Larry Johnson. 2009. "Wikis and Collaborative Inquiry." *School Library Media Activities Monthly* 25, no. 8 (April): 48–51.

Lindsay, Julie, and Vicki Davis. 2009. "Flat Classroom Project." http://www.flatclassroomproject.org/ (accessed April 2, 2010).

Loertscher, David V., and Blanche Woolls. 2002. *Information Literacy: A Review of the Research.* San Jose, CA: Hi Willow Research & Publishing.

Luongo-Orlando, Katherine. 2003. *Authentic Assessment: Designing Performance-Based Tasks.* Ontario, Canada: Pembroke Publishers Limited.

Mardis, Marcia A., and Anne M. Perrault. 2008. "A Whole New Library: Six Senses You Can Use to Make Sense of New Standards and Guidelines." *Teacher Librarian* 35, no. 4 (April): 34–38.

Martin-Kniep, Giselle. 2000. *Becoming a Better Teacher: Eight Innovations That Work.* Alexandria, VA: Association for Supervision and Curriculum Development.

Marzano, Robert J., Jane E. Pollock, and Debra J. Pickering. 2001. *Classroom Instruction That Works: Research-Based Strategies for Increasing Student Achievement.* Alexandria, VA: Association for Supervision and Curriculum Development.

Mitchell, Ruth, Marilyn Willis, and The Chicago Teachers Union Quest Center. 1995. *Learning in Overdrive: Designing Curriculum, Instruction, and Assessment from Standards.* Golden, CO: North American Press.

Mitleton-Kelly, Eve. n.d. "What Are the Characteristics of a Learning Organization?" http://www.gemi.org/metricsnavigator/eag/What%20are%20the%20Characteristics%20of%20a%20Learning%20Organization.pdf (accessed April 2, 2010).

Moreillon, Judi, and Kristin Fontichiaro. 2008. "The Dispositions: A Garden of Opportunity." *Knowledge Quest* 37, no. 2 (November/December): 64–67.

Mundell, Susan, and Karen DeLario. 1994. *Practical Portfolios: Reading, Writing, Math, and Life Skills, Grades 3–6.* Englewood, CO: Libraries Unlimited.

National Center for History in the Schools. 1996. *National Standards for History: Grades 5–12.* http://nchs.ucla.edu/standards/us-standards4–12.html (accessed March 25, 2010).

National Geographic Society Committee on Research and Exploration. 1994. "National Geography Standards, Geography Education Standards Project." *Geography for Life: The National Geography Standards.* Washington, DC.

http://www.nationalgeographic.com/xpeditions/standards/ (accessed April 2, 2010).

National Research Council. 1996. *National Science Education Standards*. Washington, DC: The National Academies Press.

Neuman, Delia. 2000. "Information Power and Assessment: The Other Side of the Standards Coin." In *Educational Media and Technology Yearbook*, ed. Robert M. Branch and Mary Ann Fitzgerald. Englewood, CO: Libraries Unlimited, pp. 110–19.

New Media Consortium. 2009. *2009 Horizon Report: The K-12 Edition*. http://wp.nmc.org/horizon-k12–2009/ (accessed April 2, 2010).

Novak, Joseph. 1977. *A Theory of Education*. Ithaca, NY: Cornell University Press.

Ogle, Doris S. 1986. "K-W-L Group Instructional Strategy." In *Teaching Reading as Thinking*, ed. Al S. Palincsar, Doris S. Ogle, Beau F. Jones, and E. G. Carr. Alexandria, VA: Association for Supervision and Curriculum Development, pp. 11–17.

O'Grady, Alice. 1999. "Information Literacy Skills and the Senior Project." *Educational Leadership* 57, no. 2 (October): 61–62.

Ohler, Jason. 2009. "Orchestrating the Media Collage." *Educational Leadership* 66, no. 6 (March): 8–13.

Pappas, Marjorie. 1997. "Organizing Research." *School Library Media Activities Monthly* 14, no. 4 (December): 30–32.

Parsons, Seth A. 2008. "Providing All Students ACCESS to Self-Regulated Literacy Learning." *The Reading Teacher* 61, no. 8 (May): 628–35.

Partnership for 21st Century Skills. 2007. *Framework for 21st Century Learning*. http://www.21stcenturyskills.org/index.php (accessed March 11, 2010).

Partnership for 21st Century Skills. 2008. "A Transition Brief: Policy Recommendations on Preparing Americans for the Global Skills Race." http://www.21stcenturyskills.org/documents/p21_transition_paper_nov_24_2008.pdf (accessed April 2, 2010).

Perkins, David N. 1992. *Smart Schools: From Training Memories to Educating Minds*. New York: Free Press.

Perkins, David. 1993. "Teaching for Understanding." *American Educator: The Professional Journal of the American Federation of Teachers* 17, no. 3 (fall): 8, 28–35.

Perkins-Gough, Deborah. 2008. "Unprepared for College." *Educational Leadership* 66, no. 3 (November): 88–89.

Perry, Nancy E., Lynda Phillips, and Lynda Hutchinson. 2006. "Mentoring Student Teachers to Support Self-Regulated Learning." *Elementary School Journal* 106, no. 3 (January): 237–54.

Pew Research Center. 2007. *Teens and Social Media*. Washington, DC: Pew Research Center.

Pink, Daniel. 2005. *A Whole New Mind*. New York: Riverhead Books.

Pinker, Steven. 1997. *How the Mind Works*. New York: HarperCollins.

Richardson, Will. 2009. "Becoming Network-Wise." *Educational Leadership* 66, no. 6 (March): 26–31.

Ronka, David, Mary Ann Lachat, Rachel Slaughter, and Julie Meltzer. 2009. "Answer the Questions." *Educational Leadership* 66, no. 4 (December/January): 18–24.

Scherer, Marge. 2009. "The World at Our Fingertips." *Educational Leadership* 66, no. 6 (March): 7.

S.C.O.R.E. Language Arts. n.d. *Schools of California Online Resources in Education: Journals.* http://www.sdcoe.k12.ca.us/score/actbank/tjournal.htm (accessed April 2, 2010).

Seitz, Hilary. 2008. "Powerful Portfolios for Young Children." *Early Childhood Education Journal* 36, no. 1 (August): 63–68.

Senge, Peter. 1990. *The Fifth Discipline: The Art and Practice of the Learning Organization.* London: Random House.

Snyder, Maureen M., and Janet Roche. 2008. "Road Map for Improvement: Evaluating Your Library Media Program." *Knowledge Quest* 37, no. 2 (November/December): 22–27.

Sprenger, Marilee. 2009. "Focusing the Digital Brain." *Educational Leadership* 67, no. 1 (September): 34–39.

Steele, Jennifer L., and Kathryn Parker Boudett. 2009. "The Collaborative Advantage." *Educational Leadership* 66, no. 4 (December/January): 54–59.

Stephens, Wendy. 2008. "Evidence of Student Voices: Finding Meaning in Intellectual Freedom." *Knowledge Quest* 37, no. 2 (November/December): 44–48.

Sternberg, Robert J. 2008. "Excellence for All." *Educational Leadership* 66, no. 2 (October): 15–19.

Stiggins, Richard. 1997. *Student-Centered Classroom Assessment.* Columbus, OH: Prentice-Hall.

Strickland, Jonathan. 2008. "How Web 3.0 Will Work." http://computer.howstuffworks.cm/web-30.htm (accessed April 2, 2010).

Strickland, Kathleen, and James Strickland. 2000. *Making Assessment Elementary.* Portsmouth, NH: Heinemann.

Stripling, Barbara K. 2007. "Teaching for Understanding." In *School Reform and the School Library Media Specialist,* ed. Sandra Hughes-Hassell and Violet H. Harada. Westport, CT: Libraries Unlimited, pp. 37–55.

Strong American Schools. 2008. *Diploma to Nowhere.* http://hub.mspnet.org/index.cfm/17122 (accessed April 2, 2010).

Tallman, Julie I. 1995. "Curriculum Consultation: Strengthening Activity through Multiple-Content Area Units." *School Library Media Quarterly* 24, no. 1 (fall): 27–34.

Thomas, Nancy P. 2004. *Information Literacy and Information Skills Instruction: Applying Research to Practice in the School Library Media Center.* 2nd ed. Westport, CT: Libraries Unlimited.

Todd, Ross. 2001a. "Evidence Based Practice II: Getting into the Action." *SCAN* 20, no. 1 (February): 1–8.

Todd, Ross. 2001b. "Transitions for Preferred Futures of School Libraries: Knowledge Space, Not Information Place; Connections, Not Collections; Actions, Not Positions; Evidence, Not Advocacy." Keynote address for the International Association of School Librarianship, Auckland, New Zealand. http://www.iasl-online.org/events/conf/virtualpaper2001.html (accessed April 2, 2010).

Todd, Ross J. 2002. "Evidence Based Practice II: Getting into the Action," *SCAN* 21, no. 2 (May): 34–41.

Todd, Ross J. 2003. "School Libraries Evidence: Seize the Day, Begin the Future." *Library Media Connection* 22, no. 1 (August/September): 12–17.

Todd, Ross J. 2007. "Evidence Based Practice and School Libraries: From Advocacy to Action." In *School Reform and the School Library Media Specialist,* ed. Sandra Hughes-Hassell and Violet H. Harada. Westport, CT: Libraries Unlimited, pp. 57–78.

Todd, Ross. 2008. "A Question of Evidence." *Knowledge Quest* 37, no. 2 (November/December): 16–21.

Tomlinson, Carol Ann. 2008a. "The Goals of Differentiation." *Educational Leadership* 66, no. 3 (November): 26–30.

Tomlinson, Carol Ann. 2008b. "Learning to Love Assessment." *Educational Leadership* 65, no. 4 (December/January): 8–13.

Tuttle, Harry G. 1997. "The Multimedia Report: Electronic Portfolios Tell a Personal Story." *MultiMedia Schools* 4, no. 1 (January/February): 32–37.

Vandergrift, Kay E. 1994. *Power Teaching: A Primary Role for the School Library Media Specialist.* Chicago, IL: American Library Association.

Weigel, Margaret, and Howard Gardner. 2009. "The Best of Both Literacies." *Educational Leadership* 66, no. 6 (March): 38–41.

Whelan, Debra L. 2004. "13,000 Kids Can't Be Wrong." *School Library Journal* 50, no. 2 (February): 46–50.

Wiggins, Grant. 1998. *Educative Assessment: Designing Assessments to Inform and Improve Student Performance.* San Francisco, CA: Jossey-Bass.

Wiggins, Grant, and Jay McTighe. 1998. *Understanding by Design.* Alexandria, VA: Association for Supervision and Curriculum Development.

Wiggins, Grant, and Jay McTighe. 2008. "Put Understanding First." *Educational Leadership* 65, no. 8 (May): 36–41.

Williams, Dorothy A., and Caroline Wavell. 2001. *The Impact of the School Library Resource Centre on Learning. Library and Information Commission Research Report 112.* Aberdeen, Scotland: Robert Gordon University.

Wiske, Martha S. 1994. "How Teaching for Understanding Changes the Rules in the Classroom." *Educational Leadership* 51, no. 5 (February): 19–21.

Zmuda, Allison, and Violet H. Harada. 2008. *Librarians as Learning Specialists: Meeting the Learning Imperative for the 21st Century.* Westport, CT: Libraries Unlimited.

Zuger, Sascha. 2008. "Build Better ePortfolios." *Technology & Learning* 29, no. 1 (August): 46–47.

Index

Action research, 14–15
American Association for School
    Librarians. *See Standards for the
    21st-Century Learner* (American
    Association for School Librarians)
Animal adaptation unit, 22
Assessment: benefits of, 17; defined, 9;
    determining standards for, 85–86;
    evaluation *versus*, 9; formative,
    9–10; importance of, 6; as integral
    to learning, 8, 12; supporting
    school-wide goals with data, 200.
    See also Critical understanding
    assessment; Dispositions
    assessment; Information literacy
    assessment; Tech-integrated
    learning assessment
Assessment for learning, 9–18;
    described, 9–10; library media
    programs and student learning,
    13–15; library media specialist role
    in, 15–18; No Child Left Behind
    Act and, 12–13; in schools, 10–12;
    student role in, 10–12; teacher view
    of, 12
Assessment tools: adapting for
    outcome-based approach, 150,
    179; creating, 19; effective use of,
    19; improving, 20; in process folio
    development, 86. *See also specific
    tools*

Backward design. *See* Outcome-based
    approach
Badke, William, 7

Berger, Pam, 135
Bias, identifying, 111–12
Bibliography, preparing annotated
    (sample lesson), 191–97;
    assessment, 192–94; learning plan,
    194–97; outcomes desired, 191–92
Big idea questions, 108
Bill of Rights unit: rating scale
    assessment, 29–31; rubric
    assessment, 26–29
Blogs, 137–38
Book creation project, 150–63;
    developing criteria to assess
    student books (sample lesson),
    155, 157–63; finding information in
    variety of sources (sample lesson),
    151–55; sample lessons, 151–63;
    summary of project, 150–51
Books, challenged, 126
Brooks, Jacqueline, 3
Brooks, Martin, 3

Callison, Daniel, 57
Checklists: assessing information
    literacy with, 22; assessing tech-
    integrated learning with, 141;
    constructing, 21; defined, 20; in
    outcome-based approach, 159–61;
    student portfolios and, 88, 90, 93;
    using, 20–21; wetlands project, 88,
    90, 93, 159–61
Civilization unit, 36–37
Civil War timeline, 102
Class profiles: Holocaust project, 209,
    211; wetlands project, 203–4

Cohen, Michael, 7
Collaboration, 5, 101–2, 103–4
College courses, remedial, 1
Colonial fair activity, 66–68
Communicating evidence of learning,
    199–224; importance of, 200–201;
    to larger community, 212–20;
    making testing connection, 220–24;
    to principals and school councils,
    206–12; to teachers, 201–6; using
    assessment data to support school-
    wide goals, 200
Communicating understanding,
    115–17
Community, communicating with,
    212–20; analyzing evidence, 214–16;
    collecting evidence of achievement,
    213–14; communicating results,
    217–20; synthesizing findings,
    216–17
Community garden project, 102–3
Community history project, 123–24
Concept maps: assessing critical
    understanding with, 114–15;
    assessing dispositions with, 126;
    assessing information literacy with,
    61–64; constructing, 60–61; defined,
    58; using, 58–60
Conclusions, drawing, 113–15
Conferences: assessing information
    literacy with, 36–37; defined, 33;
    formal, 34–35; informal, 33–34, 37;
    structuring, 35; using, 33–35
Conley, David, 4
Correspondence, personal: assessing
    information literacy with, 50–51;
    constructing, 47–51; defined, 47;
    using, 48
Costa, Arthur, 4, 100
Council for Museums, Archives and
    Libraries (Scotland), 14
Critical understanding, 99–117;
    acquiring, 101–3; assessing
    for, 105–17; defining, 99–101;
    developing through inquiry, 103–5
Critical understanding assessment:
    bias, identifying, 111–12;
    communicating understanding,

115–17; conclusions, drawing,
    113–15; connecting new learning to
    prior knowledge, 105–6; points of
    view, considering different, 110–11;
    questioning, 106–9
Cyber bullying project, 138–40

Digital landscape, defining, 133
Digital narratives, 141–43
Digital student portfolios, 78–79
Discussions, online, 136–37
Dispositions, 119–31; acquiring,
    120–21; assessing for, 121–29;
    defining, 120; using portfolios,
    129–30
Dispositions assessment, 121–30;
    flexibility, 120, 123; initiative, 120,
    122; literary appreciation, 125–26;
    openness, 120, 126; persistence,
    123–24; social responsibility, 120,
    126–29; using portfolios, 129–30
Drug education and prevention
    activity, 53

Eisenberg, Michael, 220
Election unit, 73–76
Electronic logs (e-logs), 139–40
Electronic student portfolios, 78–79
Elementary school, assessing
    dispositions in, 120–21. See also
    Outcome-based approach
    (elementary grade example); specific
    grades
Enchanted Learning, 62
Ennis, Robert, 100
Evaluation versus assessment, 9
Evidence of learning: analyzing, 202,
    209, 214–16, 222–23; collecting,
    202, 207–8, 213–14, 222. See also
    Communicating evidence of
    learning
Exit passes: assessing information
    literacy with, 53–54; constructing,
    52; defined, 51–52; using, 52

Facilitators, in learning organizations, 4
Fact-based questions, 108
Fairy tales, 120–21

Fiction writer project, 137–38
Findings, synthesizing, 203–4, 209, 216–17, 223
Flat Classroom Project, 126–29
Flexibility, assessing for, 120, 123
Fodeman, Doug, 134–35
Folios. *See* Process folios
Formal conferences, 34–35
Formative assessment, 9–10

Gallery walks, 122
Geography project, 111–12
Global warming study, 112
Gordon, Carol, 14–15
Grade 1: dispositions assessment, 122; information literacy assessment, 70–72; initiative assessment, 122; K-W-L charts, 70–72
Grade 2: checklists, 22; critical understanding assessment, 105–6; information literacy assessment, 22
Grade 3: communicating with teachers, 201–6; concept maps, 61–64; developing criteria to assess student books (sample lesson), 155, 157–63; finding information in variety of sources (sample lesson), 151–55; information literacy assessment, 61–64; process folios, 84–97; sample lessons, 151–63; summary of wetlands project, 150–51
Grade 4: critical understanding assessment, 112–15; online discussions, 136–37; tech-integrated learning assessment, 136–37
Grade 5: blogs, 137–38; critical understanding assessment, 102–3, 106–9; dispositions assessment, 123; flexibility assessment, 123; information literacy assessment, 40, 66–68; logs, 40; tech-integrated learning assessment, 137–38; webs, 65–68
Grade 6: conferences, 36–37; information literacy assessment, 36–37
Grade 7: critical understanding assessment, 111–12; dispositions assessment, 123–24; information literacy assessment, 50; persistence assessment, 123–24; personal correspondence, 50–51; podcasts and vodcasts, 138–40; tech-integrated learning assessment, 138–40
Grade 8: asking the right questions (sample lesson), 167–70; communicating with principals and school councils, 206–12; critical understanding assessment, 115–17; dispositions assessment, 125–26; information literacy assessment, 26–31; literary appreciation assessment, 125–26; rating scales, 29–31; rubrics, 26–29; sample lessons, 167–79; selecting and evaluating resources (sample lesson), 170, 173–79; summary of Holocaust project, 166; tech-integrated learning assessment, 140–41; wikis, 140–41
Grade 10: dispositions assessment, 126; information literacy assessment, 43–47; logs, 43–47; openness assessment, 126; test data, 220–24
Grade 11: critical understanding assessment, 110–11; digital narratives, 141–43; tech-integrated learning assessment, 141–43
Grade 12: dispositions assessment, 126–29; evaluating Web sites (sample lesson), 184–91; preparing annotated bibliography (sample lesson), 191–97; sample lessons, 183–97; social responsibility assessment, 126–29; summary of senior project, 182–83
Graphic organizers, 57–76; concept maps, 58–64; defined, 57; described, 57–58; K-W-L charts, 68–72; matrices, 72–76; webs, 65–68

Health care reform project, 110–11
Health education project, 140–41
High concept skills, 135, 136

High school: communicating with larger community, 212–20; critical understanding, 102; dispositions, 121; tech-integrated learning assessment, 144–45; wiki pathfinders, 144–45. *See also* Outcome-based approach (high school example); *specific grades*
High touch skills, 135–36
Holocaust project: asking the right questions (sample lesson), 167–70; communicating with principals and school councils, 206–12; sample lessons, 167–79; selecting and evaluating resources (sample lesson), 170, 173–79; summary of project, 166
Homelessness project, 144–45
Horizon Report (2009), 134, 136
Humpback whale migration project, 136–37
Hygiene project, 123

Immigrant experience project, 141–43
Independent reading projects, 125–26
Informal conferences, 33–34, 37
Information, finding in variety of sources (sample lesson), 151–55; assessment, 154; learning plan, 154–55; outcomes desired, 151–53
Information literacy assessment: checklists, 22; concept maps, 61–64; conferences, 36–37; exit passes, 51–54; K-W-L charts, 70–72; logs, 43–47; personal correspondence, 50; rating scales, 30–31; rubrics, 26–29; webs, 65–68
Initiative, assessing for, 120, 122
Inquiry, 103–5
Instructional design, 6
Instructional rubrics, 24–25
Intellectual freedom project, 126
Interviewing project, 107–9
Island of the Blue Dolphins, The (O'Dell), 40

Journals. *See* Logs

Kallick, Bena, 100
Knowledge: active production of, 4–5; collaborative building of, 5; connecting new learning to prior knowledge, 105–6
Kuhlthau, Carol, 14
K-W-H-L (know, wonder, how, learn) charts, 69–72
K-W-L (know, wonder, learn) charts: assessing critical understanding with, 105; assessing information literacy with, 70–72; constructing, 69–70; defined, 68–69; using, 69

Lance, Keith Curry, 13–14
Learning: focus on, 16; self-regulated, 11–12, 198. *See also* Assessment for learning; Evidence of learning; Tech-integrated learning
Learning organizations, 3–5; action principles, 4–5; behaviors of adult facilitators in, 4; characteristics of, 3–4
Lessons, sample: bibliography, preparing annotated, 191–97; information, finding in variety of sources, 151–55; questions, asking the right, 167–70; resources, selecting and evaluating, 170, 173–79; student books, developing criteria to assess, 155, 157–63; Web sites, evaluating, 184–91
Letters and notes. *See* Correspondence, personal
Library instruction: challenges of, 7; determining standards for, 85–86; student learning and, 13–15
Library media specialists: assessment benefits for, 17; questions for, 17–18; role in assessment for learning, 15–18; role in 21st-century schools, 6–8; student portfolio use, 77–78, 82–83; tech-integrated learning, 135–36
Literary appreciation, assessing for, 125–26
Literary response logs, 42, 173, 208

Logs: assessing dispositions with, 123; assessing information literacy with, 43–47; defined, 38; electronic, 139–40; facilitating use of, 42–43; literary response, 42, 173, 208; synthesis, 42; using as assessment tool, 38–41

Maps, resource, 155. *See also* Concept maps
Matrices: assessing critical understanding with, 112; assessing information literacy with, 73–76; communicating evidence of learning with, 202; constructing, 73; defined, 72; in outcome-based approach, 152–53; resource, 202; student portfolios and, 87–88, 90; using, 72–73; wetlands project, 87–88, 90, 152–53, 202
Media specialists. *See* Library media specialists
Middle school: critical understanding, 102; exit passes, 52–54; information literacy assessment, 52–54, 73–76; matrices, 73–76. *See also* Outcome-based approach (middle school example); *specific grades*
Monroe, Marje, 134–35
"Movers and Shakers" theme, 107–9

Narratives, digital, 141–43
National Drug Prevention Week activity, 52–54
National Geographic Standards, 111–12
No Child Left Behind (NCLB) Act, 12–13, 101, 220
Notes. *See* Correspondence, personal
Numerical scales, 29

Ohio Educational Library Media Association, 14
Online discussions, 136–37
Openness, assessing for, 120, 126
Organizers, defined, 57. *See also* Graphic organizers
Outcome-based approach: assessment tools, adapting for, 150, 179;

conventional approach *versus*, 147; steps in, 148
Outcome-based approach (elementary grade example), 147–64; described, 147–50; developing criteria to assess student books (sample lesson), 155, 157–63; finding information in variety of sources (sample lesson), 151–55; project summary, 150–51; sample lessons, 151–63
Outcome-based approach (high school example), 181–98; described, 181–82; evaluating Web sites (sample lesson), 184–91; preparing annotated bibliography (sample lesson), 191–97; project summary, 182–83; sample lessons, 183–97
Outcome-based approach (middle school example), 165–80; asking the right questions (sample lesson), 167–70; described, 165–66; project summary, 166; sample lessons, 167–79; selecting and evaluating resources (sample lesson), 170, 173–79

Pappas, Marjorie, 57
Passes, exit. *See* Exit passes
Pathfinders, wiki, 144–45
Perkins, David, 100
Persistence, assessing for, 123–24
Pet project, 70–72
Podcasts and vodcasts, 138–40
Points of view, considering different, 110–11
Pond life investigation, 102
Portfolios, student, 77–98; assessing dispositions with, 129–30; audiences for, 81–82; defined, 77; digital/electronic, 78–79; getting started with, 97; library media specialist use of, 77–78, 82–83; other assessment tools *versus*, 79–80; reasons for using, 80–81; Web-based, 78–79. *See also* Process folios

Principals, communicating with,
206–12; analyzing evidence, 209;
collecting evidence of achievement,
207–8; communicating results, 209,
211–12; synthesizing findings, 209
Process folio development, 84–97;
rating system, 87–88; samples
of student reflections, 93–94;
samples of student work, 88, 90,
93; standards for instruction and
assessment, 85–86; summary sheet,
95, 97; tools and strategies to assess
achievement, 86
Process folios: defined, 83;
developing, 84–97; planning, 84;
using, 83–84

Qualitative scales, 29
Questions, asking the right (sample
lesson), 167–70; assessment,
168–69; learning plan, 169–70;
outcomes desired, 167–68
Questions and questioning: big idea,
108; in critical understanding
assessment, 106–9; fact-based, 108;
for library media specialists, 17–18
Question webs, 122

Rain forest unit, 61–64
Rating scales: assessing dispositions
with, 123–24; assessing information
literacy with, 30–31; assessing tech-
integrated learning with, 136–37,
139; consistent, 87–88; constructing,
29–30; defined, 29; numerical,
29; in outcome-based approach,
154, 186–87; in process folio
development, 87–88; qualitative,
29; senior project, 186–87; using,
29; in Web site evaluation, 186–87;
wetlands project, 153
Read-in activity, 52–54
Reading trackers, 125–26
Reflection: fostering culture of, 5; in
schools, 6
Reflection rubrics, 144–45
Reflections, student, 93–94
Remedial college courses, 1

Research, action, 14–15. See also
Technology as tool for research
presentation
Resource maps, 155
Resource matrices, 202
Resources, selecting and evaluating
(sample lesson), 170, 173–79;
assessment, 170, 173–75; learning
plan, 175–79; outcomes desired, 170
Response sheets, 173
Results, communicating: to larger
community, 217–20; making testing
connection, 223–24; to principals
and school councils, 209, 211–12; to
teachers, 204, 206
Rubrics: assessing critical
understanding with, 117; assessing
dispositions with, 128–29; assessing
information literacy with, 26–29;
assessing tech-integrated learning
with, 137–38, 143, 144–45;
communicating evidence of
learning with, 202; constructing,
24–25; defined, 22–23; Holocaust
project, 168; instructional, 24–25;
outcome-based approach, 168,
192–94; reflection, 144–45; resource
matrix, 202; senior project, 192–94;
using, 23–24; Web site evaluation
tool, 192–94; wetlands project, 202

Salmon steward project, 105–6
School councils, communicating with,
206–12; analyzing evidence, 209;
collecting evidence of achievement,
207–8; communicating results, 209,
211–12; synthesizing findings, 209
Schools, 1–8; assessment for learning
in, 10–12; challenges facing, 1–2;
as learning organizations, 3–5;
library media specialist role in, 6–8;
reflection and assessment in, 6;
standards and their role in reform,
2; using assessment data to support
goals, 200
Science and ethics unit, 43–47
Sea turtle project, 122
Self-assessment, 11–12, 198

Self-directed individuals, 119

Senior projects, 182–97; evaluating
    Web sites (sample lesson), 184–91;
    preparing annotated bibliography
    (sample lesson), 191–97; sample
    lessons, 183–97; summary of
    project, 182–83

"Sense of Place" theme, 113–15

Skills: high concept, 135, 136; high
    touch, 135–36; library instruction, 7;
    for success in digital world, 133–35

Social responsibility, assessing for,
    120, 126–29

Solar-powered car project, 121

Standards: determining for instruction
    and assessment, 85–86; National
    Geographic Standards, 111–12; role
    in reform, 2; samples of student
    work for, 88, 90, 93

Standards for the 21st-Century Learner
    (American Association for School
    Librarians): collaboration, 101–2,
    103–4; critical understanding, 102,
    103–4, 105; dispositions, 119, 120;
    library media specialist role, 15–16;
    outcome-based approach, 148;
    student portfolios, 77–78, 81–82,
    85–86; tech-integrated learning, 135

Stem cell research unit, 43–47

Sternberg, Robert, 2

Stripling, Barbara, 104–5

Student books, developing criteria to
    assess (sample lesson), 155, 157–63;
    assessment, 158–61; learning plan,
    162–64; outcomes desired, 157–58

Students: assessment benefits for, 17;
    as audience for student portfolios,
    81–82; role in assessment for
    learning, 10–12; self-assessment by,
    11–12, 198

Summary sheets, in process folios,
    95, 97

Synthesis logs, 42

Teachers: assessment benefits for, 17;
    communicating with, 201–6; view
    of assessment for learning, 12

Teaching, need for integration of, 6–7

Tech-integrated learning, 133–46;
    acquiring success skills for digital
    world, 133–35; assessing for,
    136–45; defining digital landscape,
    133; library media specialists and,
    135–36

Tech-integrated learning assessment,
    136–45; blogs, 137–38; digital
    narratives, 141–43; online
    discussions, 136–37; podcasts and
    vodcasts, 138–40; wiki pathfinders,
    144–45; wikis, 140–41

Technology as tool for research
    presentation, 212–20; analyzing
    evidence, 214–16; collecting
    evidence of achievement, 213–14;
    communicating results, 217–20;
    synthesizing findings, 216–17

Test data, 220–24; analyzing evidence,
    222–23; collecting evidence of
    achievement, 222; communicating
    results, 223–24; synthesizing
    findings, 223

Three Rs, traditional *versus* new, 2

Todd, Ross, 4, 14, 18

Tomlinson, Carol Ann, 8, 11

Understanding, communicating, 115–17

Vandalism project, 144–45

Vodcasts, 138–40

Voting unit, 73–76

Walking tour project, 113–15

Water quality project, 115–17

Web-based student portfolios, 78–79

Webs: assessing information literacy
    with, 66–68; constructing, 65–66;
    defined, 65; question, 122; using, 65

Web site evaluation (sample lesson),
    184–91; assessment, 185–87;
    learning plan, 187–91; outcomes
    desired, 184–85

Wellness unit, 50

Wetlands project: communicating
    with teachers, 201–6; developing
    criteria to assess student books
    (sample lesson), 155, 157–63;

finding information in variety of
sources (sample lesson), 151–55;
process folio, 84–97; sample
lessons, 151–63; summary of
project, 150–51

Wiki-logs, 143
Wiki pathfinders, 144–45
Wikis, 140–41

Zoom Rainforests Web page, 62

About the Authors

VIOLET H. HARADA is a professor of library and information science in the Department of Information and Computer Sciences at the University of Hawaii at Manoa. She has been a secondary teacher, curriculum writer, elementary school library media specialist, and state library specialist with the Hawaii Department of Education. In addition to her teaching duties, she coordinates the school library specialization for the Library and Information Science Graduate Program. Her major areas of research involve inquiry-based approaches to information seeking and use and the study of teacher and librarian collaborative partnerships. She has published numerous articles in scholarly and popular professional journals on these topics and is a frequent speaker at state, national, and international conferences. She is the co-author of the following books: *Inquiry Learning through Librarian-Teacher Partnerships* (Linworth Publishing, 2004), *Assessing Learning: Librarians and Teachers as Partners* (Libraries Unlimited, 2005), *School Reform and the School Library Media Specialist* (Libraries Unlimited, 2007), *Collaborating for Project-Based Learning in Grades 9–12* (Linworth Publishing, 2008), and *Librarians as Learning Specialists* (Libraries Unlimited, 2008).

JOAN M. YOSHINA worked for over three decades as an elementary and high school teacher, a language arts resource person, and a library media specialist. Over her career she has held positions at the elementary, middle, and high school levels. Her last assignment was in a new, state-of-the-art elementary school library media center, which she helped to design. As a practicum librarian, she mentored many Hawaii library media specialists. She has also published articles on the information search process and integrated instruction. Yoshina has guest lectured at the University of Hawaii and presented her work at both state and national conferences. She collaborated with Harada to co-author *Learning through Inquiry: Librarian-Teacher Partnerships* (Linworth Publishing, 2004). In 1999, she received the Golden Key Award from the Hawaii Association of School Librarians in recognition for her outstanding contributions to school librarianship in the state.